Public Education—
America's Civil Religion

Public Education— America's Civil Religion

A SOCIAL HISTORY

Carl L. Bankston III
Stephen J. Caldas

Teachers College
Columbia University
New York and London

Published by Teachers College Press, 1234 Amsterdam Avenue, New York, NY 10027

Library of Congress Cataloging-in-Publication Data

Bankston, Carl L. (Carl Leon), 1952–
  Public education, America's civil religion : a social history / Carl L. Bankston III, Stephen J. Caldas.
      p. cm.
  Includes bibliographical references and index.
  ISBN 978-0-8077-4947-0 (pbk. : alk. paper) — ISBN 978-0-8077-4948-7 (hardcover : alk. paper) 1. Public schools—United States—History. 2. Education—Social aspects—United States—History. 3. Civil religion—United States—History. I Caldas, Stephen J., 1957– II. Title.
  LA212.B25 2009
  371.01097309—dc22

                                                                          2008055601

ISBN: 978-0-8077-4947-0 (paperback)
ISBN: 978-0-8077-4948-7 (hardcover)

Printed on acid-free paper
Manufactured in the United States of America

16 15 14 13 12 11 10 09   8 7 6 5 4 3 2 1

Only a public school?

Ah more, infinitely more;

(As George Fox rais'd his warning cry, "Is it this pile of brick and mortar,

these dead floors, windows, rails, you call the church?

Why this is not the church at all—the church is living, ever living souls.")

And you America,

Cast you the real reckoning for your present?

The lights and shadows of your future, good or evil?

To girlhood, boyhood look, the teacher and the school.

—Walt Whitman, "An Old Man's Thought of School"

Contents

An American Faith

THROUGHOUT the second half of the 1980s, one of the authors worked
in a refugee camp in the Bataan Peninsula of the Philippines, preparing people from Vietnam, Cambodia, and Laos for resettlement in the
United States. Our camp was located near a small provincial town, similar
in many respects to other small provincial towns throughout the Philippines. It held the same four major public places as those other towns. In
the very center, a plaza provided a location for people to sit and talk about
the day's events and promenade in the comparatively cool evenings. At
one end of this plaza, there was a large Catholic church. At the other end
stood the *municipio*, a town hall for the political and bureaucratic business
of the town. Finally, on the same side of the plaza as the church, stretched
a public school. Each of these typical public places was a living historical
memory. The Spanish had built the church and left the plaza. Arriving in
the late 16th century, they claimed the islands as a colony and named them
after Philip II. The town hall and the school recalled the foreign power
that replaced Spain at the end of the 19th century: the United States. Just
as the church reflected the faith of the Spanish, the buildings erected under
the Americans reflected an American creed. Both the Spanish and the
Americans had brought to their colony their own most deeply held tenets,
and the monuments of the American system of beliefs were places for
political participation and schooling.

THE UNITED STATES AND SCHOOLING

What was this faith that the Americans sought to export to its first over-
seas colony? More importantly for our purposes in this book, what does
this American export tell us about the turn-of-the-century American mind?
The American educational system had grown slowly since the nation's
founding, from highly localized and religiously based schools to a fairly

1

uniform, if still locally controlled, network of schools that had become nearly universal by the beginning of the 20th century.

These schools were responding to changes in American society. In the decades from the end of the Civil War to World War I, unprecedented waves of immigrants had arrived in the rapidly industrializing nation. By 1908, a study by the U.S. Immigration Commission found that a majority of the students in America's largest cities were from immigrant families (U.S. Immigration Commission, 1911). In response to the new waves on American shores, public schooling became widely seen as a way of "Americanizing" young people who were immigrants or children of immigrants. Not only would schools be places where new generations would acquire English as their chief means of communication, they would also be locations for inculcating beliefs about the United States. As we will argue in the following pages, through public schools American educators sought to shape their students as participants in an idealized version of American society. Social critic Neil Postman has described the vision of education that emerged from Americanization as a key part of the American civic creed. Speaking of the poem by Emma Lazarus that called for "huddled masses yearning to breathe free," Postman (1996) has written:

> Where else, save the great narrative of Jesus, can one find a story that so ennobles the huddled masses? Here, America is portrayed as the great melting pot. Such a story answers many profound questions, including, What are schools for? Schools are to fashion Americans out of the wretched refuse of teeming shores. Schools are to provide the lost and lonely with a common attachment to America's history and future, to America's sacred symbols, to its promise of freedom. (p. 14)

Immigrants would be remade into Americans through learning the tenets of the American Creed in the schools, becoming part of the new American nation. The reforming job of schools did not end with immigrants, though. This goal of remaking American society by remaking the people in it extended beyond immigrant offspring to the children of native-born citizens. Among all Americans, schooling would do more than pass on information or develop intellectual skills. It would produce a new kind of social order. As historian of education and former U.S. Department of Education assistant secretary Diane Ravitch (2000) has argued, progressive educators did not necessarily agree about the kind of social order they would create. Some believed they could bring about the better world by what we would today call liberation, by fostering the creative spirits of pupils. Others believed they needed to indoctrinate children to fit into a planned society. From both perspectives, though, the educators of the Progressive Era were committed to ". . . the idea that the methods and ends of education could be changed in ways that would reform society" (p. 60).

The increasing focus on schools of the Progressive Era derived from an insight about the nature of a society. A society is not composed of election laws, or forms of taxation, or even governmental structures in general. A society is composed of people. Those who would make a new society must make new people. To social reformers, then, the school seems to offer itself as the perfect laboratory for redesigning how people think and how they relate to each other. In fact, the great father of Progressive education himself, John Dewey, created the first "laboratory school" in 1896 as part of the University of Chicago to "experiment" on children, and try out his progressive ideas in a controlled (and one could argue "controlling") environment.

Of course, this does raise questions of power, of who should decide how people ought to think or how they ought to relate to each other. Whether they emphasized education for liberation and social justice or for socializing workers in a more efficient social order, those who would decide on how schools would be used to create new people and a new society were the educational experts. John Dewey was the best known of these experts. Tellingly, the young Dewey described his approach to schooling as his "pedagogical creed," and he characterized this creed as a belief that education was the nation's "fundamental method of social progress and reform" (as cited in Reese, 2005, p. 120). Paradoxically, Dewey (in Dewey & Dewey 1916/1962) believed that schools, as environments planned through the experimental method, would be a means of achieving progress and reform toward sacred ideals of democracy essential to the American way of life. Experts would be using the schools to make democracy.

The experts were not the only ones to see schools as a central part of a system of beliefs about the American nation. Reese (2005) quotes Nathan C. Schaeffer, Pennsylvania state superintendent of education, as exclaiming in 1906, "education is the common creed of the American people . . . [it is] the one institution in which all Americans believe" (p. 118). As the people of the nation saw their country changing rapidly, it became an article of faith among them that their deepest values could be best realized through schooling. As public schooling became nearly universal in American life, Americans increasingly came to see education as the way that they could remake themselves.

THE CREED OF EDUCATION

The comparison of the American public school with the Spanish Catholic church suggests that the school was more than a simple tool, in the United States or in its Pacific colony. It was a tool in the sense that the church was a tool for realizing core societal beliefs of the Spanish. Through schools,

Americans of the late 19th and early 20th century had begun to try to realize beliefs of their own, beliefs that were derived from some of the oldest and most deeply held ideas about their own existence as a national community. Schooling, in short, has been at the center of an American civil religion.

We recognize that we are not the first to see education in our country as a religion. Objections to education as a kind of orthodoxy providing creedal support for a society often come from those who question the society itself and therefore reject schooling as its central ideological institution. Thus, the radical critic Paul Goodman (1966) attacked compulsory schooling as a mechanistic process for enforcing conformity through bureaucracy. Goodman argued that the school system of his day had become so dominant and so widely accepted in the beliefs of his contemporaries that any new thinking about schooling had become difficult for most people. "When, at a meeting," he wrote, "I offer that perhaps we already have too much formal schooling and that, under present conditions, the more we get the less education we will get, the others look at me oddly and proceed to discuss how to get more money for schools and how to upgrade the schools, I realize suddenly that I am confronting a mass superstition" (p. 7).

In Goodman's view, the society for which schools were supposedly preparing young people was itself unworthy. In one of the most intense periods of the struggle over civil rights, he proclaimed that "the poor of America will *not* become equal by rising through the middle class, going to middle class schools. By plain social justice, the Negroes and other minorities have the right to, and must get, equal opportunities with the rest, but the exaggerated expectation from schooling is a chimera" (p. 7). For Goodman, the problem of inequality, as well as the other problems of life in corporate America, were rooted in the structure of the society. The system of compulsory education was a part of that structure and therefore contributed to the problems.

Ivan Illich, another influential anarchically inclined critic of American education, was even more explicit than Goodman in his description of education as an American religion, although his fundamental orientation toward formal schooling was quite similar to Goodman's. In the classic *Deschooling Society* (1971), Illich advanced a radical libertarian critique of formal education. He called for an end to state-supported, official education so that people could create and seek the kinds of learning that meet their own needs and desires. Illich compared institutionalized education to institutionalized religion. Established education, in his view, enabled the state to distinguish what kinds of learning constituted necessary education and to distinguish "academic" or "pedagogic" from other kinds of learning, in the same way that formal religion distinguished which aspects of human experience were sacred and which aspects were profane. He maintained that the disestablishment of religion in many countries had made it possible for people to make religious decisions for themselves and to see the worldly in the holy and the holy in the worldly according to their own lights.

The comparison of contemporary schools to institutionalized religions runs throughout *Deschooling Society*. Indeed, Illich characterized modern public education as a church:

> The school system today performs the threefold function common to powerful churches throughout history. It is simultaneously the repository of society's myth, the institutionalization of that myth's contradictions, and the locus of the ritual which reproduces and veils the disparities between myth and ritual. (p. 54)

For Illich, large-scale, state-sponsored schooling expressed and perpetuated the hierarchical, unequal structure of modern consumer society, through the organizational structure of the school and through the corporate myth and ritual carried out in the school. According to Illich, schools initiate their students into the myth of unending consumption, the myth of quantified values, the myth of packaged values (particularly through the packaged good known as the curriculum), and the myth of self-perpetuating progress. Pointing out that years of schooling were increasing more rapidly than life expectancy, he wrote that "school serves as an effective creator and sustainer of social myth because of its structure as a ritual game of graded promotions" (p. 63).

The anarchist critique of schools as an illusion of faith is similar to the Marxist objection, notably made by Herbert Bowles and Samuel Gintis (1976), that schooling perpetuates a false consciousness and maintains the inequalities of capitalist society. The Marxists, however, have largely been believers in the power of education. Bowles and Gintis maintained that schools could play a role in fomenting a necessary socialist revolution by enlightening students to the social injustice of the American capitalist system, and to the conspiratorial role that schools have played in perpetuating injustice by preparing students for their places in the oppressive capitalist hierarchy. Unlike the anarchists Goodman and Illich, Marxist critics of education have been *intra ecclesia*, inside the church of American millenarianism.

Henry J. Perkinson, in the short classic *The Imperfect Panacea: American Faith in Education* (1995), presented one of the most interesting and insightful critiques of the national belief that education can provide the answer to all public problems. In an early edition of the book, Perkinson argued that the creed of education was peculiar to America and that it stemmed from the status of the United States as the first new nation. By the time of the fourth edition in the middle of the 1990s, though, Perkinson had discovered similar creeds elsewhere in the world. In his words, "Americans are not the only people to have faith in education. People in other countries, especially developing countries, share this faith, display this outlook" (p. 7).

In this later edition, he identified the printing press as the source of the faith. This invention made formal learning and literacy more widely available than previously. At first, this extended only to the elites, who were initiated into the liberal arts, the studies that were thought to liberate them as full, free human beings. As education spread more widely, though, rulers began to consider what kind of education would be appropriate for the masses. They concluded that teachings that would make the multitudes obedient, loyal, and useful would be appropriate. Education thus split, in Perkinson's interpretation, into initiation for the elites and socialization for the masses. As a nation ideologically dedicated to being of the common people, socialization held a special attraction for Americans. Perkinson saw the American faith in education, then, as the local version of a creed that was almost universal in societies that had reached or were reaching the stage of mass literacy. As Perkinson wrote:

> With the socialization concept of education, one must start off by deciding upon the extrinsic purpose of education, what talents, knowledge, beliefs, values, skills, and understandings must be transmitted to children in order to keep society going. Thus, the construction of education as a process of socialization leads logically to the notion that education is a panacea. Americans, from the earliest colonial times, have been the unwitting captives of the concept that education is a process of socialization, a concept that lies at the heart of this enduring faith in education. (p. 9)

Perkinson's identification of the printing press as the source of modern faith in education is particularly interesting when one recalls the role of this technology in Benedict R.O.G. Anderson's (2006) account of the rise of nationalism. This first instrument of mass communication, in Anderson's view, brought people in relatively large geographic areas together into "imagined communities," held together by shared self-images. Modern mass education through socialization is a part of nationalism; schooling does not just socialize people to fit into the national framework, it also participates in the ideologies of nation-states. This observation suggests, though, that Perkinson's broad historical insight about modern nation-states, with their foundations on mass communication, can lead to a more detailed investigation of different faiths in education. While modern nations share many characteristics, each is also unique. Certainly many nations have seen socialization as a basic goal of education. So, what was "American" about the American faith in education?

Education has indeed been a central part of the modern experience of many nations, in ways that illustrate Perkinson's emphasis on socialization as a distinguishing characteristic of mass education. In modern France, for example, education has been a large part of the French attempt to create a centralized, secular state. Debates about education have therefore been about centralization and secularization, in historical episodes such as pro-Catholic, reactionary educational policies during the Vichy period to today's current controversies over the Islamic veil. We can understand French educational expectations, policies, and disagreements by looking at education within the context of modern French political culture. Similarly, asking what is American about American beliefs in education involves looking at education within the developing context of American political culture.

If we do look within the context of that political culture, we can see much more happening than the split into socialization for the masses and initiation for the elites. Indeed, from the beginning of the American political experience, the question of who are the elites and who are the masses has come up repeatedly. The earliest ideas about what education was to accomplish in this nation promoted the ideal of using education as a means for placing individuals from the masses in elite positions, rather than just maintaining two separate estates. Upward mobility and equality of opportunity have been consistent themes over the course of American history and over the course of the history of American education. But fitting individuals into slots in American society and creating national unity have also been repeated themes. Americans have also held to the idea that there is something special about their nation beyond an ancestral identity, and they have sought to realize this something special through the schools. The extent to which American exceptionalism describes reality may be open to question, but the belief in American exceptionalism is a reality in itself. In order to understand the particularly American commitment to schooling, we need to understand how Americans have seen their own nation and how they have understood schooling within the vision of the nation. We need to understand how national goals have shifted over time and how ideals of schooling shifted accordingly.

These undercurrents of heresy have suggested that the argument that schooling in America is a faith is a recurring one. But we want to move beyond decrying this faith as a superstition, arguing for its fulfillment by pushing it to an extreme, or identifying it as a strategy of social control. We think the civil religion perspective of Robert Bellah can offer a useful new way of understanding education in American life, and we want to employ this perspective to make a threefold contribution. First, we want to draw on the civil religion view to demonstrate how beliefs about education followed from beliefs about the nation, and how beliefs about education and the nation were produced by events in American history. We think good examples of this are the Progressivist ideology emerging from the late 19th and early 20th century rise of a unified, industrial nation and then the individualist egalitarian ideology emerging from the development of a postmodern, consumer society in the late 20th century. Second, we want to attempt to move our analysis beyond traditional liberal and conservative criticisms of education to show how educational initiatives thought of as "liberal" and "conservative" are often both products of a belief that an American Promised Land can be achieved by schooling. Just as we point out that child-centered education and education for social efficiency were two faces of the same Progressivist version of the faith in schooling, we also point out that Head Start and No Child Left Behind were two faces of the late twentieth/early twenty-first century version. This brings us to the third contribution of our argument to the critical discourse on education: we want to bring this discourse up to the present and show how the latest controversial initiatives in public education fit into a long tradition in American thought.

    In this book, we will argue that the best way to understand the American devotion to education as a primary means of solving the concerns of each decade is to look at schooling as a civil religion. We will be arguing that education, in particular public education, has been both a means of spreading the faith and a central part of that faith. We will trace the development of our national creed of education over the decades, identify its main characteristics, and examine how our faith may have led us to exaggerate what schools can actually do. Ultimately, we do not seek to debunk this national faith so much as to call readers to look at it with some reasoned skepticism and to consider its contradictions and limitations.

PLAN OF THE BOOK

Chapter 1 will discuss the concepts of political and civil religions in greater detail and explain how Robert N. Bellah's account of American civil religion, in particular, can help us understand the development of American faith in education. Chapter 2 will begin to trace the history of this development by looking at the early stages of American education during the first part of the 19th century, before the emergence of nearly universal public education, and at the role of schooling in the political culture of the growing nation. Chapter 3 considers a key period in our discussion of education as an American civil religion: the Progressive Era. During this time, the nation went through rapid political unification and centralization, and it underwent a rapid economic expansion that brought great waves of immigration and led to massive urbanization. We will argue that widespread education became both a means of inculcating belief in the rising nation and a central article of faith in the nation. Chapter 4 looks at the institutionalization of faith in education between the two world wars, when schooling became the established means of managing an industrial society, and when distinct varieties of the faith became clearer, with some adherents devoted to the social order vision of the creed and others devoted to schooling as a tool for designing the ideal society of the future. Chapter 5 proceeds to developments in education following World War II, when education boomed along with the American economy and the federal government began to become more involved in education. Further, it considers schooling as a means of intensifying national commitment during the Cold War, and the connection between education and the ideal of equality during the 1950s. Chapter 6 describes the time of change in American faith in education, when distributive equality moved to the center of the creed. This chapter traces the big change in the educational creed to the rise of the consumer economy and to the moral influence of the civil rights movement. Chapter 7 looks at the national anxiety about educational standards during the 1980s and 1990s and at how this concern over standards combined with the commitment to equality that became predominant during the 1960s and 1970s. Chapter 8, finally, considers recent educational developments, focusing on the No Child Left Behind legislation. We point out that although President George W. Bush's supposed conservatism may seem the polar opposite of President Lyndon Johnson's Great Society, the former historically grew out of the latter and both reflected the same underlying faith in education as a means of building an equitable society. We also look at how the theme of national solidarity, eclipsed for decades by the theme of egalitarian social reconstruction, became resonant once again in the 21st century. We conclude with an overview of our historical argument and some observations on the problems and paradoxes of a civil religion of education.

CHAPTER 1

Religions, Political and Civil

ROUSSEAU AND THE ORIGINS
OF THE CONCEPT OF CIVIL RELIGION

JEAN-JACQUES ROUSSEAU is usually credited as the author of the phrase "civil religion." In *The Social Contract*, Rousseau (1762/1972) maintained that the leaders of a nation should create and promulgate a purely civic faith, with a few tenets aimed at making good citizens. This religion would provide the state, its practices, and its institutions with metaphysical justification.

Rousseau's ideas about the proper function of religion came out of his theories of education. The Swiss philosopher understood human beings as naturally good, but corrupted by human society, particularly by the divisive institution of private property. In *Émile: Or, on Education* (1762/1961) he posed the question of how to cultivate the natural virtues of an individual, while enabling an individual to live within a corrupt society. The eponymous protagonist of *Émile* is brought up in a manner that Rousseau argued would cultivate the individual's natural inclinations in a manner consistent with social life.

In the earliest years of Émile's education, his tutor emphasizes developing the senses and reasoning on the basis of sense impressions, rather than abstract learning through books. As Émile grows older, the social part of his education begins and Émile learns a manual trade through apprenticeship, both in order to acquire a socially useful skill and to develop his ability to work constructively with others. It is only after Émile reaches adolescence and comes into closer contact with his fellows in the corrupt society that his education begins to include religion. As Mark Lilla (2007) has recently pointed out, Rousseau believed that the natural man has no need of religion; it is only in the corrupt but now unavoidable state of social existence that the religious sentiments are needed in order to guide people and give them the proper internal orientation for living together. "Emile is not a Christian, and were he never to quit his solitary existence," according to Lilla, "he would never need theology. But once he enters society, he will acquire a religious need because social interaction will confront him with hard, plaguing questions about the divine nexus and its relation to morality" (p. 124).

Rousseau handles Émile's introduction to religion through the story of "The Profession of Faith of the Savoyard Vicar" in Book IV. Émile's tutor tells this tale of a disillusioned young man exiled from his native town. Speaking in the voice of this young man, the story recounts how a Savoyard priest helps the youth find faith in the world around him. The priest tells how he himself had been disillusioned, and how he had sought certainty in a manner similar to Descartes' doubting of everything in order to find a solid foundation. The priest found that he possessed sentiments within himself that told him of basic truths, such as the existence of God, the importance of virtue, and the fact of human free will. These sentiments appear in different forms in different lands. However, to the extent that any religion preaches God and morality, that religion is consistent with the inner light of the sentiments and should be taken as true. Thus, a true religion links social ritual with nature by supporting the morality of nature, and one should follow the religion of one's own country as long as it is consistent with the order of nature.

The story of the Savoyard Vicar in *Émile* expressed at the individual level what the proposal of a civil religion in *The Social Contract* expressed at the collective level. The story's placement in Émile's life, as he emerges from childhood and comes into society, suggests the proper role of religion in Rousseau's scheme. Religion is the link between natural individuals and the artificiality of collective existence. Religions that support the morality of nature are those that coordinate interactions among people according to the inner guidance of natural moral sentiments. The religious beliefs and practices that create political unity may be based on a few basic principles, but they differ in their expressions because their polities differ. As expressions, Rousseau (1960/1758) prescribed festivals that would both provide entertainments and enable citizens to see themselves in other citizens and to identify with the public as a whole.

DURKHEIM'S CONTRIBUTION

The late-19th- and early-20th-century French sociologist Emile Durkheim developed ideas about religion and social order that recalled those of Rousseau in some respects. Much of Durkheim's work can be understood as understanding how individual–group connections come into existence and are maintained. For Durkheim (1965), one of the primary ways of binding individuals together into a community was through the sacralization of shared ideas and beliefs. Durkheim did see the solidarity of belief (in his jargon, "mechanical solidarity") as becoming progressively less important for maintaining interaction as solidarity of functional interdependence, a division of labor, became more widespread. "[I]t is an historical law," Durkheim (1947) wrote, "that mechanical solidarity which first stands alone, or nearly so, progressively loses ground, and that organic [functional] solidarity becomes, little by little, preponderant" (p. 33). While Durkheim did not believe that the integrative force of the sacred would become irrelevant, he did think that this would become less central as human beings were increasingly bound by exchange rather than by common creed.

This Durkheimian distinction between social ties of commonality and social ties of exchange can be taken as a valuable contribution to Rousseau's thoughts on what creates polities. Citizens may be united by rituals, rites, and festivals expressing common belonging, but they may also be united simply because they need one another and they all benefit from the things they can do for one another. An emphasis on one or the other source of unity continues to lie beneath many of the arguments about the nature of nationality today. Attempts to criminalize flag-burning, for example, are not produced only by emotional reactions. They also stem from a theory of citizenship in which belonging and commitment to a national community are produced by adherence to a sacred symbol, and desecration of that symbol weakens the bonds of the entire community.

Disagreements about emphases on the two different types of solidarity may also be seen as disagreements about the exercise of individual rationality versus the merging of individual thought into a sacred collective given concrete form through a credo or a symbol such as a flag. While Rousseau did describe acceptable religions as those that were consistent with the inner light of individual moral sentiment, the fundamental fact of any orthodoxy, as Durkheim realized, is that it binds together those who hold it only because they are obligated to hold the same ideas. Indeed, the sacred is something that cannot be questioned or denied. As readers of Dostoevsky will recognize, the danger of holding nothing sacred and allowing every individual to follow personal decision-making is that anything can become possible and all will move off in separate directions. With no communal faith, no rituals, and no symbols, it may be plausibly argued, there can be no polity. Rational interdependence may not be enough to hold people together, and it is unlikely to be enough to motivate them to undertake great projects together. At the same time, the merging of individual thought into great projects on the basis of sacred polities can have dangers, and these have come to concern political and social think-ers in the years since Durkheim's lifetime.

POLITICAL AND CIVIL RELIGIONS

Many of the 20th-century theorists who have looked at politics as reli-gion have seen a much darker side to it than Rousseau did in the 18th century, and they have been much less secure than Durkheim was about the steady progress toward interdependence, secularization, and rational-ity. Modern sacred polities have often been identified with extremities of political commitment and action that, in theory at least, plunged adher-ents wholly into worshipful dedication to the state. Ideologies of radical change such as national socialism, Italian fascism, and Soviet Communism, in particular, have been described as secularized millenarian religions (see Billington, 1980; Gentile, 1996; Rhodes, 1980).

The political scientist Eric Voegelin (2005) distinguished between "transcendent religions," which placed the focus of worship outside of human institutions, and "immanent religions," which made the human institutions themselves the focus of worship. A refugee from Austria after the 1938 *Anschluss* with Germany, Voegelin used the term "immanent" not to imply that the quality of transcendence was absent from movements such as Nazism, but that transcendent themes of ultimate good versus ultimate evil, the mission of a chosen people, and the end of history in an ultimate salvation had become absorbed into the worldly project of secu-lar politics. The governments of transcendent religions, such as the Chris-tian states of Europe during the Middle Ages, had derived their authority from otherworldly sources, resulting in political theories such as divine right. Immanent religions made a race or a people sacred and derived the right to rule by claiming to be manifestations of the race or people.

While the emphasis of political religions tended to fall on the extreme and theoretically all-encompassing movements such as Communism, Nazism, and fascism, Voeglin and others, including Emilio Gentile and Michael Oakeshott, also argued that the sacralization of politics had oc-curred across the ideological spectrum, in moderate as well as extreme political systems (Gentile, 1996, 2006; Oakeshott, 1996; Voegelin, 1986). Gentile, the most recent of these thinkers, summed up this general line of thinking by maintaining that modern politics in general has taken on re-ligious features, defining the fundamental purposes and goals of human life. Gentile (2006) distinguished between "civil religion," the sacraliza-tion of politics in political democracies, and "political religion," in more radical regimes.

Gentile's distinction raises the question of what civil religion and political religion may have in common and how this sacralization may differ in moderate and extreme states. The identification of Rousseau as the primary author of the concept of civil religion suggests that the sacralization of the political in democracies and in extreme forms of government stems from the same origin at the beginning of late modernity. Inspired by Rousseau's ideas, the Jacobins of the French Revolution attempted to create festivals and catechisms as rituals of public life. The historian Michael Burleigh (2005) has recently remarked of the revolutionary festivals that "all such occasions derived ultimately from Rousseau's belief that such civic festivals would counteract Christian deprecation of earthly affairs and secular government" (p. 77).

The German writer Christoph Martin Wieland described the French Revolution as a political religion, devoted to the idolization of political ideals (as cited in Burleigh, 2005). Similarly, Tocqueville wrote of the revolution as "a new kind of religion" (p. 92) that moved beyond the reform of France and aimed at the regeneration of the human race (as quoted in Burleigh, 2005). Rousseau's civil religion had slipped readily into becoming a political religion that imposed its own radical eschatological expectations on the world.

Civil religions and political religions, then, have derived from the same sources in modern history. They also continue to be closely related. The clearest distinction between the two may lie in the extent and exclusivity of the claims of mechanical solidarity on individuals. This degree of emphasis on mechanical solidarity, in turn, reflects the intensity of dedication to some project of social transformation. The more that an ideology rejects the world of the present and commits itself to another world, the greater the demands of identification and absorption it must make on its participants. While the political faiths of the extreme ideological polities have attempted to absorb individual citizens entirely into a set of sacred values and goals, civic religions have been more moderate and have tolerated more variations in adherence to the articles of faith. This is illustrated in the contrast between sect and church proposed by Roger Finke and Rodney Stark (1992): "These [churches and sects] are best conceptualized as the end points of a continuum made up of the *degree of tension* [emphasis in the original] between religious organizations and their sociocultural environments" (p. 41). Sects maintain high tension and reject their environments and nonbelievers. Churches are relatively more open. This openness to the world outside the system of beliefs is connected to dedication to goals and to control over adherents. "Churches serve the segment of the market with less need for a strict and otherworldly faith; sects serve the segment seeking those features" (Finke & Stark, p. 42).

The difference between a civil religion in a democratic society and political religion in an ideologically radical society is one of degree, not of kind. Both bind people together through common sets of beliefs, although they may differ greatly in the severity of punishment meted out to real or suspected nonbelievers. Both judge events, actions, and institutions by predetermined sacred values rather than by critical reason. If political religions and civil religions can be identified as two different branches of a single tree, divided by the histories that create different polities, then it makes sense to see each of them as, in turn, branching out. This raises the issue of what is distinctive about American civil religion.

BELLAH AND AMERICAN CIVIL RELIGION

In 1967, sociologist Robert Bellah brought Rousseau's term into current discourse about American society and brought the idea of politics as religion into an American context with the essay "Civil Religion in America." Bellah drew on Durkheim's view of social solidarity as the product of shared belief to present an argument about American civil religion that was both descriptive and prescriptive. As Robert E. Stauffer (1975) wrote several years after Bellah's essay, "working largely within a Durkheimian framework, Bellah observed that (1) it is hardly surprising that a society should sacralize its dominant values (and the events, personages, artifacts, and personages representative of these values) and (2) merely to attack this civil faith as vulgar nationalism is to overlook its profound and indispensable contribution to maintaining a cohesive and viable national society" (p. 320).

Stauffer's first point concerned the descriptive side of Bellah's theory: Americans have sacralized their dominant values. This suggests that one can analyze the events and historical characters treated with reverence by Americans in order to understand what their dominant values are and how those dominant values have changed over time. The civil religion perspective, then, offers something of a normative history of the American polity.

The second point concerned the prescriptive side. Bellah was not just saying that Americans have had a civil religion and that recognizing this can be an important part of the study of American society. Following Durkheim, Bellah argued that religion provides identity and motivation to groups and to individuals as members of groups. Therefore, the American civil religion was critical for meeting national challenges, as well as for integrating individuals into the national community. In the work published after the initial civil religion essay, Bellah emphasized this prescriptive side.

For example, in *The Broken Covenant*, published in 1975, Bellah denounced the competitive nature of modern American life and maintained that the United States needed to draw on its democratic cultural traditions to provide a new sense of national commitment to solving problems of poverty, racism, wasteful consumption, and uncontrolled economic growth. We can see Bellah, then, as acting as an advocate for his own version of American civil religion, and even as a prophet of what the "true faith" should be.

In giving his normative history of the nation, Bellah drew the idea of the sacralization of political life into a specifically American setting, and traced its stages through American history. Bellah claimed that the supposedly secular American state rested on a foundation of shared sacred beliefs that could be characterized as a civil religion that existed alongside of churches and synagogues. The assertion that the United States, with its widely proclaimed separation of church and state, had a civil religion touched off decades of discussion and debate (Cristi, 2001; Mathisen, 2006). In retrospect, it may have been the phrase, rather than the idea of a religious side to American public life, that provoked opposition. In fact, Bellah gave coherent form to the concept of an American civic faith, rather than originated it. As Marcela Cristi (2001) has pointed out, a long line of thinkers before Bellah referred to the religious dimension of American public life. Sociologist Lloyd Warner recognized the ritual qualities of Memorial Day celebrations in his classic study of Yankee City (1963) and John Dewey (1934), a character in the present book, referred to America's "common faith."

Analyzing President John F. Kennedy's inaugural speech, Bellah pointed to central tenets of American civil religion such as the rights of man and pointed out the sense of a transcendent mission in American political history. From its earliest years, according to Bellah (1967), the American republic has expressed "a collection of beliefs, symbols, and rituals with respect to sacred things . . . institutionalized in a collectivity" (p. 4).

In his article, Bellah (1967) emphasized those aspects of civil religion that had the most explicit connections to biblical religion, pointing out Kennedy's references to God throughout his speech. However, although Rousseau did argue that theism was a necessary part of a civil religion, references to a deity are not essential to make a set of beliefs holy. In the words of a contemporary sociologist of religion, civil religion can be defined as "the set of beliefs, rites, and symbols that sacralize the values of the society and place the nation in the context of an ultimate system of meaning . . . Socially, civil religion serves to define the national purposes in transcendent terms and acts as an expression of national cohesion" (Roberts, 2004, p. 356).

Many of the purposes of the American nation were expressed in transcendent terms long before its political founding, and these emerged from the Christian tradition, from which the civil religious tradition only gradually and incompletely separated. John Winthrop's famous 1630 exhortation to his fellow colonists to found a "City on a Hill" set the tone of Americans building their own Promised Land and becoming a new Israel. This idea that America was not only the New World, but the New Jerusalem, became the first and perhaps the most deeply held of national assumptions to be passed on and reworked over the centuries (Cristi, 2001).

Bellah (1967) noted that "the words and acts of the founding fathers, especially the first few presidents, shaped the form and tone of the civil religion, as it has been maintained ever since" (p. 7). George Washington designated the first holy day of the emerging civil religion in October 1789 when, at the request of both houses of Congress, he declared that November 26 would be a day of thanksgiving and prayer (Bellah, 1967). In his second inaugural address, Thomas Jefferson echoed the image of America as the new Israel. In Bellah's words, Jefferson expressed a theme that would become continuous in the American civil religion: "Europe is Egypt: America, the promised land. God has led his people to establish a new sort of social order that shall be a light unto the nations" (p. 6).

Bellah argued that the civil religion of the United States went through three trials, or critical times associated with the definition or redefinition of the nation's sacred identity. The first of these was the founding trial of the Revolutionary War. This was the source of the holy imagery that remains with us until today, with our reverence for the Founding Fathers, the Fourth of July, and the Declaration of Independence at the opening of the war and the Constitution creating American government in the wake of the war. The second crisis was the Civil War. Bellah argues that this war "raised the deepest questions of national meaning" and that Abraham Lincoln became the embodiment of this meaning. With the conclusion of this fratricidal struggle and the assassination and civil canonization of Lincoln, "a new theme of death, sacrifice, and rebirth enters the new civil religion" (p. 8).

Bellah's identification of the post–Civil War period in American civil religion is important for our consideration of the role of public schools in that faith. It was in the years following the Civil War that the nation changed in both its objective and subjective character. The rapid economic development in the late 19th and early 20th centuries created a nationwide industrial economy. Immigrants came in the millions to work in this economy. America, mainly rural in the early 19th century, urbanized rapidly, so that a majority of its inhabitants lived in cities by 1920. During the decades preceding and following the turn of the century, also, the public school rose as a prominent part of American life, charged with passing on the nation's ideals and beliefs and with responding to its perceived needs. Accordingly, public schooling became a central feature of American civic religion.

Bellah expressed concern in his influential essay that America was facing a new time of trial, writing in a period of social upheaval. In later work, Bellah (1975) maintained that the United States did, in fact, undergo a third major period of crisis of faith in the 1960s. The civil rights movement, in particular, but also deep divisions over the Vietnam War inspired doubts about the American mission in the world, and the disillusionment with politics that followed the combined experiences of Vietnam and Watergate challenged American belief in itself. Bellah saw this crisis as creating a need for a new civil religious resolution. We will argue below that some elements of a new shift in civic faith did appear, and that these were widely, although not universally, accepted. As Lincoln had been canonized earlier, Martin Luther King Jr. became a national saint in late modern America, symbolizing in his person and in his remembered words a new orientation in the gospel of the nation as the Promised Land. By the time of the civil rights crisis, though, American belief in the public school as the way to the Promised Land was already securely established in American civil religion. The survey of the development of American schools that we will undertake in the following chapters indicates that faith in the renewal of society through public education moved to the core of the civil religion during the post–Civil War period, in the Progressive Era. The faith blossomed anew during the civil rights movement.

Bellah's evocation of American civil religion seems to us extremely useful for an understanding of American society and for an understanding of the place of schooling within that society, but also deeply problematic. While the descriptive side of Bellah's three-period framework fits American education well, the prescriptive side lends itself to an uncritical celebration of American institutions. Bellah did not just argue that the United States had a civil religion, he argued that it needs this faith in order to provide the nation with a common identity and with motivation for achieving its national ends. In fact, this prescriptive side went deeper. American civil religion was not just socially useful; for Bellah it was true. It emerged from deeper sources much as Rousseau's civil religion emerged from the universal truths within each individual soul. "The civil religion at its best," he wrote in his 1967 essay, "is a genuine apprehension of universal and transcendent religious reality as seen in or, one could almost say, revealed through the experience of the American people" (p. 12).

Some of the critics of the civil religion idea, such as Thomas and Flippen (1972), have raised questions about whether America has really ever had a civil religion in the form that Bellah described it. Others from the pre-scriptive side, such as Handy (1980), have argued that by making demands on the faith of citizens, a civil religion can conflict with more traditionally recognized forms of religion. This objection echoes Voegelin's distinction between transcendent religions and immanent religions, since these critics would maintain that the idols of the state draw reverence that properly (according to one view) belongs to forces beyond state and society. Simi-larly, the fact that a modern pluralistic state consists of many different beliefs leads some to argue that the type of mechanical solidarity offered by civil religion is inconsistent with the variety inherent in a complex, interdependent, and diverse state. Moreover, the very fact that people without a common foundation of belief are so varied can be a strength of a civic order founded on the Durkheimian organic solidarity of functional exchange. As Richard Fenn (2001) writes, "Secular societies have no need for an idol that reduces the uncertainty and complexity within or around itself. Such a society refuses to reduce its awareness of the stakes and the risks of the opportunities and also the dangers that come from existing in an open, pluralistic world of rival groups and ideals" (p. 179).

In this work, we are largely following Bellah's description of the nor-mative history of American society as a sacralization of the nation's domi-nant values, and we attempt to show that schooling has come to be at the very heart of these values. At the same time, we are arguing that an at-tempt to understand public education must also involve a critical approach to this faith. The solidarity created by a common creed can indeed be a source of motivation and identity for national community, as for any other group. Functional interdependence may be fine for maintaining economic cooperation among people, although it may be possible that even economic exchange has to be founded on some ground of fundamental beliefs about individual rights and obligations, perhaps deriving from unquestioned intuitions of universal natural law. But it is difficult to commit people to achieving common goals or national purposes beyond exchange without a shared faith. This can also be a problem, though. Whether the national purposes merit the commitment may depend on how one evaluates the purposes. During the early 1930s, the National Socialist Party appeared to many observers around the world to have achieved great success in mo-bilizing the German nation. Today, of course, few would agree that the mobilization had been turned toward desirable ends.

Robert Bellah has certainly never been an extreme nationalist, nor did he ever advocate an American civil religion as a recipe for chauvin-ism. He was opposed to the Vietnam War that raged at the time of the 1967 article, and he hoped that the third time of trial would move Ameri-cans in a socialist or social democratic direction on the basis of American political traditions. Still, while social democracy is unquestionably a much more benign political theory than national socialism, both of these are nevertheless political theories. To the extent that adherence to them is based on faith, those who disagree with these theories are necessarily heretics, rather than participants in a civic debate, and placed outside the community of believers and outside the national discourse. Certainly, radical political religions deal with their heretics much more viciously than civil religions do, much as sects punish nonconformity more harshly than do mainline churches. But both establish theories as sets of necessary articles of faith.

The United States did not become a social democracy following the turbulence of the Great Society–Vietnam War era, although it did incorporate more social democratic norms and practices into its market-based society than it had contained in earlier years. We will be arguing below that this change in the normative assumptions of the nation can be clearly seen in its educational practices. The effect that faith has on limiting open and honest debate, though, goes beyond the exclusion, however gentle, of those who hold points of view at variance with the dominant values. The limitation itself is an even greater difficulty. The more we are committed by faith to a line of action, the less we are able to question whether our actions are actually toward the expected ends, much less question the ends themselves.

Following the three-period form of Bellah's description of American civil religion, then, we will now attempt to first describe how faith in schooling became part of our national system of belief before the later part of the 19th century. After discussing how education became key to our collective norms and values from the late 19th century into the first part of the 20th, we will then look at the shift in expectations during the late 20th century. Part of the goal in what follows will be to describe how education and ideas about education have been produced by changes in American society. Another part of the goal, though, will be to raise questions about just what we can and cannot do through schooling and about whether civic faith has led us to overlook these limitations.

CHAPTER 2

Before Progressivism: Belief in Education in a Divided Nation

EARLY AMERICAN SCHOOLING AND RELIGION

SCHOOLING moved to the center of American civil religion, in our view, during the time of national unification and rapid economic progress following the Civil War. However, in the earliest years of American history, one can see the first traces of a civic creed. In this chapter, we will trace the prehistory of the American civil religion of education by considering early American schooling, the links between thoughts about schooling and images of the new American nation, and the development of the common schools. We will argue that influential Americans in the early 19th century already saw schools as a way to remake the nation and their fellow citizens according to an ideal national image, but that both the country and the educational system at that time were still limited by local and regional differences and divisions.

Educational institutions have a long history in America, with complex associations to religious ideas and to ideals about the destiny of the Europeans' New World. As early as 1647, the colony of Massachusetts passed legislation requiring towns of at least 50 householders to appoint schoolmasters to teach children to read and write, and towns of 100 householders to establish grammar schools (Thayer, 1965). Thus, the American colonies became among the first Western polities to pass compulsory education laws (Perkinson, 1995), and the schools were closely associated with the idea of community. Later Americans would look back to these foundational schools as they would look back to the Puritans and Pilgrims as the sense of a national community emerged out of disparate settlements.

The early colonial New England states were explicitly theocratic and the teachings of schools were therefore Christian in purpose and in content. They were less expressions of civic faith than expressions of civic support for the faith. Efforts such as the Act of 1647, also referred to as "The Olde Satan Deluder Act," "reflected more the determination of colonial officials to insure orthodoxy in religion than the stirrings of a democratic conscience" (Thayer, 1965, p. 4).

For the interests of this book, colonial education bequeathed two major inheritances to the succeeding centuries. First, all schools continued to be invested with openly and explicitly religious teaching and religious symbolism, although later public schools were formally secularized and legally separate from biblical religion. Second, schools were local institutions, established and run by localities. This second inheritance would continue in American education into the 21st century, although, as we will see, education would become increasingly centralized with the growing centralization of American federal government.

EDUCATION AND BELIEF IN THE NEW NATION

By the 18th century, American religious ideas, especially among some members of the political elite, began to move more toward deism, toward a God who was vaguely present but had a nondenominational and distant nature (Thayer, 1965). This nondenominational deity can be recognized as one of the main components in the civil religion described by Bellah. Certainly, not all early Americans were deists; in fact, the American religious setting was highly diverse, if heavily Protestant in orientation, at the time of the nation's beginning. However, this variety encouraged the same sort of vaguely present, nondenominational God that deism did. The late 18th century was also the time when Americans began to create their political world, and the beginning of a new experiment in civic life. If schools were to be part of this new experiment, they would need to move from teaching the biblical faith alone toward teaching a political faith. They would need to be places for the formation of citizens. Thomas Jefferson, a keen reader of Rousseau, set forth one of the earliest systematic approaches to education as a means of training citizens, rather than Christians, in his 1779 essay "A Bill for the More General Diffusion of Knowledge." In this, Jefferson outlined a plan for education in his own state of Virginia that would involve every local district creating 3-year schools for white children between 7 and 10, a set of higher 3-year county schools for the top graduates of the district schools, and a state college for the top graduates of each of the district schools. Jefferson's plan was clearly intended to provide an elite leadership, a hierarchical approach to social planning that, as we will see, continues to receive support even among supposed egalitarians today. The plan was also competitive and meritocratic, with the most successful reaching the highest levels: Jefferson's "aristocracy of talent" (Church, 1976). Such an approach to schooling also continues to characterize contemporary education, although it may not always be acknowledged. Jefferson's plan, then, was for a widely available, if not universal, education for citizens, but one that was openly elitist (and one that excluded slaves).

Jefferson's plan had much in common with other ideas for education set forth in essays written in 1797 for a competition held by the American Philosophical Society for the best essay on the creation of public education for the sake of democratic government (Rudolph, 1965). These essays all tended to see education as creating literate, knowledgeable citizens who could then be left alone to run the democratic state. These early ideas about public education, then, mirrored ideas about the nature of government: government should intervene as little as possible in a society that should run itself (Perkinson, 1995). They also, however, mirrored deist ideas about the government of God in the world: the school planner should create the initial architecture for a social order and then withdraw.

Although an early proponent of public schooling, Jefferson was ambivalent about state-supported schools. The plan he proposed was a radical bottom-up approach, in which smaller communities formed the basis for most education, with progressively smaller elites emerging at each point. While his approach did include, in theory, what we would today call "equality of opportunity" leading to inequality of outcomes through competition, his goals for a broadly educated citizenry were limited to basic skills, with higher-order education strictly limited even for most men. The localism he championed also tempered his support for publicly funded schools. When Charles Mercer proposed a bill to provide free primary education in 1817, Thomas Jefferson was one of the bill's opponents. Because the bill entailed a state board of education, with matching aid from the state to localities, Jefferson was against what he saw as excessive centralization of control (Kaestle, 1983, p. 199).

The question of centralization of authority and control was, of course, one of the basic and most divisive issues of the early American republic. It later became part of a knot of disagreements about slavery, tariffs, and industrial versus agricultural systems that produced the Civil War. It was also at the heart of the debate between the two main parties of the first years of the nation, the Federalists and the Jeffersonian Democratic-Republicans. Jefferson's school plan mirrored the Democratic-Republican ideals that he voiced and symbolized. The schools would produce a nation of yeoman farmers with sufficient literacy to maintain their own affairs. Most people would live in their small localities, and the only connection to outside school systems would be the existence of similar schools in other localities. Those who ascended would, like Jefferson, be the natural leaders, and they would progressively move outside the localities, but the leadership would go no further than necessary to maintain a minimal state. All would live in a relatively static, rural society. Above all, the plan was to be a plan for Virginia.

At that turn of the century, though, Federalist ideas of education were also taking shape. While Jefferson dreamed of a rural republic of farmers, Federalist views focused on shaping the moral development of citizens in ways consistent with a different vision of the American Promised Land. The Federalist view aimed at the inculcation of a morality appropriate to an economically progressive market society and at preparing students for a political ethic consistent with that society, basing both the economic morality and the political ethic on a generalized, vaguely Protestant faith that was the ancestor of American civil religion.

The most famous schoolbook to come out of the early years of the United States, *Webster's Blue Backed Speller*, published about 1800, provided chapters such as "Lessons of Easy Words, to Teach Children to Read and To Know Their Duty" (Webster, 1800, p. 52). Many of the reading lessons were taken directly from the Bible, with a heavy emphasis on passages preaching popular behavior. In Appendices to the book, after question-and-answer passages including "What is a Noun?," "What is a Verb?," and "What is a Sentence," Webster placed "A Moral Catechism" and "A Federal Catechism." The former provides inquiries and responses beginning with: "*Question: What is Moral Virtue? Answer:* It is an honest upright conduct in all our dealings with men" (Webster, 1800, p. 138). Citations of the beatitudes and other biblical injunctions take their place alongside such characteristically American virtues as industry: "*Q.: What is industry? A.* It is diligent attention to business in our several occupations" (Webster, 1800, p. 146). Webster follows this further, making it clear that religious faith, economic industry, civic virtue, and education are all closely linked in his view:

> Q. What are the other good effects of industry?
> A. One effect is to procure an estate. Our Creator has kindly united our duty, our interest and happiness: for the same labour which makes us healthy and cheerful, gives us wealth.
>
> Another good effect of industry is, it keeps men from vice. Not all the moral discourses ever delivered to mankind, have so much influence in checking the bad passions of men, in keeping order and peace, and maintaining moral virtue, in society as *industry. Business* is a source of health; of prosperity, or virtue, and obedience to law.
>
> To make good subjects and good citizens, the first requisite is to educate every young person, in some kind of business. The possession of mil-

lions should not excuse a young man from application to business, and that parent or guardian who suffers his child or his ward to be bred in indolence, becomes accessory to the vices and disorders of society, he is guilty of not providing for his household, and is worse than an infidel. (Webster, 1800, pp. 146–7)

Webster's Federal Catechism immediately follows the Moral. The Federal Catechism defines the idea of a constitution of government, defining it into three types: as a monarchy, aristocracy, or democracy. Posing the query, *"Q. Is there another and better form of government than any of these?,"* the book instructs, "A. There is. A REPRESENTATIVE REPUBLIC, in which people freely choose deputies to make laws for them, is much the best form of government hitherto invented" (Webster, 1800, p. 148). Justifying the title, Webster ends the section and his book with a teaching on the question of federal versus state power:

> *Q. Will not this national government in time destroy the state governments?*
> A. It is not probable this w[i]ll be the case; indeed the national government is the best security of the state governments; for each state has pledged itself to support every state government. If it were not for our union a powerful state might conquer its weaker neighbour, and with this addition of power, conquer the next state, and so on, till the whole would be subject to one ambitious state. (Webster, 1800, p. 151)

By the early 19th century, many of the trends and tensions that would characterize American schooling throughout its history had already appeared. From the time of those first schools in Massachusetts, beliefs about the purpose of education reflected beliefs about the nature of community and about how individuals should be shaped for communal life. To the extent that ties among people were seen as based on biblical faith, schooling involved shaping children along biblical lines in order to make them members of a sacred polity. As concepts of that polity evolved and shifted, so did views about the role and aims of schooling. The biblical Christianity of the Puritans gradually gave way to a more generalized Christianity that could, in the minds of some intellectuals such as Jefferson, run to deism. In addition, a society that was becoming increasingly pluralistic encouraged the development of an even more generalized system of beliefs, one that would reflect and attempt to transmit changing social and political ideals.

The contrast that we have presented, between Jefferson and Webster, illustrates one of the main tensions in those ideals, between localizing and centralizing tendencies. We can see each side of this tension in ideas about education. For education to become part of a national civic faith, though, the nation would have to move toward the side of Webster, and understand schools as places where a more perfect union could be achieved, and not simply improved localities.

In addition to a tension between the idea of the United States as a united set of states and localities and the United States as a nation, the early nation also saw debates and disagreements about the readiness of ordinary Americans for self-government. These debates and disagreements were closely connected to views about the extent to which the United States ought to be a centralized state. The radical democrats, such as the Pennsylvania political prophet Herman Husband in the 1780s, argued for government built up from immediate localities. Husband's scheme for government, which reflected in many respects Jefferson's scheme for education, involved county legislatures made up from representatives of each county town. These county legislatures would, in turn, elect state assemblymen, giving the balance of power to the farmers and artisans who comprised the mass of the American people. Husband believed that the most talented ordinary people would learn the art of government through practice. He maintained that the county legislature of his plan "would prove as a school to train up a learn Men of the best Sense and Principles the Nature of all publick Business and give them Utterance to speak to the same" (Husband, quoted in Holton, 2007, p. 171).

In contrast to this localistic, democratic perspective on the desirable government for Americans, the Federalist advocates of strong central government were deeply suspicious of the capacity of Americans for self-government and wanted a centralized state in part to control what the Federalists saw as the excesses of democracy. The same Noah Webster who included the Federalist Catechism in his spelling book was also deeply disturbed by what he saw as the growing assertiveness of American farmers. "Our states cannot be well governed," Webster declared, "until our old influential characters [i.e., the traditional American political elite] acquire confidence and authority" (Webster, quoted in Holton, 2007, p. 165). Along these same lines, a 1785 newspaper essay argued that "the main body of a people cannot be politicians. They have not leisure to attend to, opportunity to be informed of, nor ability to understand all that variety of matters, which concern the community" (*Hampshire Herald*, quoted in Holton, 2007, p. 166).

In the effort to establish the United States as a centralized state, education could serve two valuable functions. First, it could serve, as Webster suggested with his catechism, a creedal function. Given divisions over what type of state the new nation should be, schooling could help to spread commitment to a set of political ideals. Second, education could serve a transformative function. While the Federalists may have believed that ordinary people were unsuited to run political and economic affairs directly, they also accepted some level of participatory government, out of either pragmatism or genuine belief. If the people were not suited to political life as they were and if widespread political participation was desirable (or at least unavoidable), the answer was to transform the people to suit the aims of the new republic. Building a new people through schools became as much a part of the American national project in the first half of the 19th century as building new political institutions and a new transportation infrastructure. If the project of creating the nation through schools did not reach completion before the Civil War, it was because the nation itself did not reach completion.

GROWTH OF THE COMMON SCHOOLS

The common school movement, usually and somewhat arbitrarily dated from about 1830, was the precursor to the educational movements of the Progressive Era. The movement entailed efforts at achieving universality and uniformity, systematization, and centralization. "The common school movement," writes Robert L. Church (1976), "had three goals. The first was to provide a free elementary education for every white child living in the United States. The second was to create a trained educational profession . . . The third goal was to establish some form of state control over local schools" (pp. 55–56).

Massachusetts, home to the religiously oriented schools at the beginning of the colonial era and later closely identified with the common school movement through Horace Mann, was a leader in education as the first full century of the United States opened. "The State of Massachusetts," observed New York's *The Balance and Columbian Repository* in 1801, "besides making legal provision for common schools, has appropriated a township of new land to each county in the State, as funds toward the establishment and support of county academies" ("Schools," 1801, p. 101). Academies, as Kaestle (1983) explains, generally fell somewhere between modern ideas of public and private schools, involving payment from students and also some public support. In 1802, the *Massachusetts Spy, or Worcester Gazette* reported of the states of Massachusetts and Connecticut that "there is perhaps, in those two States a greater number of good common schools . . . than can be found in all the other States in the union. In almost every town, new settlements excepted, decent schoolhouses are planted at convenient distances from each other" ("On Education," 1802, p. 1).

Connecticut, cited along with Massachusetts as at the forefront of publicly available education, already had a history of publicly supported education by the beginning of the republic. "Very early in the settlement of Connecticut," proclaimed a speaker in 1805, "every town consisting of 50 families was obliged by law to maintain a good school, in which reading and writing should be well taught; and in every country town, a good grammar school was instituted. Large tracts of land were given, and appropriated by the Legislature to afford these schools a permanent support" ("From the Connecticut Courant," 1805, p. 2). The Connecticut legislature passed "An Act for Appointing, Regulating, and Encouraging Schools" in 1799. Through this act, the state's lawmakers specified the duties and powers of school societies for the funding and organization of schools (*The Courier*, 1799, p. 1).

Elsewhere in the Northeast, common schools had already taken root before 1830. In March 1823, the *American Mercury* of Hartford, Connecticut, reported of Maine that "there are already two colleges and from twenty to thirty academies endowed by the State. But the greatest efforts are directed to the common schools. Every town in the state is obliged to raise an annual tax, equal at least to forty cents on each of its inhabitants . . . There is throughout the state, one school house for every 200 of its inhabitants, making about 1500 in the whole" ("Education in Maine," 1823, p. 3).

In 1851, Samuel S. Randall, Deputy Superintendant of Common Schools in the state of New York, prepared a report on the state's common schools, covering the laws and regulations governing them and the history of the schools. According to a newspaper account of Randal's work, the first appropriation for state schools was in 1795 and the first report on schools to the state legislature was in 1798. In 1805, New York had created a permanent school fund from the appropriation of vacant lands by the state ("The common school system," 1851, p. 3). The superintendent of common schools in New York estimated in 1823, on the basis of reports from 649 towns and wards, that 351,173 children aged 5 to 15 were in school, out of a total of 357,029 children in that age group ("Schools in New-York," 1823, p. 1). By 1825, the state of New York had 7,832 common schools, educating over 400,000 students, with a fund for common schools of $1,739,000 and an annual income distribution of $98,000 ("Statistics of New-York," 1825, p. 2).

The view that universal education was a foundation of the moral order of civil society had already become commonplace in the years before 1830. Thus, Samuel Fletcher, in a report of the School Committee of Concord, Massachusetts, for 1822–1823, emphasized the importance of free schooling for the moral development of society. Fletcher observed that ". . . it is to our common schools we are to look for the security and happiness of our society . . . It is at school, more than any where else, that the habits of children are formed, their inclinations are directed, and their minds take those impressions which will determine their characters and mark the extent of their usefulness" (Fletcher, 1823, p. 3). Similarly, the *Vermont Gazette*, in Bennington, editorialized in 1825 that "our common schools are the stamina for liberty and contribute to the general prosperity and moral dignity of a community, in greater degree than any other single medium." The *Gazette* gave these schools an explicitly political function within the system of a republic: "From the frailty and infirmity incident to man, a natural aristocracy must more or less exist, and the most direct corrective, is to so dispose of the means of a community, as to afford all *equal opportunities* [emphasis added] to learn and understand their equal duties and their equal rights" ("Education," 1825, p. 3).

The dating of the common school movement to 1830 is thus more of rough recognition of when an existing social trend began to intensify than it is the identification of the beginning of a new collective effort. The interest in free, universal schooling and the identification with civic ideals could be seen throughout the union, though there were fewer calls emanating from the South.

When Horace Mann became first secretary of the new Massachusetts Board of Education in 1837, he became the symbol and spokesman of this growing commitment to schooling as the route to a new future. Mann gave voice to the view that schools could make a new world by making new people, evidenced in an exuberant passage in his journal:

> Let the common school be expanded to its capabilities, let it be worked with the efficiency of which it is susceptible, and nine-tenths of the crimes in the penal code would become obsolete; the long catalogue of human ills would be abridged; men would walk more safely by day; every pillow would be inviolable by night; property, life and character held by a stronger tenure; all rational hopes respecting the future brightened. (Quoted in Perkinson, 1995, p. 18)

The reasons for this heightened interest in education are unclear (Church, 1976). It is often maintained that responding to urbanization and the first 19th-century wave of immigrants were among the chief stimuli for a new interest in schooling. The immigrants and others in the cities had to be socialized into citizens and Christians (Perkinson, 1995). These explanations sound plausible, particularly in the light of later events during America's great age of urbanization and immigration at the end of the 19th century. These are unlikely to be the sole motivating forces for the common school movement, though. Table 2.1, showing percentages of white children aged 5 through 15 in schools at the end of the common school era, in 1860, should warn us against taking merely the influx of immigrants or the urbanization of the population as reasons for the spread of schooling.

Table 2.1. Percentages of White Youth Aged 5 through 15 in School, by State or Territory, 1860

	Percent in School	Percent Urban	Percent Immigrant
Maine	90.2	16.2	5.7
New Hampshire	88.3	20.8	5.4
Massachusetts	83.4	59.8	22.2
Vermont	82.3	2.9	10.0
Connecticut	79.2	26.8	16.2
Michigan	75.1	13.0	19.2
Ohio	74.5	16.7	14.6
New York	73.3	40.5	26.3
Pennsylvania	72.3	30.7	15.0
Illinois	71.2	13.5	19.0
Wisconsin	71.1	15.7	36.7
Washington	71.0	0.0	28.4
Rhode Island	70.4	70.0	26.7
Iowa	69.5	9.4	15.5
Utah	69.4	17.4	25.7
Indiana	68.9	8.4	8.7
Delaware	64.2	20.8	7.4
New Jersey	63.5	34.7	17.7
Oregon	61.5	5.2	10.7
District of Columbia	56.4	100.0	28.4
Missouri	55.3	17.0	14.9
Kentucky	55.3	11.9	7.1
Tennessee	52.9	4.8	2.4
Minnesota	52.7	11.9	31.3
California	51.4	20.0	39.7
Mississippi	49.5	3.4	2.3
North Carolina	48.4	2.2	0.6
Maryland	48.4	40.0	13.1
Alabama	47.5	6.6	2.5
Louisiana	47.4	48.8	23.8
South Carolina	47.1	10.2	3.2
Virginia	42.8	11.8	1.9
Kansas	41.1	11.9	9.4
Georgia	40.6	7.9	2.1
Nebraska	39.7	0.0	23.4
Texas	39.0	4.0	9.9
Florida	33.9	5.4	3.5
South Dakota	33.3	0.0	62.2
Arkansas	33.3	1.4	1.3
New Mexico	7.5	5.1	8.1
Oklahoma	0.0	0.0	7.8
Colorado	0.0	14.8	13.3
Nevada	0.0	0.0	31.5
North Dakota	0.0	0.0	13.6

Source: Ruggles et al., 2008.

Vermont, a highly rural state at that time, was one of the states that enjoyed almost universal education. Minnesota, with immigrants making up nearly one-third of its population, enrolled just over half of its children in schools. Maine and New Hampshire, which had some of the highest school enrollments in the country, had relatively small immigrant populations and showed very modest urbanization. One can say that urbanized locations and places with big immigrant populations (which often tended to be the same places) were generally more schooled than places with rural and native-born populations. The common school movement, one might say, was ideologically driven, rather than demographically driven. Demographic change was significant primarily for the part it played in the development of ideology. The movement grew out of the desire to shape a national community along political lines expressed in Noah Webster's spelling book and along moral ideals recorded in Horace Mann's journal.

As would be the case in the later Progressive Era, schools were part of a wider reform movement, which included missions to urban areas and revival meetings. "The effort toward providing public education for the nation's children, the common school movement," one author has written, "stressed the universal redemptive social purpose of education. Schooling became part of a national campaign, even though most of the reform programs were organized on the state level" (Church, 1976, p. 187). Education was the means by which the disparate parts of the nation would be drawn together on the basis of shared political ideals. Encouraging the improvement of common schools, an Ohio letter writer in 1839 declared that "if there is one principle that is more than any other identified with democracy, republicanism, and liberty, it is that of universal education" ("Common Schools in the State of Ohio," 1839, p. 3).

In the geographic center of the common school movement, schooling was particularly associated with civic ideals. A Mr. Winthrop, speaking at an agricultural dinner at Northampton, Massachusetts, exclaimed, "other nations may boast of their magnificent gems and monster diamonds. Our *kohinoor* is our Common School system . . . whose pure and penetrating ray illumines every brow, and enlightens every mind and cheers every heart and every hearthstone in the land . . . of every son and daughter of Massachusetts" (*New York Daily Times*, 1851, p. 4). The stress in Mr. Winthrop's elocution should, perhaps, fall on the last word, since he was talking specifically about the schools of Massachusetts, in contrast to the glories of "other nations," raising the regional question that we will look at in greater detail below.

As the nation drew closer to the Civil War, *Harper's Weekly* gave expression to the belief that American society was undergoing a great transformation and that schools and teachers should play a fundamental part in social change:

Would that a great heart could be put into American Education! We have no fault to find with the system as an economic thing. It is, as an apparatus of utilitarianism, admirable enough; but it is so easily satisfied, so serenely complacent over multiplication-tables, logarithms, and the manipulations of chemistry. The higher utility, which takes knowledge of man's deeper wants, is so painfully ignored. There is great need of reform here, and teachers must begin it; but side influence can not do it. Teachers are God's workmen. Parents may pay them; States may pay them; but Heaven claims them and their office. Teachers, too, are always the safest reformers. If they would combine and take hold of the heart of the American people, they could soon elevate the tone of Education. This is really a great desideratum. American society is rapidly organizing its permanent forms, and it is all-important that our standard of culture should be lifted much higher. ("Opening of schools and colleges," 1858, p. 627)

The ideology of the common schools aimed both at creating citizens ideally suited to their society and at using schools to shape an egalitarian society. In his famous 1848 report, Horace Mann professed a credo of the common school movement. "Under the Providence of God," he wrote, "our means of education are the grand machinery by which the 'raw material' of human nature can be worked into inventors and discoverers, artisans and scientific farmers, into scholars and jurists, into the founders of benevolent institutions, and the great expounders of ethical and theological science" (Mann, 1848/1957, p. 79). Schooling could be "the most effective and benignant of all the forces of civilization" because of its universality, its ability to reach all members of a new generation, and because its materials (children) are "so pliant and ductile" (p. 80). In his ambition to mold the future members of American society, though, Mann did not simply want to fit individuals into the status quo. Contrasting the United States with Europe, he argued that education is a means to obtain property, and therefore universal education can prevent the development of permanent propertied and laboring social classes by promoting what we would today call social mobility. "Education, then, beyond all other devices of human origin, is the great equalizer of the conditions of men—the balance wheel of the social machinery" (Mann, 1957 [1848], p. 87).

Although he strongly opposed the introduction of partisan politics into the schools, Mann did advocate a form of basic political indoctrination. He proposed "that those articles in the creed of republicanism, which are accepted by all, believed in by all, and which form the common basis of our *political faith* [emphasis added], shall be taught to all" (Mann, 1957 [1848], p. 97). Mann did not address the apparent tautology of arguing first that a universal education should shape all citizens and then arguing that only those political beliefs universally held should be taught in schools:

it seems to follow that the common basis of political faith that should be taught is whatever has been taught. His primary concern, though, was to avoid political conflict and controversy in schools, while also preparing young people for future political involvement. His school politics were like his school religion. Both were to be built on foundations that Mann thought were essential to the kind of republican society he wanted to build, and were therefore universal in character.

By mid-century, schools had become commonly identified as central to the role of divine providence in American life. Preaching a Thanksgiving Day sermon at the Broadway Tabernacle in 1852, the Reverend Samuel D. Cochran placed schools among the institutions contributing to a sacred American exceptionalism: "When, therefore, we look with the eye of Christian patriotism over our country, more and more thickly dotted with schoolhouses and other institutions of education; and then at our free press and free Government, both so stimulant to the acquisition of learning, we are constrained to say with profound gratitude, 'God hath not dealt so with any nation'" ("Thanksgiving sermons," 1852, p. 1). At the dedication of the State Normal University in Bloomington at the beginning of 1861, Illinois Governor Yates praised "our own bright Illinois, this heaven-favored heritage, this blooming Eden, this land flowing with milk and honey" and declaimed, "I point to American school houses and meeting houses as the citadels of freedom—the rock-bound foundations of American liberty" ("Address of Governor Yates," 1861, p. 2).

The connection between belief in schooling and formal religions was complicated. Many common schools did include Bible teachings in their curricula. The question of religious instruction in common schools was hotly debated, particularly with the increase of sectarian diversity created by the influx of Catholic immigrants into Northeastern centers of common schooling. New York City Board of Education President E. C. Benedict observed in 1852 that common schools had been criticized for not giving religious instruction. However, he argued "that there is no necessary connection between the elementary branches of Education and the doctrines of religion—that the proper agencies for religious instruction are the Family and the Church—and that no other course can be pursued than that which now prevails, unless the public is taxed for support of Sectarian Schools of every kind" ("Remarks of E. C. Benedict," 1852, p. 4). In general, despite a vaguely Protestant orientation in the common schools, there was a definite growth of the idea of the schools as temples of the republic, rather than as extensions of any church. Henry Barnard, second only to Horace Mann in the common school movement, gave voice to the image of schools as civic temples. Barnard, for example, called for a ceremony after each community had constructed its school:

In prayer, and in praise to the Giver of all good an Author of all being—in song and hymn and anthem, and in addresses from those whose positions in society will command the highest respect for any object in which behalf they may speak, and in the presence of all classes in the community, of pupils and teachers, of fathers and mothers, of old and young—the school house should be set apart to the social purpose of the physical, intellectual, and moral culture of the children who will [be] gathered within its walls. (Barnard, quoted in MacMullen, 1991, p. 138)

In the Northeast, at least, schools had become centers of civic ritual during the common school period. Children and teachers from 11 local schools assembled at Capitol Park for one such ritual in Albany, New York, in the early afternoon of September 26, 1851. Headed by Mayor Eli Perry, the Board of School Commissioners, the State and Deputy Superintendents of Common Schools, and a brass band, the students and teachers formed a procession that marched through the city streets to a grove near Trinity Church. After singing and speeches by selected students, student representatives from each school presented the commissioners with gilded volumes (the contents of which have not come down to us). The news article that reported this event hailed it as "another of these annual festivals which tend so powerfully to concentrate public interest upon our inestimable institutions of elementary instruction—the pride and boast of our State—the nursery of its future citizens—and the pledge of its continued greatness" ("School celebration at Albany," 1851, p. 2).

REGIONALISM AND LOCALISM: THE LIMITS TO NATIONWIDE SCHOOLING

If schools had indeed already become centers of civic faith during the first half of the 19th century, why not date the beginning of American civil religion through education to the 1830s or even the 1820s? The answer involves intertwined strands of ideology, geography, and economic and political development. Although the U.S. Constitution contains no reference to education, ideas about education were deeply rooted in views of the nature of constitutional government in the United States. Webster's spelling book, which we discussed at some length above, presented universal education as both a foundation to the Federalist conception of a political order and as a means of expressing and transmitting belief in Federalism. A democratic central government, as Webster and other Federalists understood it, required an educated citizenry. Through schooling, moreover, commitment to a Federalist system could be propagated among the public.

Jefferson's system was localistic and oriented toward providing informed independent yeoman farmers and an elite state leadership. Jefferson often did prove to be a nationalist and a pioneer of federal government in practice, especially after he became head of that government as our third President. However, as the primary figure of the Democratic-Republicans, he became the central representative for the rival ideology to Federalism, advocating an emphasis on state and local government. Significantly, the form of education he proposed was equal and universal only at the bottom rung, intended to let a natural aristocracy rise to state leadership.

All of the states in the new American nation posed challenges to the rise of a central government. The historian Andro Linklater has observed that "given Hugo Grotius's definition that the people constituted the nation, it was significant that someone as ardently patriotic as Thomas Jefferson should have consistently referred to Virginia as 'my country' in *Notes on the State of Virginia* in 1782. Even in the deepest crisis of war, New Jersey troops reporting for duty at Valley Forge had initially refused to swear allegiance to the 'United States of America' because, as they said, 'New Jersey is our country'" (Linklater, 2007, p. 44).

While state loyalties continued to exercise their attractions throughout the United States, regional differences, especially between North and South, encouraged variations in the appeal of national government and in social systems that would promote the type of uniform and universal education that would serve the egalitarian ideology expressed by the states that came to be identified most closely with the concept of strong national government. Support for widely available education became, along with advocacy of high tariffs to promote nascent industries and commitment to a market system of labor and exchange, a characteristic of the non-slave states.

It has long been recognized that the development of public schooling in the first half of the 19th century was slowest in the agricultural South, where the class system among whites and the division between slave and free prevented the spread of education and the kind of associated civic ideology expressed by Mann. In addition, the poverty of the South made it difficult for many Southern communities to pay for schools (Thayer, 1965).

Figure 2.1 indicates that there were wide variations in the extent of schooling by the eve of the Civil War. Not only was schooling not truly universal even where it was best established, it varied greatly across a land that had not yet been effectively welded into a single nation.

Most of the black children in the United States in 1860 were held in bondage and were often specifically denied access to education by law.

Figure 2.1. Percentages of White Children, Aged 5 through 15, Attending
School in Regions of the United States, 1860

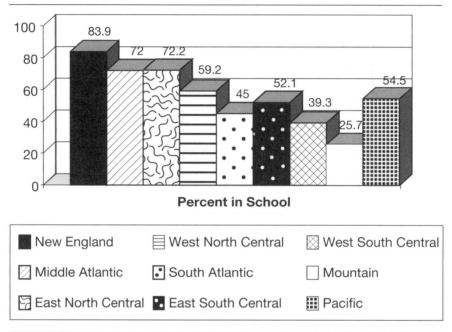

Source: Ruggles et al., 2008.

Free black children also had little presence in American schools, though.
Although it appears, in Figure 2.2, that New England had fairly large black
school enrollments, only 4.2% of school-aged free children in the United
States lived in New England in 1860. About half of the free black children
in the United States (49.3%) lived in the South Atlantic region, where only
a tiny percentage were enrolled in school. American schools not only were
legally forbidden from reaching the slave population, then, they also reached
very few children in the free black population.

Calls for common schools could be heard in the Southern states, as
well as in the others. Complaining that the academies were not reaching
all members of the poorer social classes, a writer in Georgia at the end of
1830 expostulated, "if the purity of our government, and even the government itself depends upon a free access to the door of knowledge by all
classes, a key to that door ought to be provided at the public expense and
not left to the uncertain contingency of individual providence or individual
caprice. The key is the *Common School* system" ("Education," 1830, p. 199).

Figure 2.2. Percentages of Free Black Children, Aged 5 through 15, Attending School in Regions of the United States, 1860

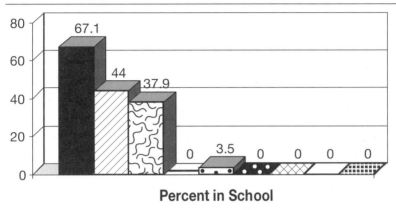

Percent in School

■ New England	☰ West North Central	⊠ West South Central
🗆 Middle Atlantic	⦂ South Atlantic	☐ Mountain
East North Central	⦂ East South Central	▦ Pacific

Source: Ruggles et al., 2008.

Still, the limited success of common schools in the South was often admitted by Southerners. One Georgia writer lamented in 1845, "the public lands of Georgia, a portion of which if applied to purposes of common school education, would have given us a system equal to any in the world in point of endowments, are all gone through the maelstrom of the lottery wheel and to the permanent benefit of few, very few" ("Education," 1845, p. 2).

As the debate over slavery intensified, the limitations of Southern education became a target for critics of the peculiar institution. The slaveholding South, argued these critics, lagged behind in widely available schooling because broad education was a trait of democratic systems. Slavery, they maintained with some justification, shortchanged poor whites as well as blacks by supporting an elite social system. Thus, the abolitionist paper *The Emancipator* declared in 1843 that "the system of Common Schools has not succeeded in a single slave State. Slavery and education are natural enemies. In the Free States, one in 53 over 21 years of age is unable to read and write; in the slave States, one in 13 is unable to write and read!" ("Slavery—the evil," 1843, p. 137).

Stressing the perceived link between democratic equality and education, "An Address to the People of Massachusetts" at the Free Soil State Convention in 1848 maintained, "in the Slave states, it is impossible that the constituencies, though mostly consisting of non-slaveholders, should be qualified for a proper exercise of the elective franchise, because it is impossible that there should be any system of general education, to prepare the elector for this momentous trust. It is not for the interest of the privileged class to open the door to their poorer neighbors for a competition with themselves, as there would be a danger of doing, if they should open common schools" ("An address to the people," 1848, p. 1).

The Southern abolitionist Cassius M. Clay remarked that he had come to the conclusion that the superiority of Connecticut over his native Kentucky was a result of "liberty, religion, and education," which were "the true foundation of individual happiness and national glory." Clay quoted Governor Hammond of South Carolina as having proclaimed in a message to the state legislature, "the Free School system is a failure. Its failure is owing to the fact that it does not suit our people or our government" ("Cassius M. Clay's address," 1845, p. 2). Accentuating the difference between North and South, the Reverend Henry Ward Beecher declared in an antislavery speech in 1855, "In the North we have *common* schools (accent on the first word in contradistinction to *select* or *class* schools). They are tending to even up society. The South may have schools but not *common* schools" (Beecher, quoted in "Anti-slavery lectures," 1855, p. 5).

Schooling, then, was closely linked historically to the idea of the Union during the Civil War. Both the real connections of the common school movement to New England and New York, and the image of schools as pillars of democracy and "citadels of freedom," made popular education one of the symbols of the republic, as seen in the non-slave states. The spread of schools became a sign of loyal participation in the social system of the Union. Writing from California in 1861, a correspondent for the *Chicago Tribune* summarized the current situation of the state. After assuring readers that Californians were solidly behind the Union in the new struggle between North and South, the correspondent described the state's economic potential and observed that schooling was important to California's progress: "Liberal provisions have been made for the support of Common Schools in this State. In this city [San Francisco], they are organized on a basis, that is calculated to make them equal in excellence to the Schools of the older cities of the Union" ("Our California correspondence," 1861, p. 2).

The associations of publicly available schooling, ideas of freedom and democracy, the unified nation, and civic rituals came together at events such as a celebration in 1864 by the New England Society of New York of the anniversary of the landing of the Pilgrims. There, a member of Congress from Baltimore proclaimed that "the immediate and uncompensated emancipation of 80,000 slaves *and the incorporation into Maryland of New-England common schools* [emphasis added] were some of the cardinal features of the reformation that was now in progress in that State" ("The Pilgrim fathers," 1864, p. 6).

The common school movement in the three decades before the Civil War helped prepare the nation for public schooling as a central part of individual and public life. It struck many of the themes that we consider articles of the American creed of education and it helped in the initial spread of schools. But this was not the time when education became vital to the national faith. Schooling did not yet have the geographic scope. It did not have sufficient reach into all areas of the country. It also did not reach very far into the lives of citizens. The great growth in education and in belief in education accompanied the rapid political and economic changes of the late 19th and early 20th century.

The United States would emerge from the Civil War, as Bellah noted in his discussion of American civil religion, with a new image of itself and a new mythology. Neither the image nor the mythology represented a complete break from the past, but a shift in national ideals. The Civil War itself became part of the national creed, *The Birth of a Nation*, as the famous and infamous D. W. Griffith film would have it. As schooling became for the first time practically universal and fairly uniform, the interconnected creedal and transformative functions of public schooling would increasingly serve a new industrial economy and an urban and immigrant society. In the Progressive Era, to which we now turn, schools would become both temples of civic traditions and vehicles for reaching out to changing visions of the Promised Land.

CHAPTER 3

Public Education
in the Progressive Era

THE PRELUDE TO PROGRESSIVE EDUCATION:
SPREAD OF SCHOOLING IN THE SOUTH

A S WE HAVE SEEN, Bellah understood the Civil War as a time of crisis that led to a new formulation of American civil religion. The decades following the war also saw enormous changes in the nation's economic and political life, and the full emergence of the public school in the form that would be familiar through the 20th century. After the war, public schooling became nearly universal in character, so that it could reach regions and elements of the population that had previously enjoyed relatively limited exposure to formal education. Given the expectations for free publicly available schooling as a preparation for citizenship and an initiation into the sacred values of the nation, which we saw growing during the era of common schools, we should not be surprised that schools became identified as the means of fulfilling the new promises of American life in the late 19th and early 20th centuries. Public schools became the institutionalized temples of American civic faith, containing and expressing beliefs that drew on earlier politico-theological traditions and reshaped those traditions in response to historical experiences of the nation.

The heightened emphasis on education and its extension to new populations began almost immediately in the postbellum years. During this time, the spread of schooling was frequently identified with the creation of a new society and new democracy in the South, as the nation faced the challenge of placing the Union on a new foundation. A California editorialist reported in 1867 that there was a revolution under way in the postwar South, where "the negroes themselves are not only permitted but encouraged to hold meetings for the consideration of public questions. In the city of Charleston—cradle of the rebellion—only a month since, they adopted resolutions in favor of the principles of the Republican party, and demanding a uniform system of public schools, to be supported by a uniform tax on all kinds of property" ("The Southern revolution," 1867, p. 2).

Reconstruction involved a missionary effort at schooling that prefigured the later American efforts in the Philippines, discussed in the Introduction. According to historian Eric Foner, for General Oliver Otis Howard, commissioner of the Freedmen's Bureau, education was the foundation of all of the bureau's efforts for the newly freed people of the South. Consequently, the bureau coordinated the actions of Northern societies, among them, notably, the American Missionary Association, which was sending teachers south to work with students directly and to train black teachers (Foner, 1988).

Foner argues that Reconstruction became "America's unfinished revolution" because it failed to provide the black population of the South with the economic basis for establishing independent livelihoods and therefore left Southern blacks vulnerable and dependent once troops were withdrawn. It is therefore interesting to note that programs for self-improvement through schooling were often favored over more radical approaches, such as redistribution of land or resources. In 1870, for example, the *New York Times* contrasted the economic plan for freedmen of prominent abolitionist Wendell Phillips with the educational plan of President Ulysses S. Grant. The view attributed to Phillips was "to furnish outright, at public expense, to each Negro or Negro family, a farm, a plough, mules, a season's supply of food and forage, seeds and agricultural supplies, [and] a thousand dollars cash." The *Times* described this plan as "preposterous." The newspaper instead supported President Grant's program, which was "to couple [education] to the freedman's vote," in order to teach "independence and the capacity for self-control," which would make the former slaves economically self-supporting and prepared for the rights and responsibilities of citizenship" ("The Freedmen's Great Want," 1870, p. 4). The idea that education was the answer to problems involved rejecting other possible answers, formulating solutions as matters of reshaping a society by reshaping individual people. In later years, much of the well-known debate between the complex and brilliant leaders W.E.B. DuBois and Booker T. Washington would revolve around the question of whether the situation of black Americans in the nation required their improvement through schooling (the answer publicly associated with Washington) or wider political involvement (the DuBois answer). Both popular attitudes toward blacks in the wider white population and the growing faith in education promoted the former response.

In addition to providing a means of preparing blacks for "indepen-dence and the capacity for self control" ("The Freedman's Great Want," 1870, p. 4), the education of the freedmen was frequently portrayed as a beginning for redesigning the whole of Southern society through the mis-sionary efforts of schools. Along these lines, while pressing for the exten-sion of public schooling to the freedmen of the South, an Iowa editorialist suggested that "the effect of educating the colored population has been to create an emulation among the white masses, who begin to perceive that without education they must soon fall far behind in the mental and moral race. It is hoped that when 'reconstruction' shall have been harmoniously accomplished, the Congress will make liberal grants of land for the en-dowment of thorough and uniform system of public schools in all the Southern States" ("Southern freedmen," 1867, p. 2).

As a result of the political goals of education, Reconstruction-era schools were often, to borrow a phrase from the 20th century, arenas of struggle. In New Orleans, on evidence from an investigation of the city's 1867 white riot against federally supported authorities, it was reported that "proscription of the friends of the Union has been carried into the public schools; teachers, male and female, have been removed where the teach-ing of the children was a framing in Union ways. Where Union songs have been taught the children and national airs sung within the schools, the teachers have paid the penalty of the offense by loss of place and employ-ment" ("The New Orleans riot," 1867, p. 3).

With the withdrawal of federal troops signaling an end to Reconstruc-tion in 1877, the schools remained. The ideological conflicts largely died out as white Southerners accepted the unified nation and the nation as a whole accepted segregation and the Jim Crow system. However, we can see education during the immediate postwar years as addressing the prob-lem of how to bring disparate populations together into a more central-ized nation through a gospel of citizenship. This effort would turn in a new direction as Americans turned to the question of absorbing new popula-tions from other parts of the world, and it would stimulate the develop-ment of new national myths and rituals.

IMMIGRATION AND AMERICANIZATION
THROUGH SCHOOLING

At the economic level, the decades from the Civil War to World War I saw the United States change from a mainly agricultural nation to a major industrial producer. In 1860, it was splitting into two warring halves, but by 1890 the United States had outstripped the leading industrial nations of Europe to become the world's foremost producer of manufactured goods (Jaycox, 2005).

The quickly developing industrial economy required workers, and the availability of jobs drew immigrants to American shores in unprecedented numbers and proportions, as shown in Figure 3.1.

This was an enormous growth in the foreign-born population that had a great psychological impact on the nation. Although the absolute number of foreign-born people was greater at the end of the 20th century, immigrants made up a larger proportion of the American population in the late 19th and early 20th centuries, when 15% of Americans were immigrants. Because of continuing immigration, moreover, another 15% of native-born Americans were children of two immigrant parents by 1910, and 7% of native-born Americans had at least one immigrant parent, so

Figure 3.1. Numbers of Foreign-Born People in the United States, 1850–1920

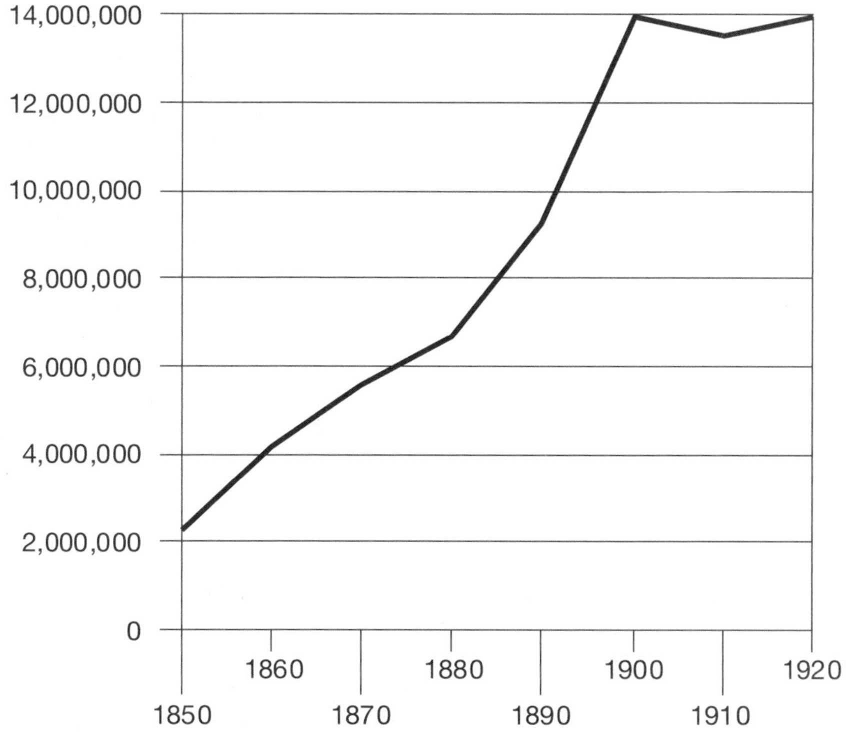

Source: Ruggles et al., 2008.

that immigrants and children of immigrants made up over one-third of the U.S. population (Ruggles et al., 2008).

The increase in the relative proportions of the immigrant population was even less notable, though, than the kinds of work they did, the places where they settled, and their countries of origin. The Dillingham Commission, set up by Congress in 1907 to study the perceived immigration problem, looked at 21 industries and found that 58% of the workers in these industries were immigrants. Immigrants were particularly predominant in construction work, railroads, textiles, coal mining, and meatpacking (Jones, 1992, p. 186).

Although immigrants to the United States came primarily from rural regions in their home countries, the concentrations in the job market drew them to the cities. As two commentators on "the immigration problem" observed in a work first published in 1911:

> The immigrants of the earlier day came to this country primarily with the purpose of becoming permanent dwellers; and a very large proportion of them, agriculturalists abroad, went to our rural districts, took up land, and became farmers here. Circumstances have so changed that the newer immigrants follow to a very great extent a different course. With the exception of the Hebrews, primarily from Russia, who are by compulsion city dwellers, the present-day immigrants likewise come from country districts where they have formed the rural peasantry and unskilled laboring class. Coming to this country, however, they find that our supply of free agricultural land is practically taken up, and that there is a strong demand for their labor, especially in our mining and manufacturing centers, at wages much higher than they have known in their own country, altho (sic) they may be low when compared with the American standard. (Jenks & Lauck, 1913, p. 27)

America in general was becoming more urban, but the new immigrants were the most urban of all in this changing society. By 1910, according to the Dillingham Commission, 79% of immigrants from southern and eastern Europe and 68% of immigrants from northern and western Europe lived in cities (Jones, 1992, p. 179). The former attracted the greatest attention from the Commission and, indeed, formed the basis of the Commission's invidious distinction between the more desirable "old" immigrants from the nations of northern and western Europe and the less desirable "new" immigrants from the nations of southern and eastern Europe. Numbers of the latter had grown dramatically during the late 19th century. In 1860, only 1.2% of foreign-born people had come from the southern and eastern countries. By 1910, this had grown to 37.5% of America's foreign-born (Jones, 1992, p. 178).

Densely concentrated in the growing cities and distinctly "alien" in the eyes of many American officials and older American citizens, the immigrant population raised the question of how they could be fit into the image of American society. Recognizing this increasingly urban concentration of immigrants, the *Chicago Tribune* told its readers in 1900 that "as these immigrants of today are going to settle in the cities and become dependent for their support on the industries carried out there, it is evident that increased responsibilities are being placed on municipal governments . . . There must be a more competent management of the public schools if all the children of the immigrants are to be Americanized. All fads must be sacrificed in the effort to make American citizens out of an increasing number of young foreigners" ("Modern immigration," 1900, p. 6).

Late-19th- and early-20th-century public statements on education consistently dwelt on the question of how foreigners in American society could be reconstructed to fit into American ideas of what that society should be. The Reverend Dr. Madison C. Peters of Philadelphia touched on this question when he preached his patriotic Thanksgiving Day sermon on the topic of "Assimilation of Aliens and the Duty of the Hour" in 1903. "There is nothing in this land that so wins the admiration of strangers and contains so much of promise for the future as our free school system. The children go in Germans, Irish, Poles, Russians, and so forth and come out Americans. There is no nation in the world where there is such a pressing need of enforcing the education and discipline of the common schools as the United States . . . The American school not only turns out men, it makes the American people" ("Patriotic Topics in Many Pulpits," 1903, p. 2).

At a time in which many officials and others in the native-born population saw the nation's immigration as a threat to its national unity, schools became the internal equivalent of restrictive immigration policies. In an article on compulsory education, the *New York Times* wrote in 1890:

> In its origin the common school system was simply the associated effort of parents who appreciated the necessity of education. With the increasing tide of immigration has come the danger of a large and alien population, ignorant of our institutions and foreign to us in all their ways of thinking. With the adult immigrants, our only protection is a greater stringency of the immigration laws. For an improvement in the second generation, which shall Americanize it, our chief reliance must be upon the common schools. That this reliance should not be vain, it is necessary for national self-preservation that the children of foreigners should become American by education. ("Compulsory education," 1890, p. 4)

Americanization through education and civic religious rituals were frequently the same. In 1901, Jewish children from Eastern Europe who were being prepared for entry into public schools by New York's Educational Alliance participated in a ceremony marking Washington's Birthday:

> The children, boys and girls varying between six and twelve years of age, filed into the hall shortly after 11 o'clock. In the procession were several large American flags, and miniature flags were pinned in front of the girls' dresses and on the coats of the boys. The exercises consisted of patriotic songs and recitations. There was a "salutation to the flag," and a little boy who had been in the country only two months gave a recitation to the memory of Washington . . . ("New York observes Washington's birthday," 1901, p. 7)

On the issue of Americanization in schools as a catechism in civic religion, one of the most illuminating sources is Mary Antin's autobiography, *The Promised Land*, published in 1912. Antin's book offers a fascinating account of national myth and ritual during the great wave of immigration at the end of the 19th and beginning of the 20th century. It also gives contemporary readers a clear view of the place of public schools in the national cult. Antin was born in the Jewish Pale in Russia, and her family suffered the hardships and persecutions of Jews in the anti-Semitic Czarist empire. Her father managed to scrape together enough for passage to America, where the family would find a better life, especially for the children. "With the children, he argued," Antin wrote of her father, "every year in Russia was a year lost. They should be spending the precious years in school, in learning English, in becoming Americans." For her part, Antin responded to her father's decision with an emotion that can only be described as ecstasy: "So at last I was going to America! Really, really going, at last! The boundaries burst. The arch of heaven soared. A million suns shone out for every star. The winds rushed in from outer space, roaring in my ears, 'America! America!'" (Antin, 1912, p. 162).

Once the family reached the new country, the schools became the route to entry into American society. Antin described her own transition from a foreigner to becoming an American by way of the public school, as a "miracle." In the school, the cult of George Washington was woven into the curriculum, as Antin's class took up the study of the life of Washington. Antin's reported response, even if it may be more exaggerated than that of the average immigrant student, illustrates the intensity of faith that American schools could sometimes instill:

> When the class read, and it came my turn, my voice shook and the book trembled in my hands, I could not pronounce the name of George Washington without a pause. Never had I prayed, never had I chanted the songs of

David, never had I called upon the Most Holy, in such utter reverence and worship as I repeated the simple sentences of my child's story of the patriot. I gazed with adoration at the portraits of George and Martha Washington, till I could see them with my eyes shut . . . As I read about the noble boy who would not tell a lie to save himself from punishment, I was for the first time truly repentant of my sins." (Antin, 1912, p. 223)

This intense sense of national feeling and worship of the nation found in Thanksgiving Day, Washington's Birthday, and other holy days of the state clearly connected with the beliefs of immigrants that they could find a kind of salvation in the new land, and the expressions of civic solidarity openly aimed at turning young immigrants and children of immigrants into believers in Americanism. While the desire to Americanize immigrants through schools was conscious and intentional, though, it was not cynical. The preachers were themselves, for the most part, adherents to a creed in which George Washington was more of a saint than a mere political and military leader, in which ordinary Americans could serve the sacred destiny of their land, and at the center of which lay the American school.

In the previous chapter, we saw that from the time of American independence until the Civil War, influential individuals from Noah Webster to Horace Mann developed ideas of schooling as ways of turning people into citizens according to ideas about the form of the ideal state. The belief in this ideal state, we argued, had a distinctly politico-religious dimension. With the rise in immigration, a large part of turning people into citizens became turning foreigners into Americans, and the politico-religious dimension of belief in the state and of the role of schooling in this belief became more intense and extensive. While immigration helped to drive the rise of public education as the center of the national cult, though, it was far from the only source.

THE SCHOOLS AND THE CULT OF THE NATION

The economic consolidation of the United States, which drew the new immigrant population and in which they participated, was matched by a growing political consolidation. It is often observed that prior to the Civil War, people spoke of the United States in the plural, as in "the United States are . . ." After the Civil War, the singular came into common usage: "The United States is . . ." Many of the political reforms of the Progressives reflect this increasing centralization. Even the basic structure of American government, the Constitution, changed in response to the growth of the American nation as a presence in people's lives and beliefs. The Sixteenth Amendment, passed in 1913, enabled the Federal government to collect income tax, since Washington, D.C. would need revenue if it were to play a more active part than it had in the past. The Seventeenth Amendment, passed in the same year, replaced election of U.S. senators by state legislatures with direct election. Washington's senators would no longer be representatives of their separate states, appointed by state governments. Instead, they would come directly from the people in their states to form a national legislative body. As national senators came to play a greater and more immediate part in the lives of citizens, the role of state legislators was accordingly reducing, shifting the power balance away from states and toward the nation as a whole (Rossum, 2006).

Economic consolidation had been stimulated by war spending, promoting the development of railroads, the steel industry, and big finance. Political consolidation had been stimulated by the expansion of federal authority required for warfare, as well as by the fact that the war had been fought, by the victors, in the name of a Union. Similarly, sacral ideas about a more unified polity began in the Civil War. The nation was seen as re-born out of the sacrifices of war. With a national economy tied together by railroads, a population growing from the influx of immigrants, and rapid urbanization, many saw this nation as reborn into a new world that faced both threats to its unity and opportunities to forge a new national existence. American civil religion sought to deal with the threats and challenges.

> Just as Thanksgiving Day, which incidentally was securely institutionalized as an annual national holiday only under the presidency of Lincoln, serves to integrate the family into the civil religion, so Memorial Day has acted to integrate the local community into the national cult. Together with the less overtly religious Fourth of July and the more minor celebrations of Veterans Day and the birthdays of Washington and Lincoln, these two holidays provide an annual ritual calendar for the civil religion. The public school system serves as a particularly important context for the cultic celebration of the civil rituals. (Bellah, 1967, p. 8)

The civil religion that came to be celebrated and expressed in the public schools was more than a ritual remembrance of sacrifice symbolizing national unity, though, and the public schools were more than contexts for cultic celebration. At the level of social organization, the schools went through the same process of expansion and consolidation as the nation's economic and political systems. At the level of culture, those who were thinking about the new phenomenon of the nationwide school system read into this school system the themes of rebirth and national integration and combined these with the much older theme of America as a Promised Land.

Indeed, the war itself was seen by many as a struggle between the darkness and social disorder of ignorance and the Promised Land of social order and political unity that could be created through schooling. Soon after the Civil War, Brown University president Francis Wayland announced to the National Teachers Association that "the Civil War had been a war of education and patriotism against ignorance and barbarism" (quoted in Perkinson, 1995, p. 35). In an address to teachers in Topeka, Kansas, in 1890, Professor J. M. Bloss proclaimed that the result of the Civil War had been not only to create a more unified nation, but also "to stimulate thought and to create a higher ideal of the possibilities of life and to give men new applications for culture." Professor Bloss attributed the growth of schooling directly to this stimulus of the war: "It is since the war that the public schools have had their growth . . . It is since the war, in this new era, that patriotism has been taught in our schools, colleges and universities. It is since the war that our high schools have been established." Professor Bloss announced to the educators that ". . . there is but one conclusion to be reached, that education gained a new birth amid the clash of arms . . ." (quoted in "Educational address of Prof. J. M. Bloss," 1890, p. 10).

New Ceremonies of the State Cult

The cult of the state, symbolized by the mythical figures of the Revolution and the Civil War, gave rise to a series of new ceremonial expressions in the late 19th century. Decoration Day, which later became known as Memorial Day, began to be celebrated in towns around the country soon after the Civil War to memorialize those who had died during the great conflict. Schools played a prominent part in the rituals. In Chicago, for example, by the 1880s, formal observance of the holiday took place in all public schools, with "essays, declamations, recitations, and songs" devoted to the ceremony ("Decoration Day," 1890, p. 2).

We have already seen the sense of almost mystical awe that the myth of George Washington inspired in young Mary Antin in the schoolroom. Proclaimed in Washington, D.C. in 1880 and 5 years later extended to the rest of the country, Washington's Birthday became the first federal holiday to memorialize an American citizen. The public schools across the nation became centers of this celebration. In the schools of Boise, Idaho, for example, by the beginning of the 20th century, on Washington's Birthday "public exercises were held . . . in all of the public schools of the city . . ." In Boise's Central School, "each of the 11 rooms carried out specially prepared programs of a patriotic nature. There were drills, recitations, compositions, debates and patriotic songs . . . In the various rooms the ceremony of repeating the pledge of allegiance to the flag was performed" ("Tribute to Washington," 1902, p. 8).

Flag ceremonies, in particular, took on a new importance in post–Civil War America, and in the schools they expressed and celebrated national ideals and unity. Indeed, as suggested by the role of the flag in the celebration of Washington's Birthday, flag ceremonies provided the core ritual for all of the civic observances. The *Sioux City Journal* in Iowa reported of the second annual Flag Day in that state that "the combination of this celebration with that of Washington's Birthday proved to be an apt one, for the life of Washington is full of incidents of patriotism and devotion to the flag, and innumerable lessons can be drawn from them. But the one feature of the observance which has made it more successful than any other is the pledge of allegiance which is given by all school children. With uplifted hands and standing erect, they unitedly vow their allegiance to the stars and stripes" ("Honor the Stars and Bars," 1896, p. 5). The myth of origin, flag worship, and the civic society of an industrial economy came together on Thanksgiving in 1890, when the Junior Order of American Mechanics presented three public schools in Philadelphia with national flags, to the accompaniment of what the *Philadelphia Inquirer* called "interesting and patriotic exercises," followed by a procession and speeches by public officials ("The turkey on top," 1890, p. 5).

The Pledge: An American Credo

Richard J. Ellis has noted in his history of the Pledge of Allegiance, "the War of 1812 and the Mexican-American War contributed to the flag becoming a more popular symbol of nationhood, but it was during the Civil War that the flag became the preeminent and hallowed symbol it is today" (Ellis, 2005, p. 3). Public schools were the primary setting for flag reverence, and the reverence was initially closely associated with a ritual that celebrated both the new economy of the late 19th century and American nationhood.

Fairs dedicated to displaying national industrial and technological achievements were national rituals that brought the idea of a newly emerging social order together with patriotism. The World's Columbian Exposition of 1893 (dedicated in October 1892), popularly known as the Chicago World's Fair, celebrated the Genesis story of the American nation by commemorating the 400th anniversary of Columbus's landing in the Americas. This event inspired American civil religion's version of the Nicene Creed, a fundamental formulation of orthodoxy, when former Baptist minister and editor Francis Bellamy wrote the Pledge of Allegiance for his Boston-based magazine *Youth's Companion* in honor of the world's fair.

The magazine had close ties to public schools. It had earlier campaigned to put an American flag atop every public school in the country. In recognition of the Fair, *Youth's Companion* organized a National School Celebration after being authorized to do so by Judge Charles Bonney, head of the fair's governing body. Bellamy set out to win support for the National School Celebration by seeking the endorsement of political and educational leaders. U.S. Commissioner of Education William T. Harris gave the project his wholehearted approval. In Albany, New York, Bellamy met with General John Palmer, Commander in Chief of the Grand Army of the Republic (GAR), underscoring the role of commemoration of the Civil War in the new national faith. Palmer gave voice to the idea of the public school as the fundamental institution of this faith when he exclaimed in support of the celebration, "The School is . . . the only thing that represents the nation to millions. It ought always to fly the flag!" (Quoted in Ellis, 2005, p. 15).

Bellamy and James B. Upham, a colleague at *Youth's Companion* who had been a moving spirit in the campaign to raise flags in schools, agreed that the flag ceremony at the celebration needed a vow of loyalty. Bellamy penned a short but stirring oath: "I pledge my allegiance to my Flag and to the Republic for which it stands—one Nation indivisible—with Liberty and Justice for All" (Quoted in Ellis, 2005, p. 19). (The phrase "under God," which brought American civic religion uncomfortably close to Judeo-Christian religion in the views of some and expressed the Judeo-Christian basis of American national life in the views of others, was added in the 1950s. It was a product of developments that will be considered in Chapter 5.) The Federal Bureau of Education was so taken with Bellamy's civic creed that it distributed it to teachers at public schools around the country. On October 12, 1892, millions of public school children participated in a national rite for the first time by reciting the Pledge. Over the century to follow, this rite would become standard. Every day at every school in the United States would begin with the Pledge (Jaycox, 2005, p. 37).

Reverence for the flag and education had become so closely intertwined by the opening of the 20th century that almost no educational activities could take place without the flag. At the 44th annual meeting of the National Education Association at Asbury Park, New Jersey, in 1905, "nothing but American flags was used for decorations, but of these there was such a profusion that the natural wood color of walls and ceilings was almost hidden" ("Thousands of teachers at opening session," 1905, p. 3).

FAITH, SCIENCE, AND THE NATION
IN PROGRESSIVE SCHOOLING

Bellamy was clear about the religious character of the pledge he created, often comparing it to the Lord's Prayer (Ellis, 2005, p. 123). His own creed, though, was a statement of commitment to the unity of a state, rather than an invocation of divinity. Bellamy, brother of the nationalist utopian writer Edward Bellamy, participated in the Progressive movement of his day. (Edward Bellamy's *Looking Backward, 2000–1887* (Bellamy, 1898) was one of the most popular books of its time. It envisions an America of the year 2000 in which society is held together by loyalty to the state and all social inequality has been abolished. It embodies one version of the Progressive dream of remaking society.) Progressivism was a complex movement, the various strands of which were twisted together by the idea that Americans should respond to the urban, industrial, economically interconnected, polyglot society they saw emerging around them by forging it into a new social order. Historian Richard Hofstadter (1955) famously argued that Progressivism was a middle-class reaction to the rise of new money. While there may be a great deal of truth to this observation from the perspective of social-psychological motivations, it is clear that Progressivism was not a reaction in the sense of denying the future or refusing to participate in social action oriented at making the future. In fact, Michael McGerr has convincingly argued that while Progressivism was indeed a middle-class movement, it was a movement by the middle class to remake all of America in its own idealized image. In McGerr's term, the Progressives aimed at "transforming Americans," at making them more abstemious, more responsible, more patriotic. Children offered a natural focus of this post–Civil War version of building a City on a Hill. "Confronting so many difficulties in changing adult behavior and transforming established social groups, reformers naturally found childhood an inviting target" (McGerr, 2003, p. 107).

Thus, the strands of reform known as Progressivism that attempted to create the new national unity expressed in Bellamy's civic creed were especially influential in the development of American public education. At the 1905 44th meeting of the National Education Association that we have referred to above, the connection of education to the rise of American nationalism came forward in a particularly aggressive form when the head of the NEA, New York City school superintendent William H. Maxwell, told his listeners that they should take Japan, newly victorious in the Russo-Japanese War, as an example of what could be achieved through education. Japan's defeat of Russia at Mukden and Port Arthur had taught "the lesson that the race which gives its children the most effective training for life sooner or later becomes a dominant race." Bringing in another strain of the Progressive ethos, Dr. Maxwell put forth schooling as the route to social reform, as well as the path to success in international competition. "The best corrective of the evils generated by the accumulation of wealth are not anti-trust laws or other repressive legislation, but a system of schools which provide a training for all that is equal to the best money can buy" ("Thousands of teachers at opening session," 1905, p. 3).

In his authoritative book, *The Transformation of the School: Progressivism in American Education, 1876–1957* (1961), Lawrence A. Cremin details how the Progressive movement shaped schooling in America. He maintains that the movement began to grow in the decades right after the Civil War. By 1900, in his account, the movement had acquired wide appeal among intellectuals. It gathered momentum around World War I and subsequently dominated the educational profession. Cremin sees the movement as breaking apart and ultimately disappearing after World War II. Our own argument, presented in the following chapter, will be that American schooling went through another transformation after World War II, but one that received, reworked, and passed on in new interpretations fundamental sacred assumptions in Progressivism.

The Underlying Unity of Trends in Progressive Education

One of the earliest trends to emerge in Progressive education was the "new education," later known as "child-centered education," which had spread widely in educational circles by the 1870s (Reese, 2005, chapter 3). Rooted in romantic ideas of nature and personal authenticity, child-centered teaching concerned itself with the liberation of the individual from binding social constraints. The child-centered advocates tended to deemphasize memorization, abstraction, and book learning.

Child-centered education was explicitly individualistic and liberationist in character, but it was profoundly oriented toward social reform and toward the efficiency of science. "Like the other reforms such as temperance and antislavery . . . the new education sought the alleviation of pain and suffering, moral and intellectual advancement, and social stability and uplift," writes William J. Reese (2005, p. 81). The individualistic orientation of child-centered Progressivism was a new version of the old teaching that the City on a Hill could be built by cultivating the virtuous natures of individuals who would make up the city (Cristi, 2001, p. 49). For all its romanticism, the child-centered version of Progressive education was also in touch with the scientific (or scientistic) orientation of an urban, industrial society. By teaching children in a manner consistent with their natures, child-centered educators sought to teach them in a way that was empirical, in the sense that teaching would be based on psychological reality, rather than on abstractions. Object teaching was the method most often advocated to achieve this pedagogy, which was at once utopian in its dream of personal liberation and concrete in its strategy. Children were to be taught by placing objects in their hands and by teaching them how to use things, rather than from books alone. This was education that was, in the truest sense of the word, manual.

The emphasis of child-centered education on manual learning linked it with another side of Progressivism in educational theory. The emerging industrial nation needed a new workforce, people who would fit into jobs in an increasingly elaborate division of labor and who would be socialized to work together in a new, efficient social order. Teaching through objects easily became vocational education. Teaching according to a child's nature easily became teaching according to a child's position in the social order.

The Faith and Science of Schooling

These philosophies of education responded to the growing centrality of public schooling in society. As we have seen, the common school movement of the prewar era enunciated the themes of American civil religion, and those active in this movement often put schools forward as the places where the ideals of the national faith could be realized. But it was only after the war that public schooling took its place as a national institution at the center of American life. Schools in the decades of the end of the 19th and beginning of the 20th century reached more children and occupied a bigger place in their lives than ever before. School attendance among both black and white children increased rapidly, so that percentages of all children in school grew from 53.4% in 1870 to 79.8% in 1920 (Ruggles et al., 2008), as shown in Figure 3.2.

In that half-century, public schooling became the common experience of people throughout the nation, and the vast regional differences had become small. The emerging theories of education were more than just ideas, they were plans for social organization that could tap into elaborate institutions.

Americans in the Progressive Era celebrated the growth of schools as the growth of the American nation itself. Along these lines, the *Santa Fe Daily New Mexican* in 1892 proclaimed both the enormously expanded role of the public schools in post–Civil War America and the greatly heightened expectations Americans placed in this institution: "Thirteen million pupils are now enrolled in the public schools of the United States—that is, *there are more than* [emphasis in the original] three times as many pupils as the entire population of the United States in 1800. The entire population in 1830 was 12,866,000; there is consequently a larger nation of children in our free schools than the whole nation of sixty years ago. These 13,000,000 pupils are one fifth of our present population of 65,000,000. There are something over a million more in private and pa-

Figure 3.2. Percentages of All Children(Aged 5–15) and White and Black
Children Attending School, 1870–1920

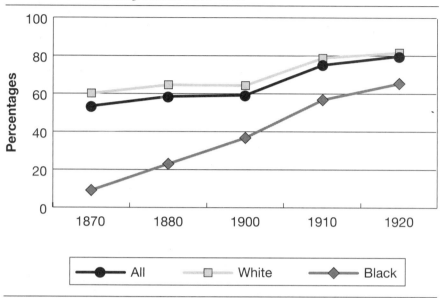

Source: Ruggles et al., 2008.

rochial schools. But it is this nation of our free school youth, this nation
within the nation, that will be controlling the republic fifteen years from
now. These 'children of the states,' imbued with our characteristic American spirit, will soon be the leaders of the people who are to solve the problems of the opening years of the coming century" ("The public school map,"
1892, p. 3).

"By 1918 elementary education was virtually universal," notes Sol
Cohen in the introduction to the Progressive Era volume of his documentary history of American education. "High schools, in 1890 confined largely
to the cities and more affluent rural areas, were by 1918 a well-accepted
part of American education" (Cohen, 1974, p. ii). Schooling had not just
become much more common during the late 19th and early 20th centuries, it had become much more uniform across the American landscape.

The growing importance of schools in American society made them
natural locations for the inculcation of the civic faith expressed in
Bellamy's pledge. The children of the immigrants, enrolled in schools,
could be incorporated into the national unity. "Education," in the words
of a pre–World War I New York high school principal, "will solve every
problem of our national life, even that of assimilating our foreign element"

(Higham, quoted in Crawford, 1992, p. 83). Non–Anglo Americans born within U.S. boundaries could also be "Americanized" through the ever-spreading school system. With the simultaneous admittance to statehood of New Mexico and Arizona, the U.S. government instructed the two new states to establish, as a part of their state constitutions, "a system of public schools, which . . . shall always be conducted in English" (Crawford, 1992, p. 52).

The social transformation of the immigrants and native minorities that we have examined above was part of the broader project of Progressive Era education that aimed at the transformation of American society itself. It was a project that grew out of an ardent faith fused with organizational and scientific rationality. Diane Ravitch (2000) has argued that child-centered and social efficiency approaches were two parts of the same underlying view of pedagogy, and she sees both as responsible for a decline in American education. The child-centered Progressives and the social efficiency Progressives continued to be two sides of emerging thought and practice in education, but the social efficiency side generally won out in application. In developing their approach to education, the most influential Progressive educators combined a belief in the power of systematization and rationalization with the religious fervor of a doctrine of social salvation. John D. Philbrick, one of the early educational systematizers, argued in 1885 that "modern civilization is rapidly tending to uniformity and unity" and maintained that these would be characteristics of an effective school system. The effective school system, in turn, would shape America's urbanizing society along the lines of a better world: "The future of our cities will be largely what education makes it and the future of our country will be largely what the cities make it" (Philbrick, quoted in Tyack, 1974, p. 40).

School administrators of the late 19th century had a passion for creating educational order that would produce social order. William T. Harris, school superintendent and the U.S. Commissioner of Education who had so enthusiastically backed Francis Bellamy and the National School Celebration, has been described as "the outstanding intellectual leader in American education in the years between the death of Horace Mann in 1859 and the emergence of John Dewey as a spokesman for the new education at the turn of the twentieth century" (Tyack, 1974, p. 43). Harris argued that the school had emphasized order and punctuality above all other virtues, since these would be traits that would improve the industrial society (see Callahan, 1962). These were precisely the kinds of virtues, inculcated through schooling, that Dr. Maxwell had seen at the flag-draped NEA meeting in 1905 as stimulating Japan's exemplary rise to international power.

Along with bureaucratic efficiency, new scientific models of human behavior and human learning constituted a parallel trend in the rationalization and systematization of education. The psychologist Edward L. Thorndike, from the very beginning of the 20th century, became one of the most celebrated exponents of a scientific approach to learning. In 1898, Thorndike published pioneering studies of stimulus and response in learned animal behavior. Based on this, he developed "laws of learning" that, with further experimentation, he extended to human students. Not only should students be taught in the ways discerned by scientific experimentation, according to Thorndike, educators should be concerned with the scientific measurement of what is learned:

> Education is concerned with change in human beings: a change is a difference between two conditions; each of these conditions is known to us only by the products produced by it—things made, words spoken, acts performed, and the like. To measure any of these products means to define its amount in some way so that competent persons will know how large it is, better than they would without measurement. To measure a product well means to define its amount so that competent persons will know how large it is, with some precision, and that this knowledge may be conveniently recorded and used. This is the general *Credo* of those who, in the last decade, have been busy trying to extend and improve measurements of educational products. (Thorndike, 1918, reprinted in Cohen, 1974, p. 2247)

Thorndike was expressing in the language of science and systematization the Progressive belief in the transformation of Americans by means of education. (The idea that science is a form and expression of religious faith is not a new one. See, for example, Noble, 1997, and Midgley, 1992.) It is revealing that he referred to his educational philosophy as a "credo," for the participation of schools in the civil religion of the Progressive Era went beyond conveying faith by means of rituals such as Bellamy's pledge. The belief that schools should change society by changing the people in the society made education a central part of the faith itself.

For all of the language of stimulus and response, the faith in education was one of intense and lasting fervor. As one scholar of Progressive education has observed, "the chiliastic hopes that characterized movements for social reform in the Progressive era survived in the 20s in the field of education. School reformers were like lay or secular preachers who sought to reform the world by means of the reeducation and training of children. School reformers were possessed with a vision of new schools producing a new American man and a new era" (Cohen, 1974, p. xix).

This vision of remaking society placed education at the core of developing American social scientific thought. In 1896, pioneer sociologist

Albion W. Small spoke to the National Education Society about the educational approach required by sociology. Approaching the issue from what he saw as the perspective of the social sciences, Small spoke in visionary and almost millennial terms. He expressed his view of teaching as a means to the radical reconstruction of society: "Sociology demands of educators, finally, that they shall not rate themselves as leaders of children, but as makers of society. Sociology knows no means for the amelioration or reform of society more radical than those of which teachers hold the leverage" (Small, 1896, reprinted in Cohen, 1974, p. 2188).

Progressive education reached its apogee in the well-known work of John Dewey. Although Dewey later criticized Progressive educators, particularly those on the extreme of the child-centered wing, he was not rejecting Progressive education, but a schooling that he felt was insufficiently systematic and, importantly, not sufficiently directed toward social goals (see Dewey, 1926, 1959). In Dewey's career, we can find the fundamental unity of the child-centered and social efficiency wings of Progressivism. "Here [in education] individualism and socialism are one," Dewey wrote in 1899. "Only by being true to the full growth of all the individuals who make it up can society by any chance be true to itself" (Dewey, 1899, p. 13). Like Thorndike and Small, Dewey maintained that the social sciences should guide education. Moreover, the school should present an education relevant to the social development of children. When Dewey established the Laboratory School at the University of Chicago in 1896, his goal was to make the school itself a community and his laboratory's experiment was to be simultaneously shaping individuals and also socializing them to become the elements of a better American society. "Dewey looked to the schools," Sol Cohen has observed. "to provide the necessary social discipline and cohesion necessary to national unity" (Cohen, 1974, p. xiii).

Dewey's belief in the school as a laboratory for designing society led him to enthusiasm for another nation's experiment in social millenarianism later in his life. In 1928, Dewey visited the Soviet Union. He was inspired by the USSR's efforts to make schools centers for the socialization of children in building a new social order (Dewey, 1928a, 1928b).

By World War I, public schooling had been established and become compulsory throughout the United States. Just after the war, in 1919, Stanwood Cobb led the formation of the Progressive Education Association (see Cremin, 1961, pp. 240–271). Teachers College at Columbia University, founded in 1887, became an institutional center of Progressive education (see Cremin, 1961). Promoted by educational psychologists, sociologists, and philosophers, progressivism obtained such a thorough predominance in American schooling during the first half of the 20th century that in 1938 *Time* magazine declared of the Progressive Education Association, "no U.S. school has completely escaped its influence" (quoted in Cremin, 1961, p. 324). As the Pledge of Allegiance had become an accepted daily ritual in American schools, so, too, had the view that schooling meant the socialization of students to create a better society become a common educational doctrine.

Although most Progressive educators intended socialization through education to serve the goal of a democratic polity, as well as a unified one, the process of socialization was clearly in the hands of elites. Diane Ravitch has described the formative period of Progressive education as "the age of the experts" (Ravitch, 2000, pp. 88–129). Americanization, child-centered development, social efficiency, and cultivation of patriotism were dimensions of social transformation all to be directed by social scientists, professional administrators, and authorities. The school plan of Gary, Indiana, was one of the most notable illustrations of professional management of the pursuit of the Promised Land of social order. Described by journalist and Progressive visionary Randolph Bourne in 1916 as the "most complete and admirable application" of John Dewey's philosophy of education, (Bourne, 1916, p. 144) the Gary plan was largely the work of a single administrator/social experimenter, Gary school superintendent William Wirt. Wirt completely redesigned the Gary schools, organizing each school as a community. Wirt's "platoon system," an idea adopted by many other school districts, involved rotating students among classrooms, workshops, and other facilities. While Wirt's plan to extend the school year to the full 12 months did not spread widely, the Gary plan was greatly admired by progressive educators, and elements of it did take root in American school administration (see Dewey & Dewey, 1916/1962; Strayer & Bachman, 1918, for contemporary views of the Gary system). While the Gary schools did not set a pattern that all schools would adhere to in the following years, they did demonstrate the kind of social order that would be pursued through public education. It would be an order pursued through the socialization of students according to the blueprints of educational experts operating as social engineers.

THE BEGINNING OF ACTIVE FEDERAL INVOLVEMENT

The final element of education as civil religion was the beginning of the active involvement of the Federal government. We have argued that the pedagogical creed that arose in the late 19th and early 20th century was explicitly directed toward a centralized state. Francis Bellamy had students pledging themselves to "one nation, indivisible." The Americanizers wanted to blend immigrants into a single political culture. Educational thinkers, most notably John Dewey, thought schooling should produce national unity. This does not mean, of course, that all those concerned with education had the same ideas about the kinds of national unity they wanted to create, but we can see a common thread running through their ideas on schools and the state.

If Progressive education contributed to the development of national unity and allegiance to a centralized state, the centralized state also began an increasing involvement in education. In the period before the Civil War, the federal government had involved itself little in matters of education, despite the nationwide ambitions of the common school movement. The Department of Education came into existence in 1867, inspired by the effort to spread education to the South that we described at the beginning of this chapter. As the war years receded and Reconstruction came to an end, the department was downgraded to the Bureau of Education, within the Department of the Interior, and its primary function became the collection of statistics on American schools (Church, 1976, p. 127). However, while education remained under local control, Progressive calls for greater federal involvement began to result in some action by Washington, D.C. as the 20th century began.

The federal involvement was limited and small-scale for the first half of the century. In 1912, Congress established the Children's Bureau, initially part of the Department of Commerce and Labor and transferred to the Department of Labor the following year [the "Act to Establish the Children's Bureau (1912)" is reprinted in Cohen, 1974, p. 2357]. The Children's Bureau, charged with oversight of matters concerning the welfare of children, proceeded in 1919 to call for minimum standards of school health, including school sanitation, adequate recreation facilities, school medical care, and maintenance of health records of students [see "Children's Bureau Calls for Minimum Standards of School Health (1919)," reprinted in Cohen, 1974, pp. 2359–2360]. Two years before that, Congress provided federal funds for the support and promotion of vocational education with the Smith-Hughes Act ["The Smith-Hughes Act (1917)]," reprinted in Cohen, 1974, pp. 2364–2368). This initial growth in federal involvement with education was modest. Even by 1930, the White House Conference on Child Health and Protection would be recommending only "the minimum essentials of a school program," still concentrating on the health of children, rather than on issues of school curriculum or administration ["The Minimum Essentials of a School Program (1930)," reprinted in Cohen, 1974, p. 2554]. This very small-scale Federal response to education, which had become a nationwide phenomenon, may appear anomalous to us today. The effort to establish the American Promised Land through schooling was still mainly an effort of national nongovernmental organizations, such as the Progressive Education Association, working through local school boards and state agencies. Nevertheless, these early Federal efforts set the stage for much greater and more ambitious activities later in the century. When the government in Washington began to play a greater part in education, the view that schooling would be the answer to all social problems and would build a better society was already well established.

SCHOOLS AT THE CENTER OF CIVIL RELIGION

In the late 19th and early 20th centuries, schools took a place at the core of the American civil religion in two respects. First, they were means of conveying beliefs about the nation. Flag ceremonies, the Pledge of Allegiance, national celebrations, and reverential narratives of the founders became standard events in American public schools, which served as churches of the American civil religion. Second, public schooling itself took a key position in the American creed. Schools would create national unity; they would enable individuals to develop their talents according to their natures; they would train citizens for a democratic society; they would socialize an efficient workforce; they would create a new and more perfect society.

The faith in education that moved to the center of American civil religion during the Progressive Era never disappeared. Schooling expanded as a part of the U.S. experience, particularly during the years after World War II, and the belief in what schooling could and should do became an even more deeply rooted part of the national creed. Nevertheless, the challenges faced by the country changed over the years, and as the challenges changed the nature of the faith shifted.

Between the two world wars, the United States went through a period of entrenchment and institutionalization. Its industries settled into established corporate organizations through the 1920s and the difficult years of the Depression. As we discuss in the next chapter, the civic faith in schooling established during the Progressive Era also became institutionalized and increasingly oriented toward socializing students toward the corporate society. Although sectarian debates about the nature of the Promised Land to be created through education appeared, the different perspectives were rooted in a common creed of schooling as the means of realizing the special American destiny.

CHAPTER 4

Public Schooling Between World Wars: Management, Design, and Varieties of the Faith

SCHOOLS IN AN INDUSTRIAL SOCIETY: A COMMITMENT TO ORGANIZATION

BY THE END OF World War I, many of the economic and social trends that had helped to create American public education had reached fulfillment. The period between the two world wars, therefore, was a time of stabilization and institutionalization of the educational system created during the Progressive Era. Since this institutionalization occurred as American society was settling into an increasingly corporate, bureaucratic form, moreover, organizational efficiency became the hallmark of interwar education.

The 1920 census was the first in American history to show a majority of Americans living in urban areas rather than rural areas (U.S. Census Bureau, 1990, Table 4, p. 5). The nation had made the transition from a republic of farmers to one of city dwellers, people who lived and worked in an organized, industrial setting. From 1914 to 1927, wage earners employed in factories producing products valued at $5,000 or more grew in number from 6,895,000 to 8,350,000 and the value added by manufacturing nearly tripled, from $9,708,000 to $27,585,000 (U.S. Census Bureau, 1930, Table 802, p. 791). By 1937, nearly 14% of all wage earners in manufacturing were working in establishments that employed over 2,500 workers, and three-quarters of American manufacturing wage earners were employed by businesses with over 100 workers (U.S. Census Bureau, 1940, Table 827, p. 803).

The immigration that had pushed the growth of American cities, industries, and public schools was now coming to an end. With immigration acts in 1917, 1921, and 1924 and two Supreme Court decisions in 1922 and 1923, the United States severely restricted the numbers of immigrants who could enter the country and implemented national origin quotas to draw the smaller numbers of new arrivals primarily from northern and western Europe. The Immigration Act of 1917 extended the earlier Chinese Exclusion Act by creating a zone of barred immigration, including Asia and the Pacific Islands. The Tydings-McDuffie Act of 1934 effectively excluded immigration from America's own colony in the Philippines. As shown in Figure 4.1, immigration to the United States dropped dramatically over 4 decades from its peak at the beginning of the 20th century.

The efforts to restrict and manage the growing variety of the nation's population had grown out of Progressive Era concerns about immigration and out of wishes to deal with these concerns through rigorous mechanisms of social control.

Similarly, the nation attempted to design mechanisms of social control to purify the lives of those inside the country. With the ratification of the Eighteenth Amendment in 1919, Congress prohibited the manufacture, sale, and distribution of drinking alcohol. The United States was going to redesign itself by planning, with ideas about achieving a better (and less diverse) society providing blueprints for the design. Even after the end of Prohibition, issues of managing and designing what was now an urban, industrial society dominated thoughts about the direction of American society.

Figure 4.1. Immigrants Admitted to the United States, 1900–1940 (in Thousands)

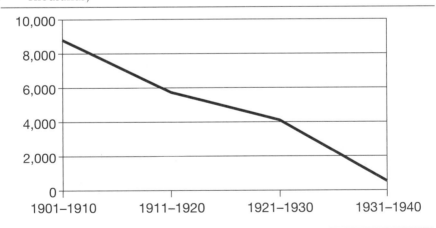

Source: U.S. Department of Homeland Security, 2003.

The commitment to management and design found expression in the movement known as Taylorism. The term takes its name from engineer Frederick Winslow Taylor, who is credited with pioneering this entirely new field of "scientific management" in business (Kanigel, 1996). Taylor believed that work tasks of specific jobs should be scientifically studied so that the optimum and most efficient way of performing a given job in the least amount of time and with the fewest motions could be determined and taught to the worker (Taylor, 1911). He advocated the time-and-motion studies that were the legacy of the efficiency movement within industry, with every motion of some factory jobs studied in intricate detail to determine how a worker could most efficiently carry out his or her job with a minimum of wasted time, movement, and energy. Taylor (1911) believed that there was only one best way to perform a particular job, "and this one best method and best implementation can only be discovered or developed through scientific study and analysis" (p. 25). Taylor also championed innovative ideas about the efficient administration of businesses, advocating for a top-down, hierarchical division of labor. Taylor argued for a clear separation of management from labor, with trained engineers and managers making all of the decisions about production goals, objectives, and methods.

Taylor's influence was felt far and wide during the interwar years and just after, not only in business, but in schooling and government as well. School administration was greatly influenced by Taylorism, and his scientific approach to efficient organization and production was incorporated into the ways schools were set up and operated (Callahan, 1962). The corporate society created by the United States, guided by planning and the elaborate division of tasks, included schools as the universal organizational setting for youth. Sol Cohen, in the introduction to his documentary history of American education, notes that "one of the outstanding achievements of the 20's and 30's was to make high school education almost as universal as the preceding 100 years had made elementary education" (Cohen, 1974, p. xxiii). Within this vast new reach, the impact of Taylorism could be clearly seen. Robert and Helen Lynd, in *Middletown* (1929), observed that "the school, like the factory, is a thoroughly regimented world. Immovable seats in orderly rows fix the sphere of activity of each child. For all, from the timid six-year-old entering for the first time to the most assured high school senior, the general routine is much the same" (p. 188).

The factory approach to schooling was a large part of American education of the interwar period, and it was accompanied by further developments of the national rituals that we saw in the previous chapter. This kind of regimented and ritualized schooling can be seen as one of the directions created for education by Progressive Era trends in planning and nationalism. Another direction, also emerging from Progressive Era trends and in many ways closer to the spirit of John Dewey, can be seen in the work of educational thinkers of the interwar period. Progressives were often critical of the regimentation and the ritualization that now characterized educational practices. Nevertheless, these thinkers shared with their more conservative counterparts a fundamental faith in educational planning as a means of realizing visions of the American dream.

TRADITIONAL AND PROGRESSIVE IDEOLOGIES IN THE INTERWAR PERIOD

The regimented schools that most closely mirrored the factory model observed by the Lynds followed what was referred to as a "traditional" or "conventional" curriculum, which focused on basic courses with few frills delivered in a standardized fashion (Aikin, 1942). Progressive schools of the era, conversely, had more varied curriculum and a more holistic, integrative approach to educating children that took into account their interests. The goal of both types of schools, however, was to produce a citizen with the requisite characteristics for participation in the American experience. Moreover, educators of both tendencies believed that the "outcomes" of both types of schools were measurable on objective instruments, such as tests of knowledge and skills.

One of the raging debates in education during the 1920s and 1930s concerned which of the two types of schools—traditional or Progressive—was the most successful in educating students. In order to gather objective evidence to answer this question, the Commission on the Relation of School and College, established by the Progressive Education Association, launched the Eight-Year Study in 1933 (Aikin, 1942). Seeing no disparity between the holistic, child-centered educational philosophy and the ability to objectively measure educational outcomes, the Progressive Education Association commissioned educator and measurements expert Ralph Tyler to help lead this famous comparative study (Tyler, 1987). Ralph Tyler's contribution to curriculum, testing, evaluation, and measurement in education during the 20th century cannot be overstated. He popularized the "Tylerian" evaluation method, which emphasized the development of clear objectives for programs that could be easily and unambiguously measured, and helped formulate the educational objective to be measured in the Eight-Year Study: how well traditional and Progressive schools prepared their students for success in college. His approach has been codified into both curriculum and program evaluation theory, and is still widely used and taught (Fitzpatrick, Sanders, & Worthen, 2004). Tyler would eventually go on to help develop the National Assessment of Educational Progress (NAEP) during the 1960s, which is still the most important K–12 test for comparing the performance of students across states and, in the 21st century, ultimately became a requirement, under the No Child Left Behind act, for all states receiving federal funding.

The two types of schools, traditional and Progressive, rooted in two ideological approaches to education, were both expressions of a large-scale, bureaucratic school system that accepted the idea of the planned society and the school as a site for social planning. They were, in addition, variations on the now-established view that the ideals of American life could be achieved through mass public education. In practice, many "progressive" ideas ran through the traditional schools and through conservative educational ideologies, since public schooling had seen so much of its growth during the Progressive Era. Moreover, there had been a strong strain of nationalism and even isolationism in the Progressive Movement, which had emerged during a time of national growth and unification. On the other side, even the most critical educational thinkers of the time between the world wars held fundamental beliefs about the destiny of American society. Most Americans, moreover, mixed the two perspectives on education that we will look at now, holding both that schools should teach adherence to a sacred state and that schools should be the means of realizing the Promised Land of America's future.

EDUCATION FOR PATRIOTISM
AND SOCIAL PROPHYLAXIS

Rituals of adherence to a sacred state became stronger and more entrenched in schools during the period between the two great wars of the 20th century. While these rituals were not widely recognized as expressing religious faith, and, in fact, were sometimes specifically denied to express any such thing, they bore all of the characteristics of a state cult. Schools and school administrations devoted themselves to canonized founders, to rites of communal belief, to holy days and sacred processions. The perception of threats from the outside intensified demands for membership of all in a community of believers. Underlying these ritual aspects of schools was a highly organized system of public education that had come to include almost all Americans from early childhood to the late teenage years, based on the planning and organizing of a corporate society. School was firmly established as the way that people became Americans and as the way that America would reach all of its collective goals.

Most schools and most school administrators adhered to what might be regarded as the traditional or conservative side of American faith in education. Schools were regarded as places where the future could be planned by imbuing the young people moving through the factorylike systems described by the Lynds with the creed of Americanism. At the same time, and from the same roots in the Progressive Era emergence of the schools, some thinkers closely associated with the Dewey tradition in education raised questions about schools as subjects and vehicles of the American faith. The intellectuals who put their credence in social education carried on the tradition of seeing schools as the places where the realities of national life could be redrawn according to plans of an ideal future.

With schools now accepted as a means of organizing American society around widely accepted beliefs and practices, the institutionalization of their rituals became ever more formal in character. School life was imbued with reverential practices and occasions. A cult of the Founding Fathers, for example, became ever more entrenched in educational practice. We can find an illustration of this in New York in 1926, when Superintendent of Schools William J. O'Shea declared something of a patriotic holy week by calling for public schools to observe "Patriots' Week" from February 12, Lincoln's Birthday, to February 22, Washington's Birthday, with special emphasis on February 17, the birthday of Thomas Jefferson. On Jefferson Day, "all students will simultaneously repeat the 'Patriot's Pledge of Faith,' bells will be rung, patriotic songs will be sung, and subjects of patriotic interest will be interspersed through the regular class work" ("Patriot's week to be observed," 1926, p. 3).

A decade later, Dr. Frank W. Ballou, superintendent of schools of Washington, D.C., released an eight-page report outlining the teaching of patriotism in the district's public schools early in 1937. The *Washington Post*, summarizing the report, approvingly told its readers that "the 90,000 boys and girls being educated here are taught to revere their country" ("Star-Spangled Banner still floats," 1937, p. 3). The numerous ways in which patriotic attitudes were inculcated in the pupils included 2 minutes of silence every Veterans Day at 11:00, "observance of special days and weeks," and "pilgrimages by history classes" to locations such as the Tomb of the Unknown Soldier ("Star-Spangled Banner still floats," 1937, pp. 1 & 3).

By the end of World War I, the nondenominational state cult of American civil religion entailed sacred objects and places (the flag and monuments), a set of rituals based on those objects and places, martyrs and holy ancestors (the dead of American wars and the Founding Fathers), sacred days of commemoration, a creed (the Pledge), and a strong sense of the transcendent nature of the nation. This cult had become firmly established in the schools, and generally raised few objections from the major denominations and sects in the country. However, there were some conflicts. Richard Ellis (2005) recounts that the clashes between dissenting faiths and the state cult centered on the Pledge of Allegiance. A small religious sect known as the Jehovites entered a legal battle with the school board of Denver, Colorado, in 1926. The Jehovites refused to let their children participate in the Pledge on the grounds that this constituted worship of an idol. The stand of the sect was highly unpopular, defying what had become firmly entrenched in the public understanding as an affirmation of commitment to national solidarity. However, defended by the American Civil Liberties Union, which had been founded 6 years earlier, the Jehovites managed to have their children quietly readmitted to school without the requirement of saying the Pledge or saluting the flag.

Other small religious refusals to participate in the state rituals continued through the 1920s and into the 1930s. Deeply ingrained as these rituals had become, the majority Christian population of the United States did not recognize the curious parallels between the religious nonconformists and the Christian martyrs of the pre-Constantine Roman Empire, who had been persecuted (albeit much more seriously) for refusing to take part in the rituals of the Roman state. The big legal battle over the Pledge only began in 1935, though, when the Jehovah's Witnesses took on the school boards that were requiring what the Witnesses saw as a form of political worship.

On May 14, 1935, Massachusetts Governor James Curley signed into law a statute requiring that "each teacher shall cause the pupils under his charge to salute the flag and recite in unison with him at said opening exercises at least once each week the 'Pledge of Allegiance to the Flag'" (quoted in Ellis, 2005, pp. 91–92). The head of the Jehovah's Witnesses, Joseph Rutherford, compared the Pledge and the salute to the flag to the legally required salute to Hitler in Nazi Germany, a comparison that was all the more uncomfortable because the American salute to the flag was at that time performed with a lifted arm. After a Massachusetts youth from a Jehovah's Witness family was expelled from school, a string of further refusals and subsequent expulsions followed around the country. Some of the students were severely beaten by their teachers. A number of teachers who refused to take part in the ceremony lost their own jobs. Government officials reacted to the Jehovah's Witnesses' stand by pushing even harder to enforce the pledge. In Pennsylvania, the refusals to salute and pledge allegiance to the flag led the state to make it mandatory that all public school teachers force their pupils to take part in the rite ("Flag salute mandatory," 1935, p. E7).

The Supreme Court eventually ruled in *Minersville School District v. Gobitis* (1940), with only Justice Harlan Stone dissenting, that states and school boards could require students to take part in the Pledge. The *Washington Post*, lauding the decision, opined that the United States did not support a state church and ". . . with our complete separation of church and state, there can be no religious or anti-religious implications in a salute to the flag." "Freedom of religion," the newspaper declared, "extends only to the realm of spiritual belief and ritualistic practice" (Oakes, 1940, p. 6). The *Post* clearly did not regard the Pledge as a "ritualistic practice."

Why would the flag ritual have become so important both to the American public and to American public officials? In the developed industrial setting of the post–World War I United States, with its limited immigration, unified national government, and large-scale corporate business practices, patriotic practices seemed ways of protecting the nation from insidious foreign influences. For many Americans, Americanization in the schools increasingly meant inculcating beliefs that would protect young people from the lure of alien heterodoxies more than bringing aliens into an American orthodoxy. The new society that Americans wanted to continue erecting following the bloodletting of World War I was not the one envisioned by their internationalist president, Woodrow Wilson, who had guided them through the Great War. Rather, most Americans wanted a society that had as little to do with the intrigues of Europe (characterized by Thomas Jefferson as "Egypt," in contrast to America as a new "Israel") as possible. Though most Americans didn't share Wilson's version of idealism with an associated vision of a new world order under multinational leadership, they were no less fervent in their belief that America should continue building its City on a Hill, only one with higher walls and a deeper moat.

The rise of the Communists in the Russian Empire, soon renamed the Union of Soviet Socialist Republics, in 1917 gave new impetus to isolationist views of American destiny. After the discovery of a plot to mail bombs to prominent American political figures in the spring of 1919, U.S. Attorney General A. Mitchell Palmer launched a series of mass arrests and deportations of immigrants suspected of being foreign radicals. Even after the Red Scare ended in 1920, the ideology of Americanism continued to be tinged by a deep mistrust of radicalism, associated with foreign ideas and influences, and by the conviction that cultivating American ideals involved protection from un-American subversion. The view of education as a way of building the ideal society became blended with perceived threats to the American political system, and the combination permeated popular culture and official statements. "There are too many Bolsheviki around teaching youth misleading and wrong things about our institutions and our country," declared New York Police Commissioner Whalen in 1930, arguing that foreign subversives were menacing American schools.

"We need no foreign propaganda here as a substitute for those things we believe in; which our Constitution guarantees and which we shall maintain" ("Whalen says reds menace schools," 1930, p. 23).

Public attitudes toward education repeatedly expressed the importance of education for creating a national orthodoxy. Along these lines, in a 1937 speech, Mrs. A. B. Conger, president of the Georgia Federation of Women's Clubs, gave voice to the blending of public education as a means of building the ideal democracy through shaping citizens and as a means of defense from threatening ideologies. Warning against socialism and Communism as "foreign born isms" that could become "dry rot" in an indifferent nation, Mrs. Conger called for "education for citizenship" that would enable Americans "to reach the promised land of a greater civilization in a real democracy." Mrs. Conger declared that "there is much to be done in establishing a planned and orderly society, and it is the youth that will help shape the society." This meant that "for the youth we must have a public school system that educates the whole child. It must co-ordinate mental, moral, and physical training to produce a worthwhile citizen" (Stafford, 1937, p. 14).

The emergence of Fascism and Nazism in Italy and Germany created another source of foreign-born isms, one that would prove much more immediately threatening than the danger on the left and eventually push the United States out of its isolationism. Indeed, this alien heterodoxy on the right pushed Justice Felix Frankfurter to vote with the majority of the Supreme Court in permitting officials to require the Pledge and salute to the flag in schools. Seeing the coming of the struggle with the right-wing dictatorships, Frankfurter believed that national solidarity would be critical for the United States to face its foreign enemies and that "national unity is the basis of national security" (Frankfurter, quoted in Ellis, 2005, p. 103).

FAITH IN SOCIAL EDUCATION:
INTIMATIONS OF THINGS TO COME

One effect of the legacy of Progressive education was to firmly establish the idea that schooling was the way in which American society could reach the fullness of its ideals. As we have seen, the Progressives, in largely creating public schooling in the United States, did not make the system *ex nihilo*, but drew on a long heritage of ideas about civic life, ideas that had taken a definite institutional form in the years following the Civil War. We can see the period between the two world wars largely as a continuation of Progressive education, and this is exactly how many educational theorists of the time, such as George Counts and Harold Rugg, saw schooling in their own day. Just as the period of the common schools contained many of the elements of the schooling that would emerge after the crisis of the Civil War, though, the interwar period contained some of the trends that would achieve greater prominence with the crisis of the post–World War II civil rights era. Among these latter trends was a certain critical stance toward a system of schooling that did not seem to be fulfilling the promise of American life, accompanied by skepticism about American institutions. This skepticism, especially provoked by the Great Depression, was frequently a part of a wider questioning of American institutions, another trait that would be seen in the civil rights era. Questioning of American institutions led critical intellectuals to see the aspect of civil religion that had become so prominent in public education. At the same time, though, this did not undermine their faith in schooling as the way to realize America's sacred destiny.

Prominent among the critical intellectuals of the interwar period, the "social reconstructionist" George S. Counts recognized and was critical of schooling as civil religion in American society during the 1920s and 1930s. In his 1930 book *The American Road to Culture*, Counts described the popular faith in the school that he saw at that time:

> This faith in the potentialities of the individual has gradually taken the form of a faith in education. The Americans regard education as the means by which the inequalities among individuals are to be erased and by which every desirable end is to be achieved. Confront practically any group of citizens with a difficult problem in the sphere of human relations and they will suggest education as the solution. Indeed this general belief in the general beneficence of education is one of the fetishes of American society. Although the processes of tuition may be but obscurely understood by the popular mind, they are thought to possess something akin to magical power. Perhaps the most striking aspect of this phenomenon, however, lies in the fact that education is identified with the work of the school. As a consequence the faith in education becomes a faith in the school, and the school is looked upon as a worker of miracles. (Counts, 1930, p. 17)

If Counts was perspicacious about belief in the school, he was equally clear-sighted, and equally critical, of the beliefs taught by the school. He observed that "during the period of the Great War and the years immediately following, the public school in the United States became a powerful engine of patriotism, spread military propaganda among the masses, and served generally to promote an intense form of national solidarity" (Counts, 1930, p. 115). Counts objected to the militarism of much of American education, to the presentation of the American nation as above criticism in all respects, to the images of the Founding Fathers as beings of superhuman wisdom and insight, and even to the saluting of the flag. He saw these kinds of reverence as turning attention away from the real conditions of life.

Counts was a keen analyst of American society, and he recognized that public schooling had become a state church by the 1920s and 1930s. His prominence in educational thinking certainly indicates that this type of criticism was not completely alien to the intellectual currents of the day. Still, the officials and administrators of schools operated as adherents of the engine of patriotism, not as skeptics. Counts and his fellow theorists were influential commentators on schools of their time, but they did not control day-to-day educational practice, which was more likely to be carried out by proponents of pledges, pilgrimages, and processions.

Despite his criticisms of faith in schooling and of schooling as a means of propagating a public faith, though, Counts still adhered to a belief in schools as the route to a social ideal. He rejected education as a means of fulfilling the unfettered potentialities of the individual, but devoted himself to education as a means of fulfilling the potentialities of society. While he took jaundiced views both of popular faith in public schools and in the kinds of patriotic rituals pushed by mainstream administrators such as Superintendent O'Shea, Counts still believed that people needed to be transformed in order to be suited to the vision of the American future, and that schools were the places for the transformation. In his pamphlet, *The Schools Can Teach Democracy*, initially delivered as an address before the Progressive Education Association on Washington's Birthday in 1939, Counts argued that the proper business of schools was to create a democratic society through cultivating "democratic habits, dispositions, and loyalties," as well as relevant political knowledge in students (Counts, 1939, p. 22). Through schooling, "the entire nation would be subjected to the most critical examination for the purpose of revealing submerged and exploited regions, occupational groups, and racial, national, and religious minorities" (Counts, 1939, p. 26). This was an ambitious educational goal for a man who questioned the general belief in the general beneficence of education. Counts maintained that educational programs should not simply reflect the social order. Instead, they should direct the social order. The belief in education that he professed on the national holy day of Washington's Birthday was of a more transcendent order than that of the conservative educators he criticized, but it was a less ritualized and more Puritan form of reaching the City on a Hill.

Counts's colleague Harold Rugg showed a similar cast of thought. The 1939 volume *Democracy and the Curriculum*, written by 10 progressive educational thinkers, including Counts, and edited by Rugg, argued for an approach to curriculum design that amounted to a redesign of American society. Rugg said of the curriculum designer that "not only must he be a sociologist and statesman, philosopher and educational technician; he must also be a competent student of individual physiology and psychology" (Rugg, 1939, p. 12). While Rugg acknowledged that this was a difficult challenge, he declared that he and his colleagues were ready to undertake it "heartened and guided by the conviction that, with the creative resources within our grasp, we can bring into existence on the North American continent a golden age of abundance . . . democratic behavior . . . and integrity of expression" (Rugg, 1939, p. 14).

Rugg continued to voice his commitment to curriculum design as a grand plan for achieving the promise of American life throughout his career. Just after World War II, in *Foundations for American Education* (1947), Rugg argued for a comprehensive approach to curriculum design that would aim at the transformation of individual Americans and their entire society by bringing together sociology, psychology, esthetics, and ethics. In Rugg's schema, curriculum design was virtually the design of a new world, and not just the planning of desirable knowledge and skills. He maintained that this should be achieved through "a nation-wide program of education which will reach from childhood to old age" (Rugg, 1947, p. xiv). Reaching into the phrases that had inspired the nation toward an earlier version of the Promised Land, Rugg declared that bringing prosperity to the entire world through cultural unity and a coherent program of life and education was the new "Manifest Destiny" of America (Rugg, 1947, p. xv).

Rugg's own foundation, then, was a transcendent faith in the complete transformative power of schooling. Although the faith was generally implicit in his writing, at times it often became explicit. In discussing "the problem of religion," for example, Rugg argued that "each of these— the religious affirmation and the scientific hypothesis—has its indispensable role in our School. Let us not fear to use them both—the realm of faith and belief and the generalizations of documented observation and of scientific thinking" (Rugg, 1947, p. 683). The religion Rugg wanted in his revealingly capitalized School was not any particular Judeo-Christian faith, though, but the non-denominational "religion of Man and the Universe . . . a religious mood that grips the sensitive man, that gives him a deep feeling of awareness of the beauty of manifold forces that, whether we are aware of it are not, play their role in moving the universe and mankind with it" (Rugg, 1947, p. 682). At heart, Rugg was more than a believer in education as a means to build the ideal society; he was a mystic of the curriculum.

One should keep Rugg's mysticism in mind when considering his teleological vision of the development of American education. Rugg saw education as moving from the subject-centered orientation of pre-Progressive public schools to the child-centered orientation of the Progressive Era. Although he acknowledged the social concerns of the latter, particularly in the Dewey School and its successors, he believed that schools through the 1920s largely lacked a sound sociological foundation. Rugg argued that society-centered foundations for schools became established by the early 1930s. The Depression, he argued, gave an impetus to social planning, and he maintained that "in the decade after 1929 the *social engineering mind* [emphasis in the original] was given a conspicuous role in government" (Rugg, 1947, p. 578). This mind flowed into education. The Teachers College Discussion Group involving Rugg, George Counts, and several others was formed in the late 1920s, and in the 1930s gave expression to the social engineering mind in education through the publication of *The Social Frontier* and the John Dewey Society for the Study of Education and the Culture. Rugg's own thought by the late 1940s was the extension of this teleological progress, extending the role of education into the design and planning of every aspect of the individual and the society.

The conservatives and the Progressives largely agreed on schooling as a way to shape citizens for the society of the future. For both, that society was corporate and bureaucratic in character. However, in a manner fascinatingly reminiscent of Catholic–Protestant or high church–low church controversies, they disagreed on whether the focus of faith should be the ritual manifestations of an existing institution or the abstract glories of a future paradise. They agreed that education should socialize students in order to inoculate Americans against dangerous heterodoxies, but the social progressives, like Justice Frankfurter, saw fascism, not Communism, as the primary ideological danger facing the nation.

THE SINGLE FAITH OF TRADITIONAL AND PROGRESSIVE EDUCATORS

Despite the criticism of the worship of the Founding Fathers voiced by George Counts and other socially progressive educators, they often called upon this same set of civic beliefs for the sacred foundations of their own version of the Promised Land. Criticizing public education for failing to meet its social obligations, nine members of the John Dewey Society of Education and Culture were reported to have declared in 1937 that "in opposition to the 'social role' intended for it by the Founding Fathers, the American public school system has supported the status quo." In addition to playing a more active role in shaping a just society, the nine educators called for teachers to help preserve civil liberties to protect the nation against the encroachments of fascism ("Schools failing," 1937, p. 19). They apparently did not detail exactly where the prescient Founding Fathers had presented intentions for the school system that did not exist in the late 18th century.

The social progressives of the interwar period often took a critical position on the now firmly entrenched state cult in the schools, but they also drew on the fundamental faith in education as the way to reach the renewed and purified society. George Counts, in particular, was a complex thinker who at once acknowledged the tendency of Americans to believe that problems could be solved through schools and argued that schools could be starting points for the reconstruction of the entire society. Above all, the social progressives were fired by an intense belief in the social role of education that evoked some of the ideas about the goals of free, publicly available schooling that had been expressed ever since the era of the common schools.

At heart, the conservative and the progressive elements of the interwar period embodied sectarian tendencies within the civic faith of public education. The former emphasized catechisms and rites that would create solidarity with the nation-state forged in the decades between the Civil War and World War I. The emphasis in this tendency was the purification from citizens of alien and subversive heterodoxies. The latter emphasized the purification of the nation-state itself, the purging of all inequalities and injustices from its ultimately ideal democratic design. The social progressives of the time certainly did not reject belief in national unity or in public ceremonies: note that Counts delivered the text of his pamphlet on Washington's Birthday and the somewhat anachronistic evocation of the Founding Fathers by the members of the John Dewey Society. But the emphasis of the progressive intellectuals of the interwar years lay on the invisible tenets of the idealized future, rather than on the fetishized ceremonies of the present. Counts, Rugg, and their associates were more conscious of the civil religious aspects of American public education than most of their contemporaries, but these followers of Dewey were also more ambitious and far-reaching in their dedication to schooling as a way of remaking the nation.

American schools would continue to be places where students learned to revere the Founding Fathers, to celebrate national holy days, and to recite Bellamy's Pledge. Formal education would extend even further through the population and dominate even more years of citizens' lives. Also, though, at the end of the 20th century, many of the visions of the social progressives would become part of the mainstream of educational thinking as the national civil religion reached its next great turning point.

The decade and a half following World War II would see dramatic expansions in American education, reworking and solidifying the belief in schooling as the way to reach the American Dream. In this period, as we will see in Chapter 5, the Cold War drove the idea of education as a way to promote national solidarity to a high pitch of intensity. At the same time, the very expansion of the role of education in the economy and society contributed to an egalitarian ethos that would begin to become paramount in the 1960s.

After World War II: The Education Boom, Cold War, and Growing Calls for Equality

THE POSTWAR ATTENTION TO EDUCATION

EDUCATIONAL critic Diane Ravitch (2000) has characterized the 1950s as the time of "the Great Meltdown" in American schooling, when the socializing approaches of Progressive thinkers finally began to lose their hold. In his classic work on Progressivism in American schools, Lawrence A. Cremin (1961) identified the 1950s as the end of the Progressive Era in education, pointing in particular to the demise of the Progressive Education Association in 1955. Both Cremin and, later, Ravitch saw popular reaction against life adjustment education, schooling as a means of socializing students to fit into an existing or ideal corporate society, as the key feature of this popular rejection of Progressivism.

There is a substantial basis to this view of the first full decade following World War II. The 1950s were indeed a time when the educational thinking of Harold Rugg and his colleagues came under steady criticism, and when the pressures of the Cold War began to push schooling in new directions. There was, however, also a great deal of continuity as well as change in the role of education in American life before and after the war. The institution of the public school remained the first answer to every problem faced by the nation, and the goal of employing schools to socialize the public for idealized futures took altered forms, rather than disappeared. Rituals of national solidarity, such as celebrations of the Founding Fathers and the Pledge of Allegiance, were carried over from the first half of the century, taking on an even greater importance.

The educational debates during the 1950s, as recognized by Cremin and Ravitch, were ultimately the result of old convictions that schooling should be the answer to all national, social, and individual problems at a time when education was particularly critical to the economic and ideological life of the nation. Schools became subject to multifarious and often contradictory expectations. Schools would make students cooperative participants in collective enterprises, but they would also promote individual upward mobility. They would promote equality of opportunity, but they would be the engines of unequal distribution of rewards. They would spread a common curriculum, but they would be sources of diverse and specialized technical skills and knowledge in a society with an elaborate division of labor. They would create a generally informed citizenry for democratic participation, but they would produce political and cultural elites. They would inculcate national solidarity and intense patriotism, but they would also foster independent and critical thinking. The 1955 report *Public Education and the Future of America*, produced by the Educational Policies Commission of the National Education Association, described the great demands to be placed on public schools:

> One prophecy can be made about the new educational cycle—its demands on both teachers and pupils will be very great. According to the report, schools will need to provide "The traditional fundamentals of knowledge. A wide range of factual information. Social know-how of living, including attitudes and skills in teamwork, initiative, honesty, personal hygiene, common courtesy, ability to use mass media with judgment. Mechanical know-how of living, including driving of motor cars and handling of all the machines and tools on which a society is materially dependent. Practice of citizenship, including the making of decisions on complex national and international questions. The schools also will be expected to do more to develop the gifted, to train leaders, and to maintain traditional moral values." (Lindsay, 1955, p. 12)

This question of how American schools could serve all of their multiple purposes simultaneously drove one of the major inquiries into schooling during the 1950s, James Bryant Conant's *The American High School Today* (1959). Conant acknowledged that the unique feature of American schooling was the fact that the development of practical skills, specialized preparation for both professional and liberal arts higher education, and universal training for citizenship all took place within the same institution, the comprehensive public high school. Therefore, how to juggle these competing demands in a manner consistent with the existing institutions of teaching and learning became the central issue for Conant.

Americans had already come to see schooling as the path to their nation's special destiny during the first half of the 20th century, but after the war their visions of that destiny were directed by new political and economic forces. Behind the tendency to see education as everything to everyone, and to fault it for falling short on any of its contradictory tasks, four interconnected developments were pushing schooling to an even more prominent part in national affairs. First, the economic structure of the nation was changing. It was shifting from a blue-collar base to a white-collar one, with increasing proportions of people involved in the technical design and management of information and in the distribution and control of resources, rather than in the factory production of resources. This created a greater demand for people with technical and managerial skills. Second, in the post–World War II environment, in which the United States had emerged as an economic and military superpower, the federal government became more actively involved in education, especially at the higher levels. This contributed to the enormous growth of tertiary education, and it tended to make higher education more than ever before the explicit goal of elementary and secondary education. Third, the postwar political environment, which consisted of an intense, global ideological rivalry between the United States and the USSR, encouraged a passionate sense of defensive nationalism, and a corresponding dedication to the cult of the nation, for which schools had become the primary temples. Finally, in the first episodes of what would soon become a major shift in perspectives on national goals, the United States began to attempt to address its legacy of inequality, especially racial inequality, through the schools.

EDUCATION IN THE ECONOMIC SUPERPOWER

The United States had become a major industrial producer in the decades between the Civil War and World War I, the time when public schooling largely took shape in this country. It emerged from World War II as the world's unrivaled economic superpower. The nations of Europe had been laid waste, but, despite some initial signs of stalling just after the war, the conflict had only stimulated American productivity. The recession of 1948–49 and two succeeding recessions during the 1950s (in 1953–54 and 1957–58) did not entail drops in output or national income, but simply slowdowns in the rate of the nation's continuous economic expansion (French, 1997).

Figure 5.1 shows the gross national product (GNP) of the United States in constant 1954 dollars. After bottoming out in 1933 at the depth of the Depression, the GNP began climbing upward again and passed the 1929 level by 1940. During the war years, as the nation poured finances and efforts into the military and war industries, productivity climbed sharply. When the war ended, many were worried that the country would plunge back into depression, or at least experience a serious recession. The demobilization of soldiers would remove a major source of employment, and

Figure 5.1. Gross National Product of the United States, 1929–1959
(in Constant 1954 Billions of Dollars)

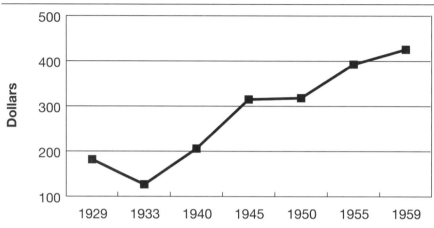

Source: U.S. Census Bureau, 1960.

a slowdown in the production of tanks, warships, planes, weapons, uniforms, and other tools of war would cause the economy to falter. As the new job seekers failed to find work in a slowing economy, they would be unable to purchase goods. An insufficient market for goods would lead producers to cut back and lay off employees, resulting in a downward spiral.

As we can see in Figure 5.1, growth in productivity did slow down from 1945 to 1950. But then it began to rise again, and shot up sharply throughout the 1950s. One answer to why this happened is that the nation embarked on something of a permanent war economy, maintaining high levels of military spending. Another answer, connected to the first, is that the Federal government grew in size and activity, stimulating the economy in its own version of Keynesian policies. A third answer, though, is that the nature of the American economy was changing. While it was still an industrial nation, with its base in manufacturing, its white-collar sector was growing rapidly. Large corporations, producing efficiently on economies of scale, along with technical advances, created new demand for specialized skills and for the management of information and people.

More Good Jobs

As an illustration, Figure 5.2 shows the percentages of Americans employed in managerial, professional, and technical occupations from 1920 to 1970.

Figure 5.2. Percentages of Americans in the Labor Force in Managerial, Professional, and Technical Occupations, 1920–1970

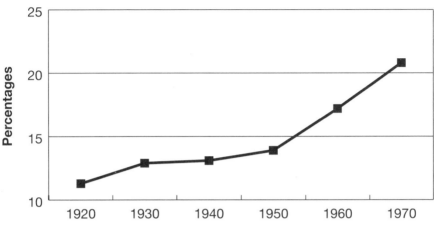

Source: Ruggles, 2008.

As we can see here, the year 1950 began a steep climb in the portions of the nation's growing workforce who were employed in these types of positions. This meant that "good jobs" would absorb more workers, increasing the general availability of employment. It also meant, though, that postwar America was going through a period of rapid structural mobility.

Individual mobility takes place when an individual gets a better job than the one she or he has previously had (intragenerational mobility) or gets a better job than the one his or her parent held (intergenerational mobility). Structural mobility occurs when the structure of the work force changes so that whole segments of the population move upward because there are a larger number of good jobs available than there were in previous years. With productivity gains and a larger part of the labor force concentrated in the professions, management, and technical work, the United States was not only succeeding in avoiding major recession or depression, it was generating high-status, good-paying jobs for more workers than ever before.

The Duncan Socio-Economic Index (SEI) is the most common means used by social scientists to measure socioeconomic status. The SEI is a composite of three things: the income earned by an individual, the prestige generally accorded to an individual's occupation, and the individual's level of formal education. These three are distinct, but also highly correlated, and social scientists combine them into a single score ranging from 1 to 96. Basically, the higher the score, the higher the occupational prestige, and the higher the mean score, the higher the average level of occupational prestige in the nation. Figure 5.3, then, can give us an idea of how structural mobility increased overall opportunity and began to systematically move Americans upward after World War II. Not surprisingly, the shape of the line is very close to that of Figure 5.2, since good jobs are the key to socioeconomic status.

Greater Demand for Schooling

Those good jobs that were becoming so much more widely available were of the sort that generally required high functional literacy, and frequently demanded specialized skills. In theory, these kinds of abilities could have been provided by means other than high school and university. Attorneys, for example, had, at an earlier stage in American history, been trained chiefly by apprenticeship in law offices. The literacy and legal abilities of Abraham Lincoln did not suffer notably from his lack of a law degree. However, the way in which Americans were to be prepared for their futures had already been established by the growth of the public school system, and it was unthinkable (and would have been completely impractical)

Figure 5.3. Mean Socioeconomic Index Score of Americans in the Labor Market, 1920–1970

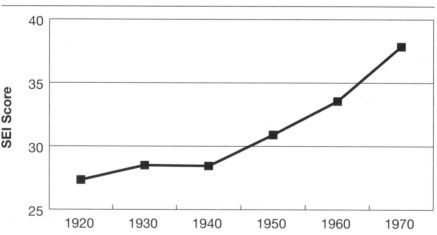

Source: Ruggles, 2008.

for the country to undo its institutional history and go back to an old way of doing things or strike out in a completely new direction.

Even highly technical preparation, such as that of an engineer, did not need to take place within the setting of a university, but could have been achieved through combinations of purely vocational instruction and apprenticeship. Moreover, a society different from that of the United States may have trained workers for a specialized and differentiated labor force by attempting to identify talents and interests early in life and channeling people into separate directions. That this last happened only to a limited degree in this country, and still became one of the nation's controversies, was a consequence of the beliefs about public education as a means of cultivating citizens, not just molding workers, and the belief that individuals should compete for goods and positions. As we will see below, these beliefs intensified tendencies that existed before the war. In the environment of the Cold War, education for citizenship intensified the demand for schooling as a way of fortifying national solidarity and building defenses against subversion. The abundance of new opportunities, and the close connection of those new opportunities to education, on the other hand, helped to emphasize the concept of America as the Promised Land of opportunity and of schooling as the way to reach that opportunity.

With the American economy booming, education became one of the greatest of growth areas. As Figure 5.4 shows, the total number of students enrolled in American schools shot up dramatically during the decade following the 1949–50 school year. Much of the growth in high schools had occurred during the interwar period, when high school attendance became a common part of the nation's life, as we discussed in the previous chapter. Secondary school enrollments did increase in the 1950s, from 5,725,000 to 8,271,000. This was to some extent a result of an increase in the high school–age population in 1959–60, born mostly during the years of the war, but it was also a consequence of the fact that young people were now expected not only to attend school, but to earn a high school diploma. The elementary school population, born during the baby boom years following the war, increased even more dramatically, from 19,387,000 to 26,911,000. Education was a growth industry during the period after the war, fed in elementary school by the baby boom and in higher education by sharp increases in rates of enrollment.

More Attention to the Educational Industry

The sheer size of the educational industry, and the requirement that it meet the needs of more students than ever before in American history and of a greater proportion of the population, while cranking out masses of people

Figure 5.4. School Enrollments, 1919–1960, for Earliest Grade Through 8th; 9th through 12th; and Postsecondary

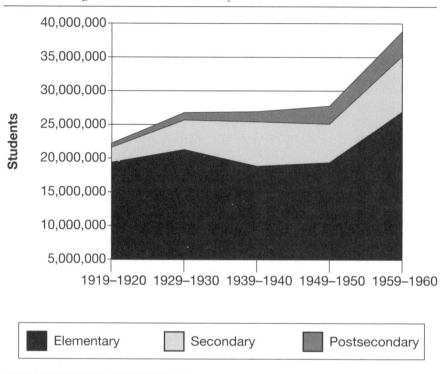

Source: National Center for Education Statistics, 2007.

with the levels of literacy required by the corporate economy, fed new debates over the quality of education. In particular, the reading skills of students became a matter of public controversy. The issue of how to teach reading has always been a matter of debate, and continues to be a source of wide disagreement and contention today. However, during the 1950s, this debate reached a particularly fevered pitch, and it became associated with Rudolf F. Flesch's 1955 book, *Why Johnny Can't Read: And What You Can Do About It*. Flesch argued that educators had taken the wrong road in teaching reading by not stressing phonics, the learning of the alphabet and the sounding out of letters. Instead, professors of education had promoted learning whole words by recognition in simply written books such as the Dick and Jane books.

Flesch's book went on the bestseller list and stayed there for weeks, a testimony to the public importance of education in the years following

World War II. "We're paying more school taxes than ever before," were the words one journalist placed in the mouths of American parents, "why can't we get our money's worth?" (Robbins & Robbins, 1955, p. G7). Schooling had become a great national investment of time and money and a determinant of who would end up where in the workforce of the future, as well as the means of producing the workers the nation would need. Getting our money's worth out of this industry was becoming a matter of controversy in part because more was going into it and more was expected to come out of it.

The Takeoff of Higher Education

One of the expected outcomes of the elementary and secondary portion of the educational industry was the production of people capable of continuing into higher education. Figure 5.5 shows the increase in college and university enrollments from 1940 to 1960. In 1940, just before the U.S. entered the war already raging in Europe, the nation's institutions of higher education enrolled a little under one and a half million people. By 1946,

Figure 5.5. College and University Enrollments in the United States, 1940–1960

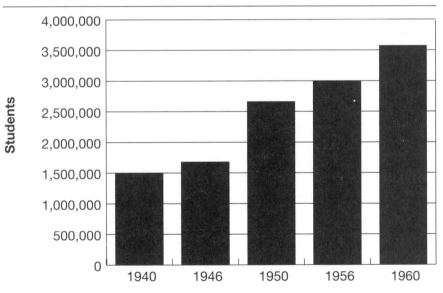

Source: U.S. Census Bureau, 1940–1960.

the year after the war, enrollment had gone up only to a little over one and a half million. Just 4 years later, though, those enrollments had reached well over two and a half million. By the end of the 1950s, they had reached more than three and a half million and enrollments were still rising. During this decade, those expanding numbers of students were coming not from the baby boom that followed the war but largely from the baby bust of the Depression years. This meant that colleges were taking in a much greater proportion of the population and a wider range of people, as well as greater numbers.

Access to postsecondary schooling was still available to "elite" or "chosen" individuals. However, unlike earlier years, the white-collar expansion of the country's labor force was, somewhat paradoxically, turning this into a mass elite, incorporating vastly greater numbers of people and people from walks of life that had previously sent few representatives to universities. Even some of the most prestigious and selective institutions expanded their class sizes and included a wider range of social backgrounds. In order to do this, tertiary education needed a new corporate system of college admissions.

The Scholastic Aptitude Test (SAT) had been a long time emerging by the middle of the 20th century. Originally developed by Carl Brigham, the foremost pioneer of IQ tests in the United States, the SAT only began to take off in the years following World War II, under the direction of Henry Chauncey. With the encouragement of Harvard President James Bryant Conant, Chauncey turned the SAT into a mechanism for making decisions about admissions in the expanding applicant pool. Essays may have worked well when universities were small shops, but big businesses required standardized procedures. The Educational Testing Service, which administered the SAT, opened on January 1, 1948. By 1957, more than half a million students were taking the test each year. The journalist Nicholas Lemann, in an excellent critical history of the SAT, observed that the large-scale college attendance that emerged from the years after World War II became the major social and economic dividing line in American society. "The placing of such a heavy load on higher education has had many other effects," Lemann wrote. "A whole industry has grown up to help people get into college and graduate school. Educational opportunity has become a national obsession" (Lemann, 1999, p. 6).

GOVERNMENT SENDS AMERICA TO SCHOOL

The increased involvement of the U.S. government in education was linked to the growing role of the schools in the American economy. The first and one of the most significant direct contributions of the Federal government to education came in the form of educational support for veterans. Economic historian Harold G. Vatter has observed that "public outlays for veterans' education were almost nonexistent before World War II; but by 1947 over $2.25 billion were already being expended for that purpose. In this matter we are dealing with both a change in economic behavior and a war-induced policy development. The contribution of veterans' education to the training level of the U.S. labor force and to future technological development was inestimable" (Vatter, 1996, p. 4).

The Servicemen's Readjustment Act of 1944, or "G.I. Bill," as it has become known, was initially an effort to avoid having the United States plunge back into an economic downturn as soldiers returning from World War II reentered the American economy and war spending went down. Among other benefits, the bill provided tuition and educational expenses to veterans who had served at least 90 days. Tuition payments were sufficient to cover costs even at elite institutions, such as Harvard University (Bound & Turner, 2002). The use of educational benefits was especially high in the cohort born in the years 1923 to 1928, half of whom drew on the G.I. Bill for schooling (Bound & Turner, 2002). In their study of the impact of the G.I. Bill on educational attainment, economists John Bound and Sarah Turner found that "the combined effect of military service and the G.I. Bill was to increase postsecondary educational attainment among World War II veterans above that of their non veteran peers, with particularly large effects on college completion . . . [O]ur estimates suggest war service increased college completion rates by close to 50%" (p. 786). Political scientist Suzanne Mettler has reported that G.I. Bill beneficiaries accounted for 49% of those enrolled in college by 1947, and that "within 10 years after World War II, 2,200,000 veterans had attended college and 5,600,000 had participated in vocational training programs or on-the-job training under the G.I. Bill" (Mettler, 2002, p. 351).

The consequences of the G.I. Bill were compounded by another war, in Korea, only 5 years after the end of World War II. On July 16, 1952, Congress passed the Veterans' Readjustment Act, which gave most of the educational benefits provided to World War II veterans to a new era of returning military service people. Veterans of the conflict in Korea who had served at least 90 days were entitled to tuition payments, as well as home loans and other benefits, for a period of one and a half times the duration of their service.

Increasing the Supply for an Increasing Demand

Although the G.I. Bill has since come to be seen as one of the great events in American history, not all commentators were enthusiastic about it at the time it was enacted. James Bryant Conant, then president of Harvard University, and Robert Maynard Hutchins, president of the University of Chicago, came out against government funding of higher education for veterans on the grounds that this would lower the quality of university education by bringing in new masses of students. That this apparently did not happen was the result of two factors that we have discussed above. First, the economic demand for people with college credentials was expanding fast enough to absorb the new college graduates. Overproduction and credential inflation would come later in American history, as the United States entered a new economic era. Second, the new filtering mechanisms, notably the SAT, reinforced the rank ordering of institutions according to prestige, with the highest-prestige institutions able to accept the highest scorers. Thus, Harvard and the University of Chicago were arguably able to obtain better students than before the war, since there was a much larger pool of applicants, and these types of institutions were able to admit on a highly selective basis.

The Impact of More Higher Education on Elementary and Secondary Schools

While the federal government poured money into higher education during the postwar years, elementary and secondary schools still continued to rely primarily on local sources of income, particularly from local sales taxes. Calls for increased federal involvement below the level of higher education could be heard through the decade and a half following the war, despite the traditional view of schools as local concerns. The *Washington Post* opined in 1950 that "there no longer remains reasonable doubt that Federal aid is needed—and needed now unless the flood of children, the crammed schools, and firetrap buildings, and the inequality of buildings in different parts of the country are to wipe out the tremendous American progress toward democracy through education" ("Many questions," 1950, p. L5). Teachers' organizations were particularly vocal in campaigns to get the federal government to share a greater part of the burden of growing school enrollments during the 1950s, but efforts in this direction were often frustrated by opposition from business and churches (Church, 1976).

For much of the decade and a half following the war, the greatest contribution of federal education spending to schooling below the postsecondary level, and to the whole of American society, was through the indirect consequences of supporting higher education through programs like the G.I. Bill. By sending to colleges and universities people from segments of the population who would not previously have set their sights on such advanced levels, the federal government contributed mightily to the idea that college was a realistic option for everyone. Author Michael J. Bennett testified to the tendency of the G.I. Bill to spread higher education far beyond the veterans for whom it was intended:

> I knew that while the GI Bill hadn't paid for the education of most of my childhood or college friends, most of us went to college because of the GI Bill. Growing up in a suburban area of Boston during and after the war, I became aware of the bill when an older boy from the neighborhood came back from the service and enrolled in college. Most of my playmates' fathers had been too old for the draft in World War II, and we were too young to be drafted for the Korean War. Our fathers, as skilled workmen, bookkeepers, and store managers, owned their own homes; they had not gone to college and saw no need for their sons to do so. But when that older boy came back and exchanged his combat boots for white bucks, every mother in the neighborhood began to say, "Well if _____ can go to college, my kid can." And we all did, just about. Somehow the money for tuition, which hadn't been in the budget, was found, because our parents thought it would be better to put off military service until we were older. Besides, with a college degree, we could become officers, not that anyone in that neighborhood had any idea what an officer did. But college graduates and engineers and doctors and teachers and social workers, even journalists, were being produced routinely by those neighborhoods by the middle of the 1950s. (Bennett, 1996, p. xii)

As Bennett and the members of his cohort began to see college as in their own futures, high schools began to prepare more of their students for entry into colleges. The linkage between levels of education became closer: elementary schools were getting students ready for secondary school, and secondary schools were getting students ready for institutions of higher learning. For vast portions of the public, schools were the route to the future, for themselves and for the nation.

This pulling together of the different levels of schooling into a single nationwide industry found support from the Federal government at the end of the 1950s. As we will describe in greater detail below, Cold War competition with the Soviet Union intensified the defensive aspects of the national faith in education that had begun to appear earlier in the century. The Soviet launch of the Sputnik satellite in October 1957 contributed to a fear already emerging that the United States was falling behind in a learning race. President Eisenhower responded to the Soviet launch by delivering a speech in Oklahoma City a month later, in which he attributed the Soviet success to the Communist power's concentration on creating an educational system that would give it an advantage in the struggle among nations. The following January, he proposed to Congress an educational program for the purpose of strengthening the nation's defense against the Communist world. The President sought greater spending on the

National Science Foundation, particularly for summer programs to train teachers in science and mathematics and to move more students into careers in science. He also wanted more money to be spent on the testing, guidance, and counseling of students in order to direct them into studies seen as strategically important for the United States (Spring, 1989).

On August 22, 1958, the U.S. Congress adopted the President's program in the form of the National Defense Education Act (NDEA). Senator John J. Sparkman of Alabama referred to this new major act of Federal support for education as a historic event, saying that it was "the first time an education bill of this magnitude has cleared both houses" (Sparkman, quoted in Furman, 1958, p. 16). The $900,000,000 4-year bill provided loans to college students identified as having special abilities; gave grants to the states to enhance the teaching of science, mathematics, and languages in elementary and secondary schools; funded testing and counseling for students; gave support and directed revenues to teacher training institutes; and paid for approaches to education that used modern technologies (Furman, 1958, p. 16).

For the sake of national defense, the Federal government was not only extending support to all levels of education, it was also creating something that would begin to move toward efforts to create a national curriculum. The NDEA aimed at reshaping American society in a new way, as a citadel against Communism, with schooling at the core of the effort at redesign. This was a different version of what life adjustment education under the Progressives had tried to do, the adjustment of individuals to a future detailed by planners. Unlike life adjustment education, though, the vision was based less on socializing individuals into teamwork than it was on systematically identifying aptitudes and cultivating individuals for placement. As education critic Joel Spring has argued (1989), this was government attempting to employ schooling as a "sorting machine," a tool for directed social stratification. The belief that planners could direct a social order through schooling had roots in the heritage of scientific systematization that we saw emerging in the social efficiency movement of the Progressive Era. Always linked to a creed of national commitment, this faith in the power of schooling took on a new form in the 1950s as Americans defined their national goal as salvation from Communism.

THE CITY ON A HILL AS CITADEL OF FREEDOM

The United States came out of World War II a political as well as an economic superpower. The Soviet Union, although devastated by the war, appeared on the world scene as a rival, having extended its control over vast reaches of Eastern Europe. As the center of Communism, the Soviet Union also represented an ideological threat to the United States and provided the major alternative to the market economy. With the rise to power of the Communists in China in 1949 and the beginning of the Korean War in 1950, it began to appear to many Americans as if their nation and their political system were under siege by this alternative, and as if the United States faced a real danger of losing a global struggle.

Schooling for a Holy War

At the beginning of the 1950s, according to historian of American religion Martin E. Marty, President Harry Truman presented the Cold War as a holy war, with America in the role of crusader for freedom. In his speech while lighting the White House Christmas tree in 1950, Truman announced, "We are all joined in the fight against the tyranny of communism. Communism is godless." Truman called on all the world's leaders to join in a "common affirmation of faith" that "would testify to the strength of our common faith and our confidence in its ultimate victory over the forces of Satan [i.e., Communism] that oppose it" (Harry Truman as quoted in Marty, 1996, p. 203). The following year, Truman spoke before the Washington Pilgrimage of American Churchmen, an organization of religious leaders devoted to the promotion of patriotism that would become a strong advocate for the inclusion of the phrase "under God" in the Pledge of Allegiance. The President told the members of the Washington Pilgrimage that it was America's national task to "preserve a world civilization in which man's belief in God can survive" (Harry Truman as quoted in Marty, 1996, p. 203). Truman's insistence on such themes was repeated to the extent that the President, in Marty's words, "was beginning to assume a priestly role, with the presidency serving as the pulpit for the nation's public religion" (Marty, 1996, p. 204). Marty points out that this was an ecumenical faith, in which Truman attempted to draw all faiths into the crusade. As we have been arguing, though, nondenominational state faith had long existed in the United States, and the ideological and geopolitical competition of the United States with the Soviet Union and China led the state religion to call more explicitly on the ultimate sources of belief.

By the time of the Eisenhower presidency, the national civil religion had reached such a high pitch that it became clearly recognized as religion by contemporaries, despite the traditional American insistence on the absence of an established church. As Marty (1996) has pointed out, the 1950s were a time of national religious revival closely linked to popular patriotism. Marty (1996) has noted that "after the Second World War and during the Cold War, the new-time religion of Protestants, Catholics, Jews and many secularists was in new ways a religion not only of the American way of life but of America itself" (p. 294). Marty cites the work of Jewish theologian and sociologist Will Herberg, whose 1955 book *Protestant-Catholic-Jew* incorporated ideas of "a common faith," "democracy as religion," "the democratic faith," and "the common religion." Herberg even used the term "civic faith" or a "civic religion of the American way of life" to describe this creed of Americanism (Herberg, quoted in Marty, 1996, p. 294).

A "Supercharged" Pledge

The central school ritual of the common American religion, which we saw first appearing during the Progressive Era, in Chapter 3, was the Pledge of Allegiance. Francis Bellamy's creed of national unity through dedication to the flag had become almost universal in public schools during the first half of the 20th century, and it had become required by law in many localities. But the Federal government did not officially adopt it until 1945. Moreover, it went through the first big change in wording in its history as a consequence of Cold War pressures. This change in wording involved an effort to draw the civic religion closer to Biblical religion and to ground the national faith in an explicitly theological faith.

If the United States was indeed in a holy war against Communism, as President Truman had suggested, then the civic faith needed to make clear its ultimate foundation in the sacred. While Communism was portrayed as godless and as satanic, the United States was rooted in the nondenominational, ecumenical holiness at the heart of all traditional religions. The desire to make clear that the American state faith flowed from this deeper metaphysical fount led to a small but highly meaningful change in the wording of the Pledge.

The question of who was the first to propose adding the words "under God" is still a matter of debate. However, Democratic Representative Louis C. Rabaut of Michigan introduced a resolution to make this addition on April 21, 1953 ("Pledge revision asked," 1953). Rabaut maintained that including recognition of the nation's dependence on a presumably nonsectarian God would help to counter the "wicked idolatry of the State impregnated into fertile young minds (sic) by Hitler and by his Soviet imitators" (Rabaut, as quoted in Gallup, 1953, p. 11). Pollster George Gallup, immediately afterward, found that 70% of respondents to a national survey favored the change (Gallup, 1953).

President Dwight D. Eisenhower approved the joint resolution of Congress, sponsored by Rabaut in the House and by Michigan Republican Homer Ferguson in the Senate, on June 15, 1954. President Eisenhower proclaimed that:

from this day forward, the millions of school children will daily proclaim in every city and town, every village and rural school house, the dedication of our nation and our people to the Almighty. To anyone who truly loves America, nothing could be more inspiring than to contemplate this rededication of our youth, on each school morning, to the nation's true meaning ... In this way we are reaffirming the transcendence of religious faith in America's heritage and future; in this way we shall constantly strengthen those spiritual weapons which forever will be our country's most powerful resource, in peace or in war." (Eisenhower, quoted in "President hails revised Pledge," 1954, p. 31)

This clear identification of American civic religion with deistic faith was supported by opinion-makers and commentators, as well as by the general public and by politicians. After a legal challenge to the revision of the Pledge by secular freethinkers was unsuccessful in the New York Supreme Court, an editorial in the *Christian Science Monitor* reprinted from the *Herald Statesman* of Yonkers opined that "never in our history has it been so essential that free America, mighty in her place of world leadership, turn to God for guidance through the maze of crisis" ("Under God," 1957, p. 16).

Progressives on the Defensive

The sense of siege from satanic forces imbued the civic faith with some of the characteristics that sociologists of religion have identified with groups known as sects. In the classic writings of Ernst Troeltsch (1931), a sect is a religious community that does not come to terms with the worldly order around it, but imposes high moral demands on its followers and requires that they overcome sinfulness. More recently, the sociologists Rodney Stark and Roger Finke (2000, p. 143) have described sects as living in a high state of "tension," or "distinctiveness, separation, and antagonism," in their relationships with the "outside" world. A corollary of this high state of tension was the tendency of sects to demand and receive passionate commitment from their believers. This requirement of commitment, in turn, can lead to perpetual questioning about the adequacy of commitment.

Recognizing this perpetual questioning of commitment during the 1950s can provide us with part of the context for understanding popular suspicion of those identified as progressive educators. One of the reasons for public discontent with life adjustment education was the proliferation of new economic opportunities combined with the fact that formal schooling, as the accepted way of addressing personal and social needs, provided the access to those opportunities. Another reason, though, was that those who had inherited the label of Progressivism during the 1920s and 1930s became associated with social criticism and redistributive ideologies. Cremin (1961) pointed out that part of the reason for the demise of the Progressive movement was simply that it had been absorbed by the mainstream: "Much of what it preached was simply incorporated into schools at large" (p. 349). As we have argued above, all of American public education can be seen as the child of Progressivism. Those who still wore the mantle of the Progressive movement were the most self-conscious, but also the most radical and most overtly social reconstuctionist heirs to the common ancestor. This characteristic was precisely what put them on the defensive. The particular defenses that they offered can give some insight into the sectlike nature of American civic religion in the schools after the war.

In addition to the incorporation of much of the Progressive program by the educational system, Cremin (1961) has given the "general swing toward conservatism in postwar political and social thought" (p. 349) as another reason for public rejection of Progressive theories in education. The term "conservatism," though, can cover a wide range of meanings, including the historical gradualism of Edmund Burke, the antisecular authoritarianism of Joseph le Maistre, and the *laissez-faire* economics of Milton Friedman. One might argue that life adjustment education can be a highly conservative approach to pedagogy, under the guidance of teachers dedicated to socializing children to fit into an accepted order.

The version of conservatism that dominated life in the 1950s was a profound sense of the holiness of the American nation in the face of a threatening and even satanic enemy. The phonics versus whole-word controversy took some of its energy from the fact that advanced literacy had become so much more important in an economy of increasing opportunities in white-collar jobs. But it also drew a large part of its energy from the fact that whole-word approaches to teaching reading, whatever their pedagogical value, had become associated with the theories of social critics in an era in which the critics of the American order had come under suspicion of undermining the creed of orthodox Americanism.

The split in the national faith in schooling that we saw in the previous chapter took on a new meaning with this setting of intense creedal orthodoxy, with its split between sacred Americanism and the godless dedication to the human reordering of social institutions. The Cold War environment strengthened the traditionalist faith in education against the social reconstructionist views of the progressive intellectuals, some of whom had looked favorably on the Soviet Communist system of the 1920s and 1930s. A letter to the editor of the *Washington Post* in 1950 expressed many of the popular views about the subversive effects of social progressivism in the schools:

Who can blame our youth for cheering the Henry Wallaces of our day when that [modern education] is all the foundation they have for citizenship, all the heritage they have to cling to? But we can blame the education policy-makers, from John Dewey, George Counts, Harold Rugg on down who have believed and taught that what America needs is a new social order; who hold a vision of an ideal society and have used the medium of the public school to bring it about. Such men and their disciples are not subversive in the sense we commonly use the term. They merely believe that they have the blue-print for a society that is nearer ideal than the one we have, and in order to bring it about, they teach our children to desire it too. Parents all over the Nation are rising in revolt against this type of education. (Anonymous Parent, 1950, p. 24)

In this time of intense and defensive nationalism, the solidarity side of American civil religion, dominant in educational practice since the creation of the public school system, became even stronger than it had been in earlier years. As we shall see, this did not preclude efforts to realize the promise of American life through distributing opportunities more widely. In fact, since the equality of citizens had long been a part of the American creed, the demand for national solidarity began to stimulate the rise of the egalitarian, redistributionist side of the civil religion. But the Progressive educators, who had become known for their emphasis on redesigning American society, came under suspicion of knowingly or unknowingly spreading subversive tendencies and of undermining the patriotic dedication of students. The Progressives responded by loudly and repeatedly declaring their own commitment to the phrases and images of the national religion.

In 1952, the newly elected secretary of the National Education Association, Dr. William G. Carr, voiced his exasperation with accusations that public school teachers were engaging in subversive indoctrination: "We fly the American flag over our schools and in our classrooms. We teach the children the pledge of allegiance and to sing 'The Star-Spangled Banner.' Then we are accused of being subversive. What more can we do?" (Carr, as quoted in Warden, 1952, p. 4). Dr. Carr's plaintive cry reminds one of Emile Durkheim's famous observation that deviance must exist in any society in order to define its rules. In a society of saints, dedicated to the strictest moral rules, even the slightest infractions are grave sins. With demands for creedal orthodoxy raised to sectlike levels by the pressures of the Cold War, even teachers, the ministers and priests of the state religion, could be suspected of denying the faith. In fact, given the importance of schools for perpetuating belief, those ministers of public education were precisely the ones who could lead the flock astray through minor infractions.

Those who defended academic freedom and critical approaches to American society were always careful to stress their adherence to orthodox Americanism and to make it clear that they were part of the holy war against Communism. Thus, Dr. Susan B. Riley, president of the American Association of University Women, justified academic freedom as part of the war against Communism, and she invoked the American creed of the assimilative virtues of education and the cult of the founding fathers. "The best defense against communism," Riley proclaimed in 1953 at the association's convention in Minneapolis, "is to be found in the fearless thinking which good teachers provoke." She declared, according to the *New York Times*, that "faith in education, expressed by our founding fathers and adhered to with devotion throughout our history has enabled our public schools to produce a literate citizenry, and a classless society assimilating millions of immigrants from all the other countries of the world" (Riley, quoted and summarized in Asbury, 1953, p. 18).

The 91st annual convention of the National Education Association, held in Miami Beach in June 1953, released results of a survey showing that teachers were avoiding controversial questions in classrooms as a result of the political climate of the times. Speakers at the convention called criticisms of free thought and speech in the name of anticommunism the true threat to the American way of life. Nevertheless, the theme of the meeting was "We Pledge Allegiance," and association president Sarah C. Caldwell declared that the teachers at the meeting "pledged allegiance to the American heritage" (Fine, 1953, p. 1). Moreover, according to some scholars, the NEA in general sided with the position that Communist infiltration of American institutions posed a genuine national security threat (Foster, 2000).

Seeking to broadcast the patriotic role of schools, the National Education Association report that we cited earlier not only gave schooling the responsibility for providing traditional knowledge, citizenship training, technical abilities, and even daily competence, it cast schools in the role of defenders of the sacred American way of life. The 98-page report maintained that public schools "must continue as supporters and guardians of the American way of life," and the historical presentation of the development of American schooling placed "the emphasis throughout the report on the vision the Founding Fathers had of a system of universal education, the struggle that led to the country's system of public schools, and the need of inculcating brotherhood in a democracy" (Furman, 1955, p. 74).

The efforts of virtually all parties in the educational debates of the 1950s to cast themselves as the true defenders of sacred Americanism against its perils and enemies raises the question of just what constituted Americanism. Like most creeds, it consisted of multiple tenets, not all of them mutually consistent. The tenet of equality, and particularly equality of opportunity, frequently came to the forefront in this time of multiplying opportunities for mobility and rising material standards. It was a precept that could contain ambiguities and varying interpretations. One could emphasize the leveling of social situations in order to achieve equality of opportunity, and this could lay one open to the charge of insufficient faith in the one nation under God and of contributing to the subversions of socialism. At the same time, though, the obsession with getting ahead by upward mobility through education, in addition to the disruptions of older ways of life, provoked an increased commitment to the ideal of equal opportunity in the mainstream and among the highest officials of the nation. If the national civic faith became more "conservative" through increased demands on national solidarity at this time, it also began to develop an opposite "liberal" tendency through the beginning of struggles to realize its belief in equality among citizens. The crusade for equality, like the campaign for creedal orthodoxy, took the campus as its battleground.

THE NEW EMPHASIS ON EQUAL OPPORTUNITY

Political equality and equality of economic opportunity were themes in American education throughout its history. James Bryant Conant (1959) maintained that the political equality that had been one of the founding concepts of the nation and the idea of competitive economic equality that had emerged during the 19th century were cultural attitudes that made American schooling distinctive. Conant observed that while working with a collaborator to translate one of his books into German, he had discovered that there was no German equivalent of "equality of opportunity" (Conant, 1959, p. 71).

In the wake of the war, this long-standing American tenet of equality, particularly in the form of equality of opportunity, took on new meaning in attitudes toward the nation's schools. With white-collar positions proliferating, and significant upward mobility from parental statuses more widely available, access to opportunity became a more vital concern. With schooling seen as the route to economic opportunity more than ever before, and the rapid ratcheting upward of educational attainments during the 1950s, accomplishment of equal opportunity through schools became a vital public matter. With a dramatic rise in higher education and more families and students looking upon elementary and secondary education as preparation for college, course work aimed at entry into higher education came to be understood as the right of the many, rather than as the privilege of the few. Among the reasons that education for life adjustment began to fall into disrepute during this decade, one of the most critical was simply that moving upward, rather than adjusting, had become more central in American life and education had become the main way to move upward.

Although elementary school had become nearly universal early in the 20th century and high school attendance became the norm in the years after World War I, the idea that everyone must complete high school and that everyone should have the opportunity to attend higher education was largely foreign to Americans before World War II. After the war, though, President Harry S. Truman's Commission on Higher Education announced that the numbers of Americans with limited amounts of education "represent a sobering failure to reach the educational goals implicit in the democratic creed, and they are indefensible in a society so richly endowed with material resources as our own" (Commission on Higher Education, 1947, p. 25).

Equal opportunity is a paradoxical concept. It entails everyone having the same chances to become unequal. Since people bring different kinds of preparation, skills, social networks, and even luck to the competition, opportunities are always ultimately unequal. The ideology of opportunity in the postwar period was also complicated by the coexisting beliefs that everyone should compete for rewards, but that everyone should also get rewards. To some extent, this problem was masked by the structural mobility we pointed out earlier. Even if everyone could not be a winner, blue ribbons were fairly plentiful. The view that all hard-working Americans should get ahead, while doing so competitively, led to serious considerations of how to make education, the primary route to mobility, more open to all. The same Commission on Higher Education report considered the question of how higher education could be made available to more Americans. Objecting to a "restricted curriculum," the report maintained that:

> we shall be denying equal opportunity to many young people as long as we maintain the present orientation of higher education toward verbal skills and intellectual interests . . . Traditionally, the colleges have sifted out as their special clientele persons possessing verbal aptitudes and a capacity for grasping abstractions . . . If colleges are to educate the great body of American youth, they must provide programs for the development of other abilities than those involved in academic aptitude, and they cannot continue to concentrate on students with one type of intelligence to the neglect of youth with other talents. (Commission on Higher Education, 1947, p. 25)

Advancement in education should be opened up to more people, but it should also be selective. It should provide better lives for all, but remain essentially a competition. Adherents of equal opportunity seemed unable to decide whether they wanted to lay the stress on "equality" or "opportunity." If credentials were to be more widely distributed, wouldn't this necessarily entail a credential inflation, scarcity being the source of market value? On this issue, James Bryant Conant argued that the American belief in equality had produced misleading representations of the meanings of the college degrees that were becoming so much more common during the 1950s. "One manifestation of this doctrine [of equality of status]," he wrote, "is our unwillingness to state frankly that a bachelor's degree has long since lost any meaning as a mark of scholastic attainment or the completion of a course of formal academic training. Whether one has a degree in engineering, agriculture, home economics, commerce, physical education, or in the arts and sciences, he is entitled to be called a 'college graduate'" (Conant, 1959, p. 6). To some extent, then, a balance between equality and opportunity could be reached by simply believing that a wider distribution of diplomas and degrees could both advance individuals in competition and also make all more equal in fact.

The difficulty posed by equal chances to become unequal could also be addressed by emphasizing the "opportunity" part of the phrase. As early as the time of Thomas Jefferson's educational schemes, the idea of equalizing life chances in order to allow inequality to become manifest was a part of the American belief system. Conant's support for strategies like the SAT to broaden the social origins of elite college students while narrowing the intellectual range of students (a strategy quietly opposite to that of Truman's Commission on Higher Education) reflected an updated, bureaucratic version of the natural aristocracy thesis.

This paradoxical idea of equality of opportunity, which would become the basis of a historic turn in the American creed, found expression in responses to an old, deep-rooted, systematic contradiction of national ideals. The most significant product of the doctrine of equality of educational opportunity during the 1950s was the effort to obtain racial equality in education. This effort would, in the following decade, become the center of the crisis of civil religion in American education. World War II marked an increasing awareness of enforced inequality among African Americans, and the war fueled their struggle for racial equality and full inclusion in American society. In the military, blacks demanded, and were ultimately granted, legal rights equal to those of their white comrades-in-arms. In 1948 Truman signed Executive Order 9981, which mandated the racial integration of America's armed forces. The Korean War of 1950 to 1953 saw the first racially integrated combat units since the Civil War, and served as a model for how blacks and whites could successfully integrate in other social spheres.

In 1950, the Supreme Court, following this postwar trend, rendered a decision that began to turn the nation's educational system away from the "separate but equal" doctrine that had held sway since the end of the 19th century. Because there was no Texas law school for blacks, a black man named Herman Marion Sweatt sued for admission to the University of Texas law school. The state of Texas responded by hastily slapping together a woefully inadequate black law school in the basement of a building. The NAACP and its lead attorney, the future Justice Thurgood Marshall, brought Sweatt's case before the U.S. Supreme Court, and argued for his admission to the white University of Texas law school. The high court agreed with the persuasive arguments of the skillful Thurgood Marshall, and ruled that the new black law school was hardly "equal" to the white law school (*Sweatt v. Painter,* 1950). Sweatt won the case, setting a high court precedent acknowledging that separate educational facilities for blacks were not necessarily equal. The reality was that they were almost never equal, and indeed were usually grossly inadequate. The successful rationale used in the Sweatt case would become ammunition in Marshall's assault on the Topeka Board of Education just 4 years later.

Brown v. Board of Education was one of the nation's most ambitious attempts to seek both competitive opportunity of individuals and actual equality of life chances through education. Following the Supreme Court's decision in this case, a district court, on remand, proclaimed, "School children irrespective of race or color shall be required to attend the school in the district in which they reside and that color or race is no element of exceptional circumstances in warranting a deviation of this basic principle" (*Brown v. Board of Education II,* 1955). This statement appears to be a requirement that each pupil be treated according to identical procedures in school assignment, regardless of race, and it has led some scholars to characterize *Brown* as "a study in color blindness" (Caldas, 2006, p. 78). Such color blindness would mean that the chance to enter the natural aristocracy of achievement had simply been extended to include individual African Americans, without any effort at racial leveling.

While *Brown* did focus on the problem of discrimination against individuals in procedures, it also brought an explicit concern with larger questions of societal structure into judicial deliberations. As Kenneth K. Wong and Anna C. Nicotera have pointed out, the opinion of the majority in *Brown* set a precedent for its use of social science research in legal considerations of educational inequality (Wong & Nicotera, 2004). A statement by Kenneth Clark, Isidor Chein, and Stuart W. Cook was particularly influential. This statement, summarizing their research and signed by 32 noted social scientists, argued that racial segregation was one of the most serious problems facing the American people and that social science could contribute to the resolution of this problem. Clark, Chein, and Cook (1952) reported that social scientific research indicated that segregation promoted feelings of inferiority within the minority group, and that it contributed to a social context that maintained racial inequality.

Was *Brown*, then, primarily a commitment to extending individual opportunity in educational competition or an assertion of the role of schools in shaping a more desirable society? The best answer is probably that the early proponents of school desegregation and integration were devoted to both of these rationales, but saw little difference between them. By ending racial discrimination against individuals, the courts would eliminate the institutional structure of segregation and therefore of systematic racial inequality. While commenting on the Supreme Court's decision in 1954, Thurgood Marshall said that he expected it would take "up to five years" to eliminate segregation in education throughout the United States. Further, the *New York Times* reported that Marshall "predicted that, by the time the 100th anniversary of the Emancipation Proclamation was observed in 1963, segregation in all forms would have been eliminated from the nation" ("N.A.A.C.P. sets advanced goals," 1954, p. 16).

Political and social resistance to removing racial barriers to individual movement through schools soon became evident. In 1956, 101 Southern senators signed a manifesto proclaiming that the Court itself had made an illegal declaration by ordering racial integration (Bergman, 1969). The following year, President Dwight D. Eisenhower was forced to activate the Arkansas National Guard to escort seven black children through an angry mob to integrate all-white Little Rock Central High School. In that same year, officials of Virginia's Prince Edward County announced that they would close public schools in response to a desegregation order (Muse, 1956), a promise that they kept.

Beneath the conflict over the free access of individuals to educational institutions, and therefore to the upward mobility assumed to be the consequence of educational attainment, lurked much deeper problems. If the legal blocks to enrollment and attendance were removed, would this, in fact, eliminate racial inequalities in American society? Indeed, if all Americans could compete equally as individuals for ascension in a meritocratic educational hierarchy, would this eliminate the influence of differences in family backgrounds, neighborhood and community characteristics, and social networks? Since the opportunities of individuals are heavily shaped by the social structures surrounding them, a commitment to equality of opportunity could easily become a commitment to equalizing the whole of society. Since equality of opportunity produces inequality of outcomes, the effort to give all individuals the same life chances can lead to continuous, circular attempts to redress the consequences of individual competition for the sake of individual competition. In the following decades, as the problem of racial inequality drove egalitarianism to become the central article of American faith in education, schools would become defined as places where the society is transformed into a state in which no one is ever left behind, while everyone always strives to get ahead.

THE POST–WORLD WAR II YEARS:
AN END AND A BEGINNING

In the decade and half following World War II, then, the end of one period in the American civil religion of education saw the earliest beginnings of a new period. Americans still saw schooling as a way to build the Promised Land that had become more than ever the land of opportunity. Adaptation to life meant getting ahead in an environment of economic growth, more than adjustment. Schools were still seen as ways of fitting individuals into the society, but as mobility became more the meaning of adaptation, enhancing the competitive preparation of students received greater emphasis than making them team players. At the same time, the Cold War intensified the existing tendency to make the school the focal point of the nationalist side of the American creed, and the nationalism itself reached the point of a sectlike defensiveness and commitment. This nationalism also tended to turn Americans against educational theories and practices that seemed to be critical of the nation, and to be adjusting pupils for a relatively collectivist vision of the future. Both the individual mobility orientation and the fear of subversion raised suspicions of the social reconstructionist wing of educational thought.

At the same time, the emphasis on opportunities and mobility, and the postwar changes in American society, planted the seed of a new kind of social reconstructionism in American education. The ideology of equality followed from the pursuit of individual opportunity. Americans believed both that everyone should be better off in the surrounding abundance, and that people should get ahead by free competition. The incipient struggle of African Americans, systematically and legally denied many of the nation's benefits and excluded from the competition, moved to the center of the question of equal opportunity. But opportunities can only be truly equalized by leveling the starting places in the competition. The competition itself then results in inequalities of outcome, so that the starting places, the positions in the society, have to be perpetually readjusted. With the long history of national faith in education, many Americans would come to attempt to employ schools simultaneously as fields of meritocratic competition and as arenas of equalization. This would bring a new crisis to American civil religion and to the schools.

CHAPTER 6

Education for Equality
and Education as Redistribution
in the 1960s and 1970s

A TURNING POINT IN THE FAITH

THROUGH the first half of the 20th century, the American civic religion continued in the schools, often with a tension between the vision of education as a way of changing the nation into its ideal self-image and that of education as a means of propagating membership in the state and adherence to it. Immediately following World War II, in the threatening environment of the Cold War, the solidarity side of American civil religion seemed to be uppermost in the nation's institutions of learning. At the same time, although the transformationist views of the social reconstructionists seemed to many at best out of touch with the need for assimilation of individuals to a new economy of mobility or at worst downright subversive, there was a strong undercurrent of belief in using schools to achieve an egalitarian society. Since this last was a matter of faith, the problems and paradoxes of achieving equality through educational competition generally received little attention.

During the 1960s, this undercurrent of egalitarianism moved to the surface of American education. So much has been written in praise and condemnation of the 1960s that anyone who attempts to address this decade as a distinctive period runs the risk of falling into one of the competing mythologies. Arthur Marwick (1998) portrays this time as a cultural revolution, a renaissance that gave birth to new and imaginative artistic forms, as well as intellectual and social experimentation. Conservative critic Roger Kimball (2000) also describes the 1960s in America as a cultural revolution, but maintains that the revolution overturned fundamental American social values in a spirit of heedless antinomian self-indulgence and fantastic utopianism. The very fact that there is this debate over the significance of the decade, though, points to it as a critical time from all perspectives today.

The Crisis in Civil Religion

In earlier chapters, we have followed the American civil religion through the decades, pointing out its fundamental unity in commitment to political institutions, in reverence for national saints and martyrs, in rituals and ceremonies, and, above all, in the recognition of the American nation as consecrated to a special destiny. The first great turn, or crisis, in this faith came in the late 19th and early 20th century, when America emerged as a politically unified and economically expanding power. At that time, schools, which had long been associated with beliefs about the nation, moved to the center of our civil religion, becoming both articles of faith and means of conveying it. Beginning in the 1960s and continuing into the 1970s, we saw a second great turn, with redistribution of opportunity and inclusion of formerly excluded groups moving to the forefront of beliefs about the special American destiny.

While historical change is complex, it may be possible to identify two sources of the American cultural revolution and the great shift in civic faith during the 1960s. One of these sources was economic. The upward movement of the American economy reached a general level of affluence that had turned high consumption into an expectation. In this setting, it seemed unjustifiable that some would not share in the general high standard of living. An orientation toward consumption, rather than production, also worked a subtle transformation in American views of the nature of economic justice. With goods and services so widely available, attention tended to move from individual contributions to the commonweal toward the distribution of benefits. The question of who gets what took on increased importance.

In a consumer economy, moreover, the main problem is maintaining sufficient demand for all that can be produced. Profits and employment levels depend on having sufficient buyers. Since the poor are, by definition, those with the least buying capacity, increasing their purchasing power means pumping up overall demand. Corporate interests combine with general expectations to draw attention to the relatively underprivileged.

The second source of the shift lay in the realm of collective interpretation. Human views of the world are not deterministic consequences of material environments. These views also derive from the shared narratives that people employ to make sense of their lives. We saw earlier how events such as the Civil War and the Cold War became narratives about morality and destiny. During the 1960s, the civil rights movement became part of the grand account of American life. The movement was, as Robert Bellah realized, as critical for the national faith as the Civil War had been 100 years before. The televised African American struggle for equal rights and equal citizenship became the morality play of the second half of the 20th century. In using this term "morality play," we are not being dismissive. Rather, we are suggesting that the images of peaceful marchers attacked by dogs, the murders of civil rights workers, and the inspiring speeches of the leaders of the movement gave Americans a drama of moral values that helped to redefine the normative interpretation of social relations. Since the civil rights movement aimed at equality for the systematically excluded, the dramatization helped to make equality and inclusion the major themes of civic values. The moral perspective of the civil rights movement, as well as the orientation toward increasing the purchasing power of the poor, contributed to a definition of social justice as the state of affairs that would most benefit the least advantaged in a society.

A martyrology contributed to the moral drama of the decade. The extent of President John F. Kennedy's actual support for the civil rights movement is unclear. However, many of the programs in the crusade for social and economic uplift of the excluded under his successor, President Lyndon B. Johnson, began as initiatives in President Kennedy's administration. The shock of Kennedy's assassination made him a national martyr in modern American civil religion, much as President Lincoln's assassination had made him a martyr in the American belief system for the post–Civil War period. The slain 20th-century president became a symbol for a wider distribution of the benefits of American life and for the inclusion of excluded groups, as the 19th-century president had been a symbol for national unification. President Kennedy's martyrdom was followed by that of his brother, Robert F. Kennedy, and, perhaps even more importantly, by that of the foremost spokesman of the civil rights movement, the Reverend Dr. Martin Luther King Jr. Significantly, the United States later adopted Dr. King's birthday as a national holiday, ranked alongside Washington's Birthday, Memorial Day, the Fourth of July, Labor Day, Veterans Day, and Thanksgiving Day.

Joel Spring (1989) has observed that the concern about the disadvantaged from the 1960s onward represented a shift in emphasis from the previous decade. Studying and criticizing the social-sorting function of schools for placing students in the labor market and stratification system, Spring argued that "the early 1960s shifted the major concern from the talented to the disadvantaged but still kept within the framework of the social-sorting process" (p. 141). This is a valuable insight, and it is precisely this movement of emphasis toward those at the bottom of American society that we identify as the primary characteristic of this time of crisis in American civil religion. However, the assimilation of those at the margins into the nation's economic and social structure through education for purposes of sorting was only part of the great shift at this time. High expectations for standards of living also provide another, less overtly manipulative motivation for socializing everyone into a single American Dream. Concerns with those at the bottom of the nation, whom we might consider the domestic aliens, were also driven by the need of a consumer economy to keep consumption high, as well as the need to fit people into the workforce. At the same time, dramatic, disturbing, and inspiring events on the national stage transformed the moral discourse of the country and rearranged traditional elements of American civil religion, still keeping education at its center.

The Consumer Economy and the Shift in Expectations

Despite occasional economic downturns, most notably, the recession at the end of President Eisenhower's term in office, the American economy continued to move upward throughout the 1950s and 1960s, with marked benefits to individuals. As Figure 6.1 demonstrates, disposable personal income and personal income expenditures increased dramatically during these two decades, so that by 1969 real per capita consumer spending power was more than double what it had been in 1950. With each passing year, the average consumer could expect to enjoy significantly more goods and services. By 1958, economist John Kenneth Galbraith was characterizing the United States as an "affluent society." In this new economy, according to Galbraith, the fundamental issue was no longer how to achieve sufficient production, but how to distribute what was being produced. Galbraith argued that the nation was spending too much on private consumption, to the detriment of public goods and public interests. Galbraith, later an associate and advisor of President Kennedy, maintained that the production of private consumer goods without government guidance left corporations pursuing profits through advertising to increase demand for luxuries, while roads fell into disrepair and children attended badly maintained schools. This high private consumption also left the poor behind the rest of society. Galbraith proposed steering more investments toward public spending, especially through human investment in education.

The state of the economically disadvantaged in high consumption America also concerned Michael Harrington, another writer on social and economic affairs who influenced President Kennedy. In *The Other America* (1962), Harrington argued that the poor had become invisible to much of

Figure 6.1. Disposable Personal Income and Personal Consumption Expenditures, 1950–1969 (in 1958 Dollars)

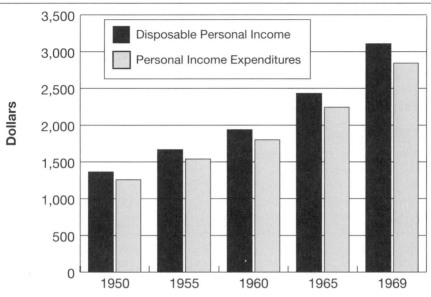

Source: U.S. Census Bureau, 1970.

America. The movement of non-poor people to the suburbs physically separated the economic levels, and mass-produced clothing made it difficult to recognize the poor by dress. At the same time, poverty had become even more of a problem as the isolated poor developed cultural perspectives that made them aliens in the mainstream of their own nation, and as modern jobs increasingly demanded skills that the poor simply did not have.

President Kennedy identified the underprivileged segment of the country as a growing area of attention at the beginning of his own administration. When he took office, the nation was coming out of recessions in 1957 and 1960 that had slowed the remarkable rate of postwar economic growth. In his February 1961 message on the economy to Congress, President Kennedy announced an economic recovery plan that would "sustain consumer spending and increase aggregate demand now when the economy is slack." Among other measures to increase demand, the President announced his intention to distribute the nation's surplus food to the poor. One of these steps involved increasing the school lunch program, then a small-scale effort, later to grow into the enormous Free and Reduced Price Lunch Program. Kennedy also recommended expanding the Aid to Dependent Children Program (later renamed Aid to Families of Dependent Children), then available only to children with absent fathers, to include children with unemployed, needy fathers present. Thus, in a key speech foreshadowing President Johnson's War on Poverty, Kennedy explicitly identified boosting demand through government spending, including spending on the poor, as an economic strategy ("Text of the President's message," 1961, p. 10).

The following year, in his economic message of January 21, 1962, President Kennedy announced his own expectation that rising standards of living should erase poverty. "Increasing in our lifetime," he declared, "American prosperity has been widely shared, and it must continue so. The spread of primary, secondary, and higher education, the wider availability of medical services, and the improved post-war performance of our economy have bettered the economic status of the poorest families and individuals. But prosperity has not wiped out poverty. In 1960, 7 million families and individuals had personal incomes lower than $2,000 [a little over $14,000 in 2007 dollars]. In part, our failure to overcome poverty is a consequence of our failure to operate the economy at potential" (quoted in "Goal of growth," 1962, p. C6).

President Kennedy, then, expressed some of the basic themes that began to turn attention in an economy of high consumption toward the economically and socially marginalized. Spending could reverse economic slowdowns. Since the poor had the least to spend, government could boost economic growth by improving their spending power and by targeted government investments that would ultimately bring them in from the margins and create full employment. Following Galbraith's logic, public spending would go toward benefits such as health and training so that human resources could be developed with full efficiency. When all were employed and enjoying salaries, demand would push the country's productive capacities to their maximum. Kennedy saw education as a key to this kind of strategic development. "Our progress as a nation can be no swifter than our progress in education," he proclaimed in 1961. "Our requirements for world leadership, our hopes for economic growth, and the demands of citizenship itself in an era such as this all require the maximum development of every young America's capacity" (Kennedy, 1974 [1961], p. 3348).

At the same time, Kennedy's attention to the poor reflected distributional expectations, as well as ideas about the relationship between demand and production. In the land of plenty, there should be no shortages for anyone. Prosperity must not only be widely shared, but it must completely wipe out poverty. One of the difficulties with this expectation was that poverty is relative in a society of rising expectations. The policymakers who prepared the way for the Great Society/War on Poverty were attentive to the relative nature of poverty. These individuals saw the problem not as the danger of widespread starvation, but as subgroups that were falling behind in the general abundance of American life. As historian Allen J. Matusow (1984) describes the deliberations of President Johnson's Council on Economic Advisors, the Council recognized that real standards of living had been rising for all Americans, including the poor, over the course of the 20th century. It followed, then, that relative poverty was the problem, because rising consumption meant rising expectations and the poor were those who fell behind as all expectations rose. However, as economic advisor Ralph Lanham observed to Walter Heller while they were planning their program, openly advocating the redistribution of wealth from those who had more to those who had less would have been completely unacceptable to much of the American public (Matusow, 1984, p. 220). Therefore, the War on Poverty opted to raise the poor relative to the rising consumer standards of the nation without acknowledging that anyone else could possibly be worse off, either in relative or absolute terms. The nation would be remade in such a way that it was still a competitive field, but there would be no losers.

In fact, the American economy had been becoming more equal, as well as more abundant, for most of the postwar period before the federal actions of the 1960s. The Gini coefficient is a common measure of inequality in income distribution, ranging between "0" (all incomes are perfectly equal) and "1" (a single individual or family has all of a society's income). The coefficient for American family incomes dropped steadily from 1950 to 1957, only moving sharply upward in the recessions at the end of the 1950s and the beginning of the 1960s. By 1962, before the Great Society/War on Poverty that we describe below, the Gini coefficient had begun to drop dramatically once again (Jones & Weinberg, 2000, p. 2, Figure 1). The situation of the American poor had not only been improving in absolute terms before the social campaign that began under President Johnson, it had even been improving in relative terms. Judged in terms of expectations, though, this may have made the subjective problem of poverty even greater. Just as when all standards of living rose, deprivation became even less acceptable, inequality in a setting of abundance became even more objectionable at the same time that the amount of inequality was decreasing. The very fact that the conditions of the poor were improving increased the perception that any gap at all between their conditions and those of others was unjust.

Beyond expectations, demand-side logic focusing on the poor did make sense, even after the recession at the beginning of Kennedy's term. The corporations that John Kenneth Galbraith saw advertising luxuries were doing so because they needed to keep demand high. A tendency toward overproduction is a constant problem for a modern market economy. Karl Marx had argued that the ultimate crisis for capitalism would be one of overproduction and underconsumption, in which an underpaid proletariat could not buy all the goods of profit-seeking businesses. In response, the businesses would cut back and lay off workers, exacerbating the problem of an insufficient market, pushing the industrial economy into a downward spiral.

The Great Depression was, at its core, a crisis of overproduction that ultimately ended through war spending. The federal assistance programs of the New Deal era, the Social Security Act of 1935 and its welfare provisions (Aid to Dependent Children, Aid to the Blind, and Aid to the Disabled), and the Federal Housing Act of 1934 were, at least in part, efforts to stimulate the economy by increasing demand. As demand-side policies became institutionalized in the American economy, putting the least advantaged into jobs and directly subsidizing them to increase their buying power became ways of ensuring that everyone participated fully in a consumption-driven economy. Because the economy could never be judged to be fully "recovered" until it reached a potential of full employment and eradication of poverty that it could never actually attain, the concentration on bringing up the standards of those at the bottom would become institutionalized in policy.

If the ideas of Galbraith and Harrington represented a new emphasis on the excluded and the disadvantaged in a consumer society at the beginning of the Great Society years, those of philosopher John Rawls represented the adoption of this emphasis as orthodoxy after the War on Poverty had officially ended. At the risk of oversimplifying a sophisticated and complex argument, Rawls, in *A Theory of Justice* (1971), essentially attempted to define the nature of social justice by asking what would be fair for all individuals, regardless of social position. To answer this question, he posited an Original Position, before entry into a society, in which no one knows what position she or he will occupy. What social arrangement would rational people choose? According to Rawls, they would choose what would be best for them if they happened to land at the bottom of that social order. This means that the just social order is the one in which there is the least possible inequality in distribution of goods and opportunities, and any amount of inequality is justified only to the extent that it benefits those at the bottom.

The Rawlsian view became entrenched in American thought, perhaps because it expressed the dominant values of its time in a coherent intellectual form. The political scientist Peter Berkowitz (2002) has argued, in a manner consistent with the theme of this book, that beneath the rational surface Rawls's ethics were founded on a secular religion, a liberal faith. We would suggest that the appeal of Rawls for social policy in the late 20th century was precisely that he provided a highly systematized expression of the newest turn in American civil religion. Some version of his theory arguably lies within most uses of the phrase "social justice," even on the lips of those who have never read him or even heard of him. The most interesting characteristics of this view are, first, that it is almost entirely concerned with distribution and seems to assume a state of abundance to be distributed. As we have pointed out elsewhere in a discussion of the implications of Rawls for education (Bankston & Caldas, 2002), there is little consideration in his work of production or the claims of producers on the results of their own labor. The goods, services, and work relations that the occupants of the theoretical Original State consider when deciding on the best society are simply there, and social justice is distributive justice. It is, in other words, a consumer orientation on fairness. The fact that those at the bottom become the most important players in this thought experiment follows from that consumer orientation. If social justice is at bottom a question of how abundant resources are distributed, then one would have to justify why some get more than others, and the greatest justification is required for those who get the least. As we will see in the rest of this book, policymakers and commentators of the late 20th and early 21st centuries tended to view all educational questions in terms of what would be best for those at the bottom, to see any inequality in education as a matter of unjust distribution of an available product, and the distribution of education to those at the bottom as the way to achieve the highest American ideals.

The Moral Drama of the Civil Rights Movement

The previous chapter looked at the stirrings of the civil rights movement during the 1950s, and we saw that schools, seen as the key institutions in American life, played an early part in attempts to achieve racial equality. Injustice and inequality could and should be corrected through the schools. Throughout the 1960s the quest for civil rights became wider in scope as activists moved into many areas of effort, beyond lawsuits. In the age of television, the drama of the civil rights movement played out before the eyes of the entire American public.

　　The year 1960 saw the passage of a new Civil Rights Act. This bill strengthened penalties for obstructing Federal court orders, required state election officials to keep voting records for Federal inspection, and authorized Federal courts to appoint voting referees who could enroll black voters in areas where voting discrimination had been proven. Voter registration became a major part of the drive for civil rights. The Southern Christian Leadership Conference (SCLC), meeting in Nashville, Tennessee, in September 1961 under the leadership of Martin Luther King, made plans for a registration campaign. The campaign aimed to double the number of registered Southern black voters in a 2-year period. Opposition to voter registration also became violent, with burnings of churches and shootings.

The movement reached its highest point in the 1963 March on Washington. In August over 200,000 marchers from all over the United States gathered in the capital to demand immediate equality in political rights, employment, and other areas. There the Reverend Dr. Martin Luther King Jr. gave his most memorable speech, in biblical cadences with echoes of both Judeo-Christian religion and the tradition of American civil faith. Delivered in the shadow of the Lincoln Memorial, Dr. King began by evoking the memory of President Lincoln and of the martyred President's signing of the Emancipation Proclamation, thereby situating the civil rights struggle within the framework of the American faith. He then called up the Founding Fathers, describing the "magnificent words of the Constitution and Declaration of Independence" a "promissory note" of "the unalienable rights of life, liberty and the pursuit of happiness" and observed that by denying these to black citizens, the United States had defaulted on its note. He called upon his listeners to work to get the nation to fulfill its promise, and he proceeded to give vivid images of his dream of freedom and equality around the nation. At the end he brought the language of civil religion together with that of biblical religion in a crescendo of faith in the future (King, 1993/1963).

Dr. King's "I Have a Dream" speech was eventually to become part of the civic catechism in America's classrooms, taking its place alongside the Gettysburg Address. If one had to choose a specific point in time for the symbolic turning of American civil religion, one could probably point to that August 28 oratory before the Lincoln Memorial. This was, moreover, the time of the widening of the movement. Until 1963, the civil rights movement was primarily a struggle against legal discrimination in the South. During that year, however, the struggle also spread to the North, as it became a broader struggle for equal treatment and not simply a battle against discriminatory laws.

Finally, in 1964, Congress, pushed by President Johnson, passed a strong Civil Rights Act that banned discrimination in most public accommodations. This was followed, the next year, by a Voting Rights Act that banned the use of voter qualification tests and authorized Federal voting examiners in places that failed to meet voter participation requirements. Even before passage of the Voting Rights Act, the Reverend King had begun a new voter registration campaign in Selma, Alabama, in January 1965. Alabama officials attempted to stop the campaign with arrests, harassment, and violence. After the passage of the Voting Rights Act, Alabama Governor George Wallace attempted a court challenge of the now federally backed registration, but the courts dismissed his efforts. These and other conflicts kept the movement continuously before the eyes of American policymakers and the American public.

The movement lost possibly its most important unifying leader on April 4, 1968, when the Reverend Dr. King died from an assassin's bullet in Memphis, Tennessee, where he had gone to support the calls of black sanitation workers for better working conditions. Even in death, however, Dr. King furthered the civil rights cause. The rioting and anger that erupted in many American cities after the assassination pushed Congress to pass the Fair Housing Act of 1968, which prohibited discrimination in the sale or rental of housing. Dr. King also joined the pantheon of American fallen heroes, including Lincoln and Kennedy, giving an added aura to his cause.

The civil rights movement worked a deep change in the social vision of Americans. Although the civil rights movement was primarily a movement for equality for African Americans, it served as a model and an inspiration for other groups. The movement became a model for Native Americans, Hispanics, and other ethnic and racial groups. Legislation protecting and promoting the rights of women and the disabled, following the model set by governmental responses to the movement, took the form of civil rights laws.

The civil rights era, seen by Bellah as a turning point in American beliefs, reshaped even American policies on immigration, opening the way for the largest wave of immigration since the Progressive Era that we considered earlier. By the mid-1960s, social norms had led Americans to identify racial discrimination as a fundamental flaw in American society. Thus, Democrat Philip Hart, one of the sponsors of the 1965 Hart–Cellar immigration reform, declared that efforts to maintain the American creed and to protect the American political heritage "require that our immigration policy be brought in line with the moral and ethical principles upon which our democracy is based" (quoted in Shanks, 2001, p. 170). The Hart-Cellar Act of 1965 consequently turned the nation away from the national origins quota system, heavily biased toward northern and western Europeans, that had dominated American immigration policy since the 1920s, and opened the way for the massive wave of Latin American and Asian immigration of the late 20th and early 21st centuries.

By the 1970s, the civil rights perspective had become established as a vision of core American values. It was based on the old idea of individual rights, but understood individual rights as threatened on the basis of group membership. Therefore, rights were to be protected on the basis of group membership. Most importantly for the thesis of this book, groups that were excluded had to be included. The turn toward the disadvantaged was a turn toward disadvantaged groups, so that equality of opportunity was increasingly understood as equality across racial or socioeconomic categories. Although the equalization was to occur throughout the society, it was in the schools, more than anywhere else, that it was to be achieved. Driven by the distributive orientation of a society of high consumption and by the moral vision of civil rights, the American government began a new campaign of assimilation in earnest under the administration of President Lyndon B. Johnson. The assimilation of the disadvantaged became the idea underlying most educational changes from the mid-1960s onward.

THE WAR ON POVERTY AND THE NEW ASSIMILATION

At the end of 1963 the National Association of Intergroup Relations (NAIRO) met in Cleveland. The members devoted a special memorial session to the recently assassinated President Kennedy and to the meaning of his death for the civil rights movement. Giving voice to the turn of attention to the marginalized as the new center of American civil religion, Edward Rutledge, director of housing for the New York State Commission for Human Rights and president of NAIRO, declared in December 1963, "I believe that programs for more public housing for low-income families, retraining programs for our technologically unemployed, intensified programs in public schools and other such social and economic measures geared to redress the grievances and reduce the problems of almost one-fifth of the American population—the disadvantaged whites and Negroes, Puerto Ricans, Mexicans, and Indians—are all in the interest of establishing the American dream of equality for all" (Seeger, 1963, p. 10).

President Kennedy's successor began to translate this moral vision into governmental action. President Johnson's package of social welfare legislation became law in the faith that the United States "would end poverty in our time." In proposing his program, the President assumed the mantle of the slain Kennedy, and then launched his War on Poverty. In his State of the Union address at the beginning of 1964, President Johnson drew on the memory of President Kennedy to present his plan for a crusade against poverty. "Let us carry forward the plans and programs of John Fitzgerald Kennedy," Johnson urged, "not because of our sorrow or sympathy, but because they are right. And in his memory today, I especially ask all members of my own political faith, in this election year, to put your country ahead of your party" ("Text of Mr. Johnson's State of the Union Message and His Earlier Press Briefing," 1964, p. 16).

The War on Poverty was based on the ideas that a culture of poverty existed among the poor, that this culture created a vicious cycle that maintained people in a state of poverty, and that government programs could eliminate poverty by changing the poor. Kennedy and Johnson economic advisor Walter Heller, one of the chief architects of the War on Poverty, moved education to the center of the Federal government's attempt to change the culture of the poor, declaring, in the opening words of his 1964 report "The Problem of Poverty in America," "equality of opportunity is the American dream, and universal education, is our noblest pledge to realize it. But, for the children of the poor, education is a handicap race; many are too ill-motivated at home to learn at school" (quoted in Spring 1989, p. 127). Heller's remarks reveal, first, the continuing paradox of equality of opportunity. He saw the problem as the disadvantage of the poor in the race to move forward among unequal positions, although poverty is itself part of the inequality of positions. Second, Heller specifically identified the problem as one of motivation, of the cultural orientation of the poor. Third, he was suggesting that government had both the obligation and the ability to change motivations. Finally, Heller saw education as the reason for governmental intervention in the mental orientations of the poor and as the means for this intervention. The War on Poverty, as Walter Heller presented it in this founding document, had a great deal in common with the Americanization movement of the early 20th century: if we substitute "children of immigrants" for "children of the poor," the remark could easily be attributed to the advocates of national assimilation.

THE EDUCATIONAL FRONT IN THE WAR ON POVERTY

Schools were seen as the logical and most important front in America's newest quest, since education was viewed as the poor's ticket out of their collective misery. As educational critic Joel Spring has noted,

> the major emphasis given in the strategy against poverty was education. The report [of the Council on Economic Advisors] flatly stated, "universal education has been perhaps the greatest single force, contributing both to social mobility and to general, economic growth." No data were presented to support this statement nor was there any discussion of the complexities involved in linking mobility and economic growth to education . . . Without supporting data, the statement must be viewed as one of belief, and

not fact. And it was this belief that was incorporated into the battle plan. (Spring, 1989, p. 130)

Citing the Continental Congress of 1787 and pronouncing that America had been "strong and prosperous and free" since that time because of the nation's commitment to education, President Johnson proclaimed in January 1965, "We are now embarked on another venture to put the American dream to work in meeting the new demands for a new day. Once again we must start where men who would improve their society have always known they must begin—with an educational system restudied, reinforced, and revitalized" ("Johnson's message to Congress," 1965, p. 20).

Accordingly, one of the most important planks in Johnson's far-reaching legislative package was the Elementary and Secondary Education Act (ESEA) of 1965. A key provision of this core effort in the War on Poverty was Title I, which distributed funds to schools and school districts with high percentages of low-income students. Schools at risk (also known as Title I schools after this section in the ESEA) would ultimately be flooded with funding from ESEA programs falling under this title in the legislation. Title I later became the cornerstone of the No Child Left Behind legislation. Ultimately, one of the ironic consequences of the ESEA was that many schools actively sought the label "Title I." Even relatively high achieving middle-class schools maneuvered to be reclassified as "poor schools." (One school seeking the designation of Title I so that it would be eligible for as much as $600,000 in additional Federal funding contacted the second author of this book to help with the mountain of paperwork. One of the co-authors' best graduate students, who teaches at a very desirable middle-class school with relatively high test scores, lamented that they did not *yet* have enough poor students to qualify as a Title I school.)

The logic behind the ESEA was essentially that both poverty and the substantial racial achievement gap could be lessened through programs to help compensate for historically produced disadvantages of specific groups in the United States, including disadvantages produced by hundreds of years of public neglect of African Americans. Thus, for example, ESEA programs such as Head Start were viewed as compensatory efforts to help underprivileged preschoolers begin the educational race closer to the starting line.

The compensatory education movement of the 1960s, which lay behind the ESEA, had as its goal the provision of schooling that would compensate for the deficiencies of the culturally deprived. According to a 1965 report on *Compensatory Education for Cultural Deprivation*, "we will refer to this group as culturally disadvantaged or culturally deprived because we believe the roots of their problem may in large part be traced to their experiences in homes which do not transmit the cultural patterns necessary for the types of learning characteristic of the schools and of the larger society." While the primary focus of compensatory education was on the cultural reorientation of poor children, early compensatory education also displayed some of the ambitions at social redesign. "Integration will contribute most effectively to better attitudes and relations," wrote the authors of the 1965 report, "when there are a great variety of ways in which children of both races engage in common activities on a one-to-one basis" (Bloom, Davis, & Hess, 1965, p. 32).

Following in the assimilationist tradition of American education, the educators of the emerging War on Poverty saw the poor as the "internal foreigners," to be Americanized through the educational system. "Predominantly Negro, Puerto Rican, Mexican, and southern rural or mountain whites, these people [the poor] are the bearers of cultural attitudes alien to those which are dominant in the broader communities they now inhabit, and their children come to the school disadvantaged to the degree that their culture has failed to provide them with the experiences that are 'normal' to the kinds of children the schools are used to teaching" (Gordon & Wilkerson, 1966, p. 2).

Ambitions for transforming the lives of the poor reached well outside the usual boundaries of the campus and into personal and family lives. In 1963, President Kennedy began a program intended to combat dropping out of school. Earlier, the decision to leave school before completion of a high school diploma had been seen as a matter of individual choice or as a consequence of an individual's own economic needs. By the early 1960s, though, leaving school was seen as demanding a response from the Federal government. Kennedy's campaign, overseen by the U.S. Office of Education, concentrated on 63 of the country's large cities. In those cities, school counselors and other local personnel went to the homes of dropouts, called them on the phone, and wrote to them to encourage them to return to school (Gordon & Wilkerson, 1966, p. 40).

Ypsilanti, Michigan, ran an experimental program in the 1960s laboriously titled the Intervention in the Cognitive Development of the Culturally Deprived and Functionally Retarded Negro Preschool Child. Gordon and Wilkerson (1966), in a contemporary description, observed that "the Ypsilanti project is most notable . . . for its method of extending the school program into the home. During a two-hour afternoon period each week, a classroom teacher goes into each child's home . . . There, in a kind of private demonstration lesson, she continues the education of the child on a one-to-one basis with the cooperation and participation of the mother" (p. 50). The school was not simply attempting to correct the putative cultural defects of the internal aliens, it was incorporating their family lives into the state-run institutions. "Many programs," reported the same document from that era, "also provide for parent discussion groups, parent education on matters of child guidance, and individual parent meetings with professional psychiatric personnel for consultation on behavior or other emotional programs. In New Haven, no child is accepted in the public school prekindergarten program unless a parent will consent to participate in a parallel but separate program" (Gordon & Wilkerson, 1966, p. 51).

In order to build the Great Society through changing the culture of the disadvantaged, the federal government created its most ambitious and most long-lasting program of compensatory education, Project Head Start. The Office of Economic Opportunity had been created by the Economic Opportunity Act of 1964 (PL 88-452) to direct the War on Poverty. The OEO's first director, Sargent Shriver, was the initial prime mover in creating a national intervention program. The program provided publicly subsidized preschool care for children living near the poverty level. The theory behind Head Start was implied in its name: it is an educational program designed to move disadvantaged children closer to the starting line from which more advantaged children already begin the academic race. According to the Office of Head Start, the program "was designed to help break the cycle of poverty by providing preschool children of low-income families with a comprehensive program to meet their emotional, social, health, nutritional, and psychological needs" (Office of Head Start, 2006).

In the summer of 1965, a Project Head Start operation brought early learning to 560,000 children enrolled in 13,000 centers in 2,500 of the nation's communities (Gordon & Wilkerson, 1966). Following the design statement of Head Start, the centers that spread around the country sought to provide disadvantaged children services that are normally obtained in families. "Since in discussions of the disadvantaged, the home and family were considered the major causes of deprivation," wrote education critic Joel Spring, "it was only logical to gear part of the program toward family intervention. Supposedly the introduction of intellectually stimulating toys and objects into the home plus training and education of the parent would be one major step in the direction of changing family life" (Spring, 1989, p. 146).

Project Head Start has been one of the longest-lasting initiatives of the War on Poverty. Its efficacy is a hotly debated topic. The official Head Start Web site maintains that the program "has had a strong impact on communities and early childhood programs across the country" (Office of Head Start, 2006). Janet Currie (2007), somewhat more modestly, has reported that Head Start does not appear to close the gap between disadvantaged and other students but that it does show long-term benefits for students. Other independent program evaluations of state-funded preschool have generally found only modest positive effects for programs like Head Start (Gilliam & Zigler, 2001), or initially positive effects that diminish as the child moves through elementary school (Lee, Brooks-Gunn, Schnur, & Liaw, 1990).

While cultural assimilation, through programs such as Head Start, formed part of the focus on bringing domestic outsiders into the mainstream, President Johnson's project included "better health" for the bottom fifth of Americans, as well as "better schools . . . and better homes and better training" (Text of Mr. Johnson's State of the Union Message, 1964, p. 16). Just as education served as a means of creating better homes, through interventions such as Head Start, educational institutions were pinpointed as places for improving health. At the time the Great Society legislation was being formulated, many poor children were coming to school hungry. As we saw, President Kennedy had identified the redistribution of surplus food as a means to simultaneously address the problem of poverty and stimulate economic demand. Social scientists in the Great Society period rightly saw hunger as a handicap to optimal learning, and used this justification to push for the inclusion of the Free and Reduced Price federal lunch program to be part of the ESEA. The program would eventually be expanded to include free breakfast as well.

The era of the Great Society and the War on Poverty drew to an end, and the nation entered the troubled decade of the 1970s and the more conservative Reagan years of the 1980s. But the legacy of the era was greater than the survival of programs such as Head Start and government-supplied meals in schools. The ESEA, with its assimilationist orientation and its concentration on schools as a means of uplifting the disadvantaged, continued to be the foundation of American school policy even into the 21st century, when the No Child Left Behind program of President George W. Bush, a leader with a political orientation quite different from that of President Johnson, emerged from the continually renewed ESEA. In the decades following the 1960s, American policymakers and scholars accepted the assumption that the nation could remake itself and realize its destiny through the schools by transforming its least advantaged so that all would compete and none would lose.

Meanwhile, the United States did not eradicate poverty. The War on Poverty years did indeed show a dramatic drop in percentages of Americans below the poverty line, as shown in Figure 6.2. However, this is somewhat misleading, when we recall that the Federal government's estimates of proportions of the population above or below poverty only date back to 1959, between the recessions of 1957 and 1960, when inequality was increasing sharply in the United States. During the 1950s, moreover, the general trend of decreasing income inequality had seen reverses each time an

Figure 6.2. Percentages of People in the United States Below the Poverty
Level, 1960–2003

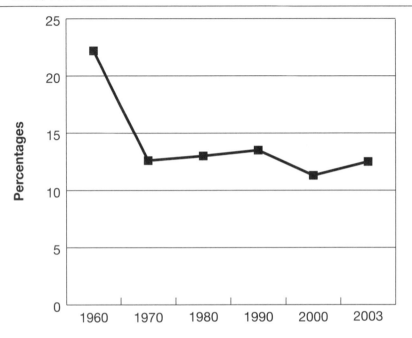

Source: Ruggles et al., 2008.

economic downturn occurred (Jones & Weinberg, 2000, p. 2, figure 1).
Both the War on Poverty and the most commonly used indicator of poverty apparently began when relative poverty was at a high point and when
the economy was about to pull out of a slump and go into a boom. Although any contribution the War on Poverty made to improving the conditions of poor people was highly desirable, it is difficult to separate the
consequences of the distribution of governmental funds and services from
those of a strong 1960s economy.

In 1967, the United States changed its unit of measurement of income
inequality from the family to the household, due to changes in living patterns of the population. Using the household, "measures of income inequality traditionally used to study the income distribution of the United States
suggest that the 1967–1980 period was one of relatively stable inequality" (Jones & Weinberg, 2000, p. 4). In fact, the lowest fifth of Americans
actually gained in their share of the nation's wealth during the decade

following the War on Poverty, from 4.0 percent of the nation's aggregate income to 4.4 percent in 1977 (Jones & Weinberg, 2000). President Reagan's economic policies during the 1980s may well have contributed to increasing income inequality, although the decrease in the share of income going to the poorest fifth began in the late 1970s.

Although the contribution of assimilative programs such as Head Start and the provision of federally funded school meals to antipoverty efforts continue to be debated in academic and policy circles, they enjoy continuous political support and are popularly assumed to be successful. Whatever their virtues, these programs certainly have not ended poverty. Nor have they assimilated the disadvantaged.

One of the main goals of projects such as Head Start, as we have seen, was to make the families of the marginalized more like idealized middle-class families, and thereby move the children of the domestic outsiders into the middle class. These types of programs, as we have seen, attempted to reach out into the families of children. However, from the Great Society period on, the poor became less like the non-poor in some critical ways. Figure 6.3 shows the prevalence of single-headed family households among those below and above the official poverty level from 1960 through 2000. This type of household became more common throughout the late 20th century. More importantly, though, the household structures of the poor became steadily less like those of the non-poor. The question of whether poverty programs contributed to changing family structure among poor families is a highly controversial and difficult one. But for our purposes, it should suffice to observe that the new developments in family life were entirely outside of the control of educational programs such as Head Start.

African Americans have constituted an important segment of the marginalized. The civil rights movement, in addition to changing the moral discourse of the nation, was also followed by marked material achievements. From the 1960s onward, the black middle class expanded, and with the lowering of the explicit barriers of discrimination, the numbers of African American professionals shot up. It was a testament to the abilities and determination of many minority members that individual mobility did proceed so quickly once the legal impediments were removed, in spite of the prejudices and historical burdens that undoubtedly still remained. However, again the Great Society years were followed by new differentiations, rather than by large-scale assimilation. As Douglas Massey and Nancy Denton detailed in their book *American Apartheid* (1993), American society has followed a steady trend in racial segregation in housing throughout the course of the 20th century, including the years of the Great

Figure 6.3. Percentages of People in the United States Below the Poverty Level and Above the Poverty Level Living in Single-Headed Family Households, 1960–1980

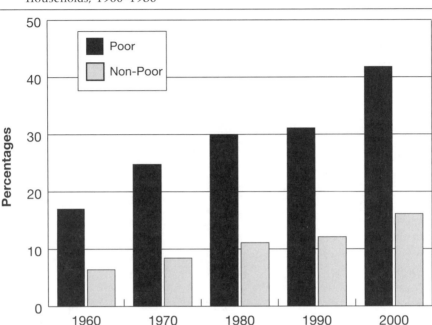

Sources: Ruggles et al., 2008 for years 1960 through 1980; U.S. Census Bureau, 1990a and 2000 for 1900 and 2000.

Society. In the last part of the century, in particular, a majority of white Americans settled in the suburbs, while a majority of black Americans lived in the central parts of cities.

In retrospect, attempts to assimilate the marginalized through cultural redesign appear to have been overly ambitious, if not hubristic. While the educational and training programs that made up much of the War on Poverty may have held out some opportunities for some individuals, they did not fulfill their stated goals of eliminating poverty. As we look at the most long-lasting and determined efforts to assimilate the marginalized and ultimately change the shape of American society, through judicial direction of education, we want to ask readers to think more about whether we as Americans have not put too much faith in education and expected more than schooling can deliver.

EQUALITY, THE JUDICIARY, AND THE SCHOOLS

In the early stages of the efforts to achieve racial equality in the United States, the federal judiciary, especially the Supreme Court, was the most active part of the government. The legislature is entrusted with making policy, often proposed by the executive branch, but the judiciary is ultimately responsible for protecting the rights of citizens, including and even especially minority rights that majority democratic procedures may infringe. Since judges do not live outside of their society, the same perceptions and currents of belief that affect others affect judges as well. The judiciary therefore tended to share in the view that the historic wrongs of American society, brought into sharp relief by the civil rights struggle, could be righted through the school system.

As we saw, many, including Thurgood Marshall, believed that segregated schools would end with the death of segregation by law. Though *de jure* segregation largely did come to an end not long after 1965, over the course of the late 1960s it became evident that racially segregated schools were not simply maintained by law, but by social class, residential patterns, and other deeply rooted characteristics of American society (*de facto* segregation). If schools were to create real equality of opportunity, and not simply equality of current legal status, American society itself would have to change. Black schools, even after the end of *de jure* segregation, truly were inequitable in just about every sense of the word, from inferior facilities and books to overcrowding and underqualified teachers (Bankston & Caldas, 2002). As inequitable as black schools were on these educational characteristics, a major study, *Equality of Educational Opportunity* (Coleman et al., 1966), often referred to as the *Coleman Report*, demonstrated that black schools were even more disadvantaged in terms of the backgrounds of their student bodies. The *Coleman Report* linked the quality of an individual's schooling to the average socioeconomic level of a school's student population.

Using extensive schooling data, the *Coleman Report* made a convincing case that students from socially and economically disadvantaged backgrounds who were isolated from the mainstream were not likely to rise above their group's low educational and occupational levels. Separate black schooling, in essence, was helping to perpetuate a separate black social caste. For America to build its equitable society without poverty or socioeconomic disadvantages, the separate, grossly inequitable system of black schooling would need to be dismantled, and black students integrated into middle-class white schools. The *Coleman Report* would become one of the primary social science justifications for the judicially mandated desegregation that would soon follow its publication.

The logic of moving isolated students into the mainstream was essentially assimilationist. Excluded, separated groups of students could be included in the mainstream, where they would eventually become full participants in American prosperity and opportunity, by moving them into schools attended by relatively privileged majority group members. To point out that this reasoning is assimilationist is by no means to say that it was therefore erroneous. But simply acknowledging legal rights of access will not bring the excluded into the institutions of the larger society. If the society is organized so that real access is not available, then the attempt at assimilating the historically marginalized can easily become an effort to reorganize the society itself. Thus, in the late 1960s and early 1970s, the attempt to transform the disadvantaged through schools moved to the center of the old goal of transforming the entire society through schools.

In the volatile social atmosphere that followed Dr. King's death in 1968, the Supreme Court handed down its watershed *Green* desegregation decision (*Green v. County School Board*, 1968). The Virginia school district's freedom-of-choice desegregation plan at issue in this case had not resulted in even one white student transferring to a majority black school, and only 15% of blacks transferring to majority white schools. The court ruled that since the district's schools were not meaningfully integrated, the district was still operating an unconstitutional dual school system. The court did not want to see "a 'white' school or a 'black' school, but just schools" (*Green v. County School Board*, 1968, p. 442), as the decision tersely put it. The school system was ordered to immediately come up with a plan that created truly integrated schools. Three years later, the *Swann* Supreme Court decision of 1971 upheld the constitutionality of busing to create racially mixed schools in a still largely racially separate society (*Swann v. Charlotte-Mecklenburg Board of Education*, 1971). These cases marked the beginning of judicial efforts at desegregation that eventually swept across the entire South and, beginning with another landmark case in Denver in 1973 (*Keyes v. School District Number 1*, 1973), to the rest of the nation as well (Caldas & Bankston, 2008).

By the 1970s, then, education moved beyond being only a way to assimilate the excluded. It had become a way to remake American society to end exclusion. "If we want a segregated society," remarked the eminent social scientist Christopher Jencks (1972, p. 106), "we should have segregated schools. If we want a desegregated society, we should have desegregated schools." The comment sounds incontrovertible: what reasonable person, especially in the post–civil rights movement era, wants a racially segregated society? But it betrays the belief that it is possible to change an entire society by changing its schools.

Educational Inclusion through Affirmative Action

The courts also pursued the twin goals of incorporating the excluded and creating a society in which everyone would be included through rulings on affirmative action. During the second half of the 1970s, cases regarding affirmative action plans in both employment and education began to reach the Supreme Court. The essential question in all of these cases concerned the possibility of a contradiction between the protection of individuals from discrimination and the goal of including members of historically excluded groups into the main body of American society. Did attempting to address historic discrimination or to produce desirable social ends through promoting opportunities for some categories of people involve discriminating against other categories of people? If so, should equalization and inclusion trump antidiscrimination?

The Supreme Court provided an answer to the dilemma with its 1978 *Bakke* decision (*Regents of the Univ. of Ca. v. Bakke*, 1978). In this case, four justices supported the use of race in admissions to university programs in order to provide a remedy to minorities for the present-day consequences of past discrimination and racial prejudice. Four justices opined that compensatory admissions violated the individual rights of members of the racial majority under the equal protection clause of the Fourteenth Amendment and the Civil Rights Act. Justice Lewis Powell provided the tiebreaker with his argument that treating individuals differently on the basis of race requires a compelling state interest, and that creating diverse student bodies provides such a compelling interest.

Justice Powell wrote the opinion of the Court, which the four justices who favored race-conscious admissions joined in part. Although part of Powell's argument involved the assertion that racially or ethnically diverse learning environments would presumably be beneficial to all students who had been fortunate enough to be admitted, a large part of it also involved a goal of restructuring American society through institutions of education, so that the society would be more inclusive of historically excluded groups. Thus, in the 2003 *Grutter v. Bollinger* decision, Justice Sandra Day O'Connor began her opinion for the majority with a restatement and analysis of *Bakke*, expressing nearly millenarian expectations for the consequences of affirmative action in education.

In the *Grutter* case, Justice O'Connor reiterated the idea that only a compelling state interest could justify treating individuals differently on the basis of race, explicitly recognizing that the racial categorization of individuals is constitutionally problematic. Only the compelling interest of increasing the diversity of a student body provided a sufficient state interest to outweigh the differential treatment of individuals according to race. Justice O'Connor held out high, if not utopian, expectations for the consequences of educational affirmative action. The problematic character of racial categorization led Justice O'Connor to one of her most widely publicized assertions: race-based programs cannot continue forever, either in specific institutions or within the American polity. They must be limited in time, and O'Connor gave 25 years after her decision as the date by which American society would be reconstructed to the point that racial preferences would no longer be needed or acceptable.

The diversity rationale for affirmative action turned to elementary and secondary schools shortly after the *Grutter* decision. The 1968 *Green* decision had introduced the concept of unitary status to determine when school districts had actually reached the state of true integration. But since the goal of desegregation was a truly integrated society, and not just conformity with legal processes, how could schools avoid slipping back into *de facto* segregation after the accomplishment of unitary status?

While the *Bakke* and *Grutter* decisions concerned admissions to higher education, they shared an important characteristic with new cases on elementary and secondary education at the beginning of the 21st century. Earlier cases at the elementary and secondary levels had dealt with whether schools would be compelled to redistribute students in order to undo the effects of past discriminatory policies. The new trend in elementary and secondary education, like the higher education cases, dealt with whether schools would be permitted to engage in race-conscious policies to achieve social ends, even though the school systems were not charged with discriminatory practices.

The Supreme Court began to hear the cases of *Parents Involved in Community Schools v. Seattle School District* and *Meredith v. Jefferson County Board of Education* together in 2006. This case dealt with two school districts, neither currently under a desegregation order, that engaged in assigning students to schools on the basis of race. Social scientists supporting race-conscious school assignment filed briefs that racial diversity promotes cross-racial understanding and reduces prejudice, enhances student achievement, avoids the harm to minority students produced by racially isolated schools, and helps to create desegregated communities (American Educational Research Association, 2006; 553 Social Scientists, 2006). Their arguments were, then, both assimilationist, in viewing racial assignment as a means of inclusion, and social reconstructionist, in viewing such policies as means of moving the country more closely to an ideal society.

Ultimately, the Supreme Court ruled against the school boards' practices of race-conscious assignments, in a split decision. However, for the first time the Supreme Court in the Seattle/Louisville decision explicitly legitimized the diversity rationale in K–12 education, as it had earlier in higher education. The split in the Court may be taken as representing a tension between different tendencies in the American civic faith. On the one hand, a dedication to individual upward mobility through education has long been one of the tenets of this faith, and the years immediately following World War II reinforced this tenet. On the other hand, education had also long been seen as a way of assimilating the marginalized and as a way of transforming America into an ideal society. These two goals had become united in the new turn in American civic faith. While events such as the Court's decision in the Seattle-Louisville case suggested that the individual mobility orientation remained strong, an examination of other developments after the 1970s, in the following chapters, will offer evidence that the change wrought by the crisis of the 1960s became institutionalized in all ideological tendencies of American civil religion.

Consequences of Judicial Efforts to Change Society through the Schools

What were the fruits of the long efforts at employing the courts to make American society more inclusive by means of educational institutions? Most observers would agree that the schools themselves have actually grown more segregated over the past few decades, although the reasons are matters of contention. One reason minority concentrations in schools are increasing, in spite of all the attempts at redistribution of students, is due simply to mathematics: minority members constitute an increasing proportion of all students. This is especially true in urban schools. Black and Hispanic students, although minorities in the American population, made up over 60% of central city public school students in 2000 (U.S. Census Bureau, October, 2000). This last point should remind us of the limits of the power of schools. They clearly cannot determine the demographics of their communities, but rather reflect them.

Beyond this, some observers have contended that the Federal government, and particularly the courts, did not have a sufficiently clear image of schools to impose on American society, and this resulted in a conflict over strategies. This line of thinking has also maintained that the lack of purpose and direction from Federal authorities encouraged those who were seeking to subvert or avoid desegregation through white flight (see, for example, Orfield, Eaton, et al., 1996). It is true that by 1990, a relatively conservative Supreme Court began to deemphasize the more coercive aspects of school desegregation and to cede power to lower courts. This decentralization was especially notable in the court's affirmation of the concept of "unitary status," allowing lower courts to decide if individual school boards had made good-faith efforts to comply with desegregation orders and, if such efforts had been made, to release school districts from judicial supervision. But one must ask why there has been so much pressure to seek release from the supervision of the courts and why perpetual control should be needed to maintain desegregated schools.

In previous books that examined in detail the history of desegregation in a single state (Bankston & Caldas, 2002) and surveyed school desegregation experiences around the nation (Caldas & Bankston, 2007), we found that school districts did not just resegregate after the end of court supervision. They also tended to quietly segregate by race and social class while under desegregation orders, since first whites and later members of the black middle class moved out of desegregating districts or into private schools. The reasons they did this were the same reasons that the Federal government tried to redistribute students.

The idea behind James Coleman's influential argument for equalization of educational opportunity was that schools were not just places where learning was distributed, they were also social environments. Moving minority students into schools with members of the majority was a way of sharing the social resources that more advantaged students brought with them. These resources included parental familiarity with the school environment, high educational expectations, social network links that would prove useful in later life, and other benefits that are loosely called "social capital." However, logically and empirically, increasing a school's proportion of students who lacked these kinds of resources meant decreasing the advantages offered by the school.

The turn in American civil religion meant that racial prejudice and discrimination became much less socially acceptable during the late 20th century than it had been earlier. But even while proclaiming their rejection of racism and their support for ideals of equal opportunity, white and even black middle-class Americans deserted school systems that were trying to include the increasingly concentrated and largely African American or (toward the end of the 20th century) Hispanic urban poor. We believe that one should take three points from this process. First, however much we may celebrate schools as the foundation of American democracy, the social system has much more power to change the schools than schools have to change the social system. Second, if we take a Rawlsian social justice perspective and concentrate only on what appears to be in the interest of the disadvantaged or marginalized, we lose sight of the fact that all others also have interests, and that they will act on the basis of those interests. Third, although a consumer orientation encourages us to see schools as places where education is distributed to the students, schools are also places where learning is produced by students from the assets that they bring with them from their homes and communities. Readers should keep this last point especially in mind as we look later at programs such as No Child Left Behind, which assume that variations among schools are matters of some serving students well and others failing to serve their students.

We have examined the connection between desegregation and affirmative action. One big difference is that judicially mandated desegregation has been explicitly compensatory. School districts have been required to make up for their own past wrongs in excluding minority group members by coming up with plans for inclusion through redistribution. The *Bakke* decision that emerged from Justice Powell's strange one-justice pivot rejected compensation. Institutions could use race-based decision-making only to create a better future through diversity. There again, though, the faith in schools seems to lead policymakers to assume that educational institutions are primarily instigators of social change, rather than recipients; that the society somehow exists inside the schools and colleges, rather than the colleges and schools inside the society.

The stated goal of affirmative action in education was to create a more diverse society, in the sense that all members of excluded groups would be included, and a more equal society, without variations among groups in educational achievement or attainment or in occupational status. The American middle class by the early 21st century did indeed include a wider range of physical appearances than it did in the 1960s, although it is difficult to say how much of this was due to affirmative action rather than to the lessening of legal barriers and increasing immigration. Despite Justice O'Connor's prophecy of the withering away of race-conscious programs by 2028, there is no evidence that group differences in educational or socioeconomic outcomes will disappear at any time in the foreseeable future. In fact, the large-scale arrival of new groups of immigrants, mainly from Asia and Latin America, has tended to magnify these differences in recent years (see Bankston, 2006). In short, whatever affirmative action in education may have done for some individuals, it has not been an effective tool for redesigning American society.

IMPACT OF THE CRISIS IN AMERICAN
FAITH IN EDUCATION

We have argued in this chapter that the American civil religion went through a major shift about the time of the 1960s, that schooling was both a vehicle of faith and an article of faith in this shift (as it had been in earlier periods), and that the turn in attention to the inclusion of disadvantaged categories of people was the defining characteristic of the shift. In itself, no part of that particular argument constitutes a criticism. Robert Bellah, whose writings we have taken as a framework for our analysis, saw civil religion as a valuable means of creating national identity and motivation. Writing around the time of the civil rights movement, Bellah also saw the new shift in faith as offering the potential for realizing the shared moral value of equal rights for all American citizens.

The second part of our argument, though, leads us to a more skeptical view of the change in the civic faith of American schooling. While belief can mobilize adherents, it also tends to silence doubt. In our minds, as Americans, using education to include the excluded and to realize visions of equality has become linked to sacralized memories of Kennedy and King and to televised images of the moral drama of the civil rights movement. These memories and images, in turn, have become part of a broader heritage of icons and rituals, including the Founding Fathers, the Pledge of Allegiance, Memorial Day, and Thanksgiving. It seems to verge on sacrilegious to ask if education really can create the Promised Land of equality and inclusion. When it hasn't, it must be because the schools have failed or the teachers are inadequate or we as a nation just haven't shown enough dedication to the new promises of American life. In the concluding chapters, we will concentrate more on this second, more critical part of our argument, as we consider the quandaries and contradictions created by the American faith in education at the end of the 20th century and the beginning of the 21st.

CHAPTER 7

Anxiety and Standards: *A Nation at Risk* and the Equity–Excellence Dilemma in the 1980s and 1990s

LAMENTING THE QUALITY OF EDUCATION

THE 1980s and 1990s can be characterized as a period of anxiety over educational quality and a period of emphasis on standards. In 1983, the National Commission on Excellence in Education published *A Nation at Risk*. This influential and widely cited volume proclaimed that the educational foundations of the nation were being eroded by "a rising tide of mediocrity." The report stressed the importance of basic education for the functioning of the American economy in the information age. The report further emphasized the importance of a high shared level of education for realizing American social and political ideals, and expressed a commitment to enabling all Americans from all backgrounds to fully develop their abilities through schooling. American schools, though, had failed to fulfill these expectations. The condition of public education in the United States had eroded so badly in the preceding 20 years, the report lamented, that "[i]f an unfriendly foreign power had attempted to impose on America the mediocre educational performance that exists today, we might well have viewed it as an act of war" (NCEE, 1983). While the report did make some distinction between students who were bound for college and students who were not college-bound, it argued against a "differentiated curriculum" providing different kinds of instruction for students with different backgrounds and with different goals.

The new back-to-basics movement of the 1980s arose as the commitment to the inclusion of the historically marginalized became more deeply institutionalized in the national faith. President Ronald Reagan signed a bill creating a federal holiday to commemorate Dr. Martin Luther King on November 2, 1983. President Reagan had earlier expressed reservations about the new holiday, and some lawmakers and citizens, led by conservative North Carolina Senator Jesse Helms, opposed and even denounced it. By the end of the decade, though, parades and public events around the nation memorialized Dr. King. Schools were especially involved in Martin Luther King Day events, frequently centered around recitations of the moving "I Have a Dream Speech" that had so skillfully employed the traditional themes of American civil religion in the service of the civil rights perspective.

The phrase "equity and excellence" became, during this time, a shorthand for efforts to employ schools to simultaneously achieve visions of social justice and ensure mastery of those basics that concerned the authors of *A Nation at Risk*. Through standardized curricula and standardized testing, the United States could create equality of opportunity for all and redesign its own citizens to meet all perceived threats to its economic and political preeminence.

Calls for Standards

The alarm over the quality of education in the 1980s intensified calls for standards. But if all American children had to be brought up to specified standards, how could we determine that this was actually happening? Engineering social outcomes requires social measurements, so the answer seemed to lie in testing at all levels, not simply at the level of college admissions, where tests such as the SAT and ACT had been guiding policies in higher education since the end of World War II. The tests of the late 20th century, moreover, were not intended to rank students, but to serve as tools in the provision of quality schooling to all.

The new age of reform and accountability would have some striking parallels with the efforts to standardize education during the efficiency movement in the early 20th century, as well as echo the "Why Johnny Can't Read" controversy of the 1950s in the emphasis on basics. However, unlike the country's first infatuation with the nascent field of psychometrics in the early 1900s, measurement statistics had advanced considerably since Alfred Binet and Edward Thorndike first tried to take the measure of the mind around the turn of the 20th century. Advances in testing theory, statistics, and computing capacity had drastically improved the reliably and validity of standardized assessment. Very complex mathematical models now permitted the creation of value-added statistics that purported to measure how much of a child's learning (an "output") was due to the unique contribution of the individual classroom and school environments ("inputs"), controlling for a multitude of measurable extraneous environmental variables. Value-added techniques were econometric measures originally developed to measure business inputs and outputs (Kay, 1993), but would now be enthusiastically applied to the realm of education (Caldas, 1993; Caldas & Bankston, 1997; Hanushek, 1986).

Computing power had increased exponentially from the 1980s onward. This allowed for processing the digitized information on hundreds of thousands of students simultaneously at very high speeds, and for performing the mind-boggling mathematical wizardry underlying the new complex statistical procedures in mere seconds. Value-added scores could now easily be computed from student data and assigned to schools. Classrooms, schools, school districts, states, and even nations could now be compared on a variety of standardized academic achievement measures. Moreover, private testing firms would accommodate the states' burgeoning assessment needs and develop into a multibillion-dollar industry staffed with hundreds of Ph.D.-bearing psychometricians with the expertise to develop just about any kind of assessment instrument to measure any kind of learning outcome. At first, there were either no stakes or only low stakes tied to the educational statistical comparisons being made. But as we'll see in the next chapter, these newly developed statistical techniques in conjunction with the technical capabilities to apply them to an entire state's school-aged population would ultimately be used to reward or punish teachers and schools in the new climate of educational accountability.

During this new age of efficiency, the pendulum would swing much farther in the direction of standardized accountability than it ever had in the past. Growing in tandem with this sophisticated retooling for educational standardization was a much more profound (and blind) faith in the Progressive premise of the ability of schools to help fashion the ideal society. Whereas this idealism had earlier been most evident in efforts to racially desegregate schools during the late 1960s and 1970s, it would now soar to new heights as schools would be expected to not only erase all racial inequality, but also solve the most intractable of family and social problems. Schools were increasingly expected to assume the roles and responsibilities formerly associated with families and communities. Classrooms were quickly filling with children coming from more complex and often more troubled family lives, and teachers were expected not only to act as educators, but also as parents, psychotherapists, and social workers. Moreover, teachers were expected to assume all of these new social responsibilities and increase their students' test scores at the same time. Adapting the distributive ideas about education that became much more prominent during the 1960s and 1970s to the growing demand for mastery of basics, testing became a way of determining whether schools were handing out the same high-quality products to all consumers.

A Nation at Risk in some respects, such as the concentration on basic academic subjects, seemed to introduce a less experimental and ambitious tone than had become common in educational deliberations during the free-thinking 1960s and 1970s. However, it was well within the long-term, overarching civic faith in education as a means to constructing the City on a Hill, and it echoed the egalitarian goals of recent decades. The report maintained that all students should receive essentially the same education through high school and that the education could and should be of uniformly high quality. In these goals, the report echoed a perspective that was becoming commonly summarized in a phrase that some might regard as oxymoronic, "equity and excellence." The report recommended that high schools implement the following, decidedly academic curricula for *all* students: "(a) 4 years of English; (b) 3 years of mathematics; (c) 3 years of science; (d) 3 years of social studies; and (e) one-half year of computer science" (p. 22).

The only curricular difference for college-bound students stipulated in the report was that they should pursue 2 years of a foreign language in high school in addition to following the basic plan recommended for all students.

The idea of equity implied standardization and uniformity in schooling. To be measurably "equitable," the education provided to each student had to be on the same scale. The idea of excellence was essentially outcome-based. Students needed to have a high level of performance for education to be regarded as "excellent." The combined concepts of equity and excellence assumed that all students, of all backgrounds and interests, could and should show high levels of achievement on the same measurements. Educators were not to give excuses for differences in family backgrounds as justification for why some students performed better than others. To do so meant that one had "low expectations" for the at-risk students, and this was unacceptable within the assumptions established in the 1960s.

The call for standards sought both high, definable, and measurable levels of accomplishment and the redistribution of opportunities and resources to those at the bottom. E. D. Hirsch attempted to balance this simultaneous pursuit of elite knowledge and egalitarian outcomes in his 1987 bestseller, *Cultural Literacy*. Hirsch argued that specific areas of cultural knowledge are necessary in order to operate in contemporary society. The items of cultural literacy that concerned Hirsch were often of the sort traditionally identified as "elite" knowledge. However, Hirsch argued that it was the knowledge that made the elites. If we could distribute this cultural literacy more broadly, we could serve the cause of social justice by giving the culturally disadvantaged the educational background formerly possessed only by the advantaged. Hirsch's argument indicates the extent to which the standards movement of the 1980s was operating within the orientation toward national goals that came out of the 1960s. The ultimate justification for cultural literacy was Rawlsian: it would serve the interests of those at the bottom. Moreover, following the culture of poverty views of the Great Society, it assumed that inequality was primarily a matter of education, not a matter of the social and economic structure, of community and family backgrounds, or of the historical formation of class-based worldviews. By giving everyone an elite education, educators could give everyone access to elite membership.

Testing and the Demand for Accountability

During the 1980s, following the recommendations of *A Nation at Risk* for high-stakes testing at transition points, many states began implementing more rigorous assessment programs, including graduation exit examinations. In response to the report's recommendations for higher education, many universities also began raising entrance requirements and demanding that college applicants follow the strict state high school curriculum recommended by the influential report. It would seem that given this increasing rigor, ACT and SAT test scores should have risen markedly as better-prepared students took these college entrance exams. But this was not the case. Data indicate that from 1980 to 2000, average scores on these two exams remained flat.

The stagnation in scores on these two college entrance exams corresponded with a lack of upward growth in test results on the country's only nationally standardized achievement test for elementary and secondary students, the National Assessment of Educational Progress (NAEP). Figure 7.1 shows that there was little change in math or reading scores from the early 1970s to the early 2000s.

The achievement gap between whites and blacks did diminish over this roughly three-decade period on the NAEP, but interestingly, the greatest advances for blacks took place in the decade *before* the school accountability movement. The bulk of the hundreds of millions of dollars spent for educational programs targeted to at-risk students was spent *after* the most significant narrowing of the achievement gap. This is clearest in reading, the most foundational of academic skills, and the area that has perhaps received the greatest sustained efforts at improvement, with the federally funded reading programs Success for All and Reading First. As shown in Figure 7.2, the average reading scale score for blacks in 1971

Figure 7.1. NAEP Mathematics Scores for 17-Year-Olds, by Race and
Ethnicity, 1971–1999

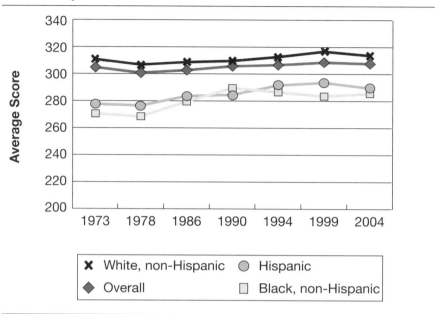

Source: National Center for Education Statistics, 2005.

was 239. This score rose dramatically, to 264, by 1984, the year after *A
Nation at Risk* came out. After that time, black scores ceased to rise and
Hispanic scores actually declined.

Why, with all of the emphasis on higher standards and more rigorous courses, following the new concern with testing in the 1980s, are students not performing better, and in some instances groups of students are
performing worse? The simplest, most logical answers are: 1) In general,
the quality of education provided during the 2 decades following the release of *A Nation at Risk* did not improve in the United States, and for some
subgroups, like African Americans, it may have actually deteriorated, and/
or 2) other factors outside of the school, which negatively affect how children perform academically, were increasing in importance during the
school reform movement, and trumped any school reform efforts. The
second explanation raises questions about the extent to which we can
actually plan and control our nation's future, even its educational future,
in the classrooms. The fact that much of the apparent decline in test scores
came after *A Nation at Risk*, during the periods of Goals 2000 and No Child

Figure 7.2. NAEP Reading Scores for 17-Year-Olds, by Race and Ethnicity, 1971–1999

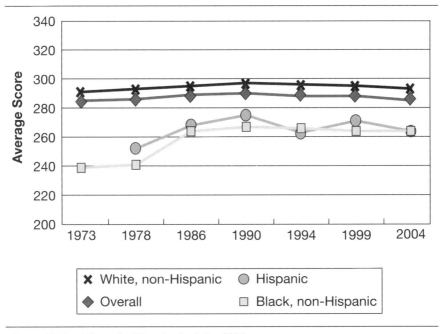

Source: National Center for Education Statistics, 2005.

Left Behind, raises the issue of why we sounded the alarms over educational rigor in the early to mid-1980s. To address this last point, we need to return to the idea that schooling plays a central symbolic role in our system of beliefs about the nation, and consider the threat in that symbolic report.

THE THREAT OF DECLINE AND THE QUEST FOR RENEWAL

During the 1980 presidential election, candidate Ronald Reagan famously asked voters if they were better off than they had been 4 years earlier. Since unemployment and inflation were then high, and gas prices were high relative to earlier levels, this was clearly an effective campaign issue. The American malaise ran deeper than current economic problems, though, and it ran even deeper than concerns over the Iran hostage crisis that was then in progress. The 1960s had proven to be a turbulent as well as a socially significant period. The great change in civic faith that we discussed earlier had raised expectations for social equality and for universal prosperity. Although the nation did make some advances toward equality, each advance brought evidence of how far short of our national ideals we remained. Not only had we not eradicated poverty, but simultaneously fighting a war on poverty and a real war in Southeast Asia had overtaxed the economy.

The disillusion caused by the widespread dissatisfaction with the latter war and its unsatisfactory end had undermined faith in our political institutions. This faith suffered even further when President Richard M. Nixon left office following the Watergate scandal, avoiding probable impeachment. Under the administration of President Nixon's unelected successor, President Gerald Ford, the country saw a period of "stagflation," a combination of economic stagnation and inflation, two ills that had earlier been thought to be opposites. Ronald Reagan's successful election came from his ability to convince the American public not just that they had been better off before the term of President Carter, but that the nation needed to recover itself and to rediscover its sense of national mission.

In the debates leading up to the election, Reagan harkened back to Winthrop's phrase, and spoke of building "for all mankind a shining city on a hill" (Shogan, 1980, p. 7). This evocation of American civil religion touched a special note in much of the American electorate because they felt that the nation had not just failed to fulfill its promises, but was in a deep state of decline. Interestingly, President Reagan ran for the leadership of his nation, and praised the possibilities of the nation, while running against its major institutions, including its system of public education. This was effective in a nation that wanted to believe in its own possibilities, but had become deeply cynical about its own existing realities. A Gallup Poll in 1983, for example, found that public confidence in American institutions was still affected by post-Watergate attitudes. "The sharpest decline in public confidence, according to the poll, came for the public schools, which sank to 39 percent from 58 percent in 1973" ("Esteem for public institutions," 1983, p. B13).

Seen in the context of the perception of social and political decline and the hope for reinvigoration, the call for standards in schools can be understood as, in part, an effort to reform the institution at the heart of the nation's belief in the future. To say that we should all acquire a uniform standard of knowledge was to call for a kind of solidarity in a country that had lost its standards and that many felt needed to rediscover its identity. There was a profound similarity between trying to establish what all Americans needed to know and what all Americans needed to believe: both were ways of bringing the nation together to meet the threat of decline.

Americans were concerned over a real or perceived decline of their polity, and they were looking for ways to bring their greatest dreams back to life. They turned to finding common standards of knowledge or belief in their schools, seeing a link between the quality of their schools and the quality of their nation. That nation was felt to be at risk because of its standing in the world, as well as because of its internal disorder.

GLOBALIZATION AND THE JAPANESE THREAT

Author, economic theorist, and Clinton administration Secretary of Labor Robert B. Reich acknowledged that the United States had been doing an excellent job of educating top intellectuals, but falling short in the education of those at the bottom, reiterating the focus on the least advantaged inherited from the great turn in orientation of civic belief in the 1960s and 1970s (see Reich, 1989, 1993). Revealingly, Reich made these observations as part of his plans for a national industrial policy that would redesign and reinvigorate the American economy for an age of globalization. As we progressed in that age of globalization, though, it began to appear that the nation that had been so seriously at risk in the 1980s had actually not done too badly. In 2006, education commentator Gerald W. Bracey pointed out that many of the Americans who were still bemoaning the failure of schools to educate graduates up to basic standards ". . . were members of the senior class of 1983. They received their diplomas a mere two months after *A Nation at Risk* warned us about that 'rising tide of mediocrity.' Today, these seniors are 40 and bear substantial responsibility for making the U.S. the most globally competitive of the 117 nations ranked by the World Economic Forum. And the class of 1983 scored lower than today's students on the National Assessment of Educational Progress, the SAT, and the Iowa Tests of Basic Skills" (Bracey, 2006, p. 93).

A Nation at Risk had "awakened" the country to the plight of our troubled schools and inspired some early reform efforts, like the institution of minimum competency testing and increasing graduation requirements, and in some states the institution of high school exit exams. But throughout the decade of the 1980s there was mounting public dissatisfaction with schools in some sectors. *New York Times* stories of college athletes who couldn't read and functional illiteracy rates of 25 to 30 percent among high school athletes (Nyad, 1989) fed suspicions that schools were little more than glorified day care centers. The business sector, in particular, decried the quality of American public schools and blamed America's slipping competitiveness in the world market on the country's education system (Vinovskis, 1999). A 1988 *New York Times* series on illiteracy in the U.S. captured well the deep malaise in the business community over the quality of American schools: "The schools are the best place to forestall illiteracy, but are falling far short of meeting the needs of a challenging work force. To do so, the nation's system of public education needs to be thoroughly revamped" (Daniels, 1988, p. B8).

As the Cold War entered its last phase, Americans saw themselves in a peaceful economic war that did not threaten our survival, as the nuclear arms competition with the Soviets had, but that appeared to put our nation at risk of losing its economic preeminence. Schools became the focus of our sense of risk. Businesses were complaining about the low quality of partially literate workers graduating from American high schools, and many business, academic, and government leaders were pointing to countries like Japan, a major economic competitor to the United States, and holding up this Asian country's schools as paragons of educational excellence to be emulated back home (Vinovskis, 1999). For example, the Committee for Economic Development (1985), a think tank comprised of 200 business executives and educators, published a report scathingly critical of American education's failure to prepare students to be competitive in the workplace against our country's chief economic rival, Japan.

Few of those who pointed to Japanese education as a model for realizing American ideals considered how peculiar this was for our national belief that schooling could be the way for us to bring our national aspirations to fruition. Whatever the successes of the Japanese educational system, these were not intended to produce equality of outcomes or equality of opportunity. Entry into Japan's top schools was, and is, extremely competitive, and Japanese elitism still mirrors its feudal past. Moreover, to the extent that Japan has remained successful in economy and education even after its modern glory period of the 1980s, this has apparently been the result of the society surrounding the schools as much as a result of educational policy. While Japanese schools were getting all the credit for producing such highly educated workers and American schools were being excoriated for their abject failure to teach even basic literacy skills well, few were attributing the international education gap to more obvious cultural and, even more fundamentally, familial factors.

Family structure and family attitudes toward education figure prominently among the influences on school performance. In 1980, 3 years before the United States embarked on its quarter-century of school reform, America had a divorce rate five times higher than Japan's (United Nations, 1984). In the words of one sociologist (Stack, 1992), Japan had "a relatively low divorce rate, a relatively highly extended kin network in its family structure . . . and a cultural emphasis on conformity" (p. 324). Indeed, whereas at the time only approximately 0.5% percent of America's elderly lived in extended families, fully 37.5% of the Japanese elderly lived with their children and grandchildren (Japan Ministry of General Affairs, 1987). By the 1990s Japanese families were spending five times as much as American families on educational resources for their children (*Japan Times*, September 18, 1994, p. 3). Commenting on Japanese family goals, one expert noted that "the academic achievement of their children is by far their foremost priority" (Bossey, 2000, p. 77). Japanese children were infused with deep-seated guilt that failure in school would tarnish the family reputation (Hendry, 1995). Japanese school performance, in short, was not a matter of good curricular planning as much as a reflection of the society surrounding the schools.

The 1980s were not the first time that Americans considered the Japanese model. Readers will recall New York City Superintendent William H. Maxwell's 1905 praise of Japanese education as a source of their victory in the Russo-Japanese War. Because schooling is so central in our national system of beliefs, our immediate response to the success of every other nation is to say: it must be their schools. Readers should, though, also remember the Cold War with the Soviet Union and our response to the launching of Sputnik. We do not simply explain every success in the competition among nations through education, but the reform of education becomes our reaction to the threat of national competition. Seeing education as an abstract blueprint for an ideal future, we, as Americans, believed that if the Japanese were besting us in some areas of intellectual or economic achievement, it must have been because they had drawn up a better blueprint, which we could study and use in our own standardized plans.

THE EQUITY AND EXCELLENCE DILEMMA

The phrase "equity and excellence" achieved increased circulation during the 1980s as a consequence of the concern with uniform mastery of educational basics. This particular term had been in usage since the great turn of the 1960s, and the University of Massachusetts School of Education journal *Equity and Excellence in Education* had begun publishing in 1963. In response to generally politically conservative calls for excellence through standards in the early 1980s, such as those in *A Nation at Risk*, politically liberal equity reformers increasingly tied their own concern to that of educational excellence (Berube, 1994). In 1991, the equity and excellence movement achieved permanent institutional standing through the establishment of the Center for Equity and Excellence in Education at George

Washington University (2008). The mission of the GW-CEEE was "to advance education reform so that *all* [emphasis in the original] students achieve high standards" (http://ceee.gwu.edu/About_CEEE.html).

Theorists of the equity and excellence movement argued strongly against any differentiation in the schooling experience. Educators and advocates particularly condemned ability-group tracking because it conflicted with the idea of equity, as measured on a single scale. First "mainstreaming" and later "inclusion" became accepted practices of combining students of all ability levels, including students with mental, behavioral, and, increasingly, emotional disorders, in the same classrooms. These practices did ensure that earlier abuses of excluding handicapped students from an appropriate public education were curtailed. Another benefit to including lower-functioning students within the same classrooms as more advanced students is the exposure of the weaker students to more positive role models and higher standards. So, at least for a minority of students, inclusive practices have probably been beneficial.

However, mainstreaming and inclusion also meant that the special needs of students performing at much lower levels academically might have to be addressed by a single classroom teacher also charged with challenging her most accelerated students. In a classroom with 30 students spread out across the entire continuum of needs and abilities, almost any teacher will point out the logical impossibility of providing the best instruction possible to students at both ends of the spectrum simultaneously. This doomed exercise in futility would be no more successful than trying to create a single university program charged with producing both the best medical researchers and the best constitutional attorneys—with the same curriculum. The necessary division of effort and resources would ensure at best a mediocre program producing poorly trained students in both specialties.

These new pedagogical approaches also meant that disruptive students with behavior disorders were more likely to be included in regular education classes. In our earlier research, we documented the exasperating effect on teachers of increasing the numbers of students in their classrooms with learning and/or discipline problems. The majority of the teachers in our study admitted that this practice hurt the academics of all children more than it helped the students needing additional assistance. (Ostensibly, the "benefit" to the inclusionary exercise would come from the atmosphere created in the classroom from the higher functioning students. See Caldas, Bankston, & Cain, 2007.) In the words of one outstanding teacher (nominated for teacher of the year in her urban district) who had to include in her classroom a group of low-achieving students lacking in many basic social skills (due to a desegregation order), she spent more time teaching these students basic social skills than academics. She felt like by the end of the first year [after they were included in her classroom], she had finally taught her students such basics as how to respect one another, but that when these same students moved on to the fifth grade, negative peer influences [of other included students] countered much of her hard work. (C. Broussard, personal communication, January 29, 2003, cited in Caldas, Bankston, & Cain, 2007, p. 21)

In short, increasing equity, at least in terms of providing all students with the same instruction at the same time and in the same place, of necessity meant decreasing excellence, as the most capable students received less attention.

To suggest that equity and excellence might be contradictory goals seemed heretical within the context of the belief in education as a means of creating an efficient, egalitarian society where all children were both equal and excellent. Such utopian idealism eventually built into the second wave of the education reform movement in the late 1980s and early 1990s, beginning with the Charlottesville Education Summit of 1989, and cresting with the Goals 2000 Act of 1994. The Charlottesville Education Summit took place in September 1989 in the 1980s atmosphere of urgency to train a more highly qualified workforce to increase America's global competitiveness, while simultaneously distributing opportunities and outcomes more equitably. The purpose of this influential bipartisan meeting was to pound out a national education reform agenda. President George H. W. Bush, championing himself as "the education president," met with the nation's governors, led by men like Lamar Alexander (R-TN) of Tennessee and Bill Clinton (D-AR), and set forth six broad, largely impossible-to-attain national goals for American schools to achieve by the year 2000. "Goals 2000" was born. These six goals, which were espoused by "the education president" during his 1990 State of the Union Address, were:

1. All children in America will start school ready to learn.
2. The high school graduation rate will increase to at least 90 percent.
3. American students will leave grades four, eight, and twelve having demonstrated competency in challenging subject matter, including English, mathematics, science, history, and geography; and every school in America will ensure that all students learn to use their minds well, so they may be prepared for responsible citizenship, further learning, and productive employment in our modern economy.
4. U.S. students will be first in the world in science and mathematics achievement.
5. Every adult American will be literate and will possess the knowledge and skills necessary to compete in a global economy and exercise the rights and responsibilities of citizenship.

6. Every school in America will be free of drugs and violence and will offer a disciplined environment conducive to learning.

(Vinovskis, 1999, p. 44)

These six national goals were incorporated into the Goals 2000: Educate America Act of 1994 (P.L. 103-227), where they were supplemented by two additional goals:

7. By the year 2000, every school in the United States will be free of drugs, violence, and the unauthorized presence of firearms and alcohol and will offer a disciplined environment conducive to learning.
8. By the year 2000, every school will promote partnerships that will increase parental involvement and participation in promoting the social, emotional, and academic growth of children.

(Goals 2000, 1994, sec. 102)

These ambitious statements clearly display a faith in the capacity of American education to solve all social and economic problems, and the insistence that it do so. In retrospect, the nation's executive leadership seemed to be aiming a bit high in assuming it could by governmental fiat order schools to not just fix, but *perfectly* fix all of these mostly societal-level problems, much less fix them in 6 years. But this was precisely the mandate handed to bewildered teachers and schools in the later part of the 20th century, and through the progeny of Goals 2000, NCLB, at the beginning of the 21st century as well.

These proclamations in the early 1990s grew out of developments in the previous decade. In a report describing well the events leading up to the 1989 Charlottesville Education Summit, it was agreed by all parties that "Goals should reflect desired educational outcomes . . . such as 100% high school graduation" (Vinovskis, 1999, p. 34).

The standards movement that began in the 1980s had committed educators and policymakers to the faith that we could identify standards of achievement and attainment that were both high and universally applicable. There would be no underachievers, outsiders, or marginalized groups or individuals. Schools could meet the internal and external challenges to our society by pursuing policies that would distribute educational benefits widely and abundantly. But if we placed such high expectations on schools, then the schools, and the teachers who carried out the mission, would receive the blame for failing to deliver.

The anxiety over education and the consequent standards movement of the late 20th century, then, were expressed in terms of a long-standing American faith in education as a means of reaching the ideal society. The nature of that ideal had shifted toward egalitarian inclusion during the great turn of the 1960s and 1970s. The outwardly conservative curricular developments of the century's end followed from premises established by the prominent educational front in the War on Poverty. As we will see in the concluding chapter, the high and at times contradictory expectations placed on schools continued into the 21st century, reaching expression in the No Child Left Behind legislation.

CHAPTER 8

Where All the Children Are Above Average: Entering the 21st Century

NO CHILD LEFT BEHIND

ALMOST immediately after entering the presidency in January 2001, President George W. Bush announced an educational reform program intended to (in his words) "express my deep belief in our public schools and their mission to build the mind and character of every child, from every background, in every part of America." Derived from the long-standing place of education in American civil religion, the No Child Left Behind bill (No Child Left Behind [NCLB], 2002) was a clear product of the historical evolution of this growing faith in American government to cure all social (and even foreign) evils. NCLB reauthorized the Elementary and Secondary Education Act (ESEA) of 1965, setting the educational program of the 21st century on the foundation laid in the era of the Great Society. In fact, as we will argue in this chapter, NCLB was one more consequence of the turn in American civil religion toward education as primarily a means of building an equitable society, a turn that can be traced to the time of President Johnson's administration.

This reauthorized Federal bill was also a logical continuation of the unfulfilled Goals 2000 agenda established under President George H.W. Bush. Both the Goals 2000 manifesto and then the NCLB Act were shaped by the desire for standards and equity from the preceding time of the *Nation at Risk* report. All children, the movement maintained, could achieve at equally high levels of academic performance as measured on the same empirical assessments. The governmental determination in Goals 2000 evidenced in statements about every child entering school ready to learn continued in NCLB, where the government declared that all third graders would be on grade level by 2014—or else. Schools that failed to move toward this goal in a consistently upward, linear fashion would be slapped with increasingly heavy sanctions, including being shut down completely.

No Child Left Behind prescribed the annual administration of standardized tests to children in grades 3 through 8 and required that all states develop progress objectives to ensure that all groups of students would reach proficiency (which is another way of saying at or above average) by 2014. The test results and the progress objectives were to be broken down by classifications of poverty status, racial and ethnic groups, disability status, and English proficiency. All groups were to advance at the same rates on essentially the same measures of achievement.

Following in the direction set by the civil rights era, the administration of President Bush took keen interest in closing the achievement gap by using tests to identify groups that were lagging behind and measure success in eliminating group differences in performance. Indeed, closing the racial and ethnic (Latino) achievement gap and achieving universal equality among categories seemed to be a primary focus of No Child Left Behind. While the Bush administration opposed affirmative action in education, it made racial and ethnic categories a key part of its strategy for using testing and corrective measures in schools to eliminate group variations in outcomes.

One of NCLB's key concerns, then, was with the idea of equity on a single scale, with school, district, state, and Federal efforts concentrated on the historically disadvantaged or educationally weakest groups. There were penalties for any school that failed to meet goals for any group, including special education students and students who did not speak English (on English-administered tests). Students could transfer out of schools that had failed to meet standards for any group. In addition, school districts had to use Federal Title I funds to pay for extra tutoring or other educational services for students in schools that consistently failed to meet overall goals or goals for specific groups. The idea that uniformly high educational achievement could be distributed by schools to all children had left schools with the responsibility, and the blame, for any shortcomings. One of the greatest challenges to this goal came from special education.

NCLB, Inclusion, and the Problem of Special Education

The move toward unification that eventually took the form of NCLB was reflected in the inclusive classrooms movement, which has both legal and philosophical underpinnings. In 1975, Public Law 91-142 ordered that all children, regardless of handicapping condition, be provided a "free and appropriate public education" in the "least restrictive environment." This very much needed legislation had the positive effect of ensuring that children who might otherwise have received no education at all were finally admitted into public educational facilities.

As can be seen in Figure 8.1, following the passage of P.L. 91-142, the percentage of public school students classified as special education shot up from just over 8% in 1976 to almost 14% by 2000 (Parrish, Harr, Wolman, Anthony, Merickel, & Esra, 2004). At first, though, children with severe mental, physical, psychological, or behavioral handicapping conditions were often educated together, apart from the mainstream of students. It is indeed documented that students with disabilities are more likely to be abused than students without disabilities (Sullivan & Knutson, 2000). Also, when students with disabilities are educated in isolated environments they are more at risk of being abused by predatory caregivers who can abuse more flagrantly since fewer protective checks are in place (Hindelang, Gottfredson, & Gaofalo, 1978; Sobsey, 1994). So while on the one hand including an increasing number of students with disabilities in mainstream environments may have reduced their risk of exposure to abuse, the at-

Figure 8.1. Percentages of Public School Students in Special Education, 1976 to 2001

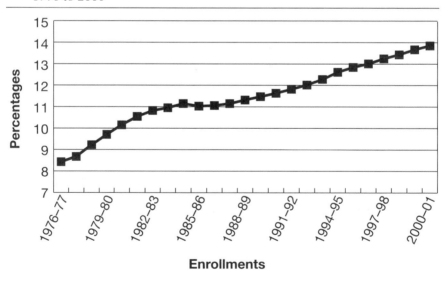

Source: Parrish et al., 2004.

tention to the increased needs of this group may have shifted resources and energy away from teaching students without disabilities.

Not only were human resources like regular educators' time and energy being diverted to help special education students, but in exponential fashion so were material resources. According to the Center for Special Education Finance, "between 1977–78 and 2002–2003, *federal* special education appropriations increased from approximately $252 million to nearly $7.5 billion. According to the 42 states that provided data on the CSEF/NASDSE survey, *state* special education funding rose by 36 percent between 1994–95 and 1998–99, or 24 percent when adjusted for inflation. The actual state revenue per special education student rose by 23 percent, or 12 percent when adjusted for inflation" (Parrish et al., 2004, p. 17).

The ratio of spending on special education students to spending on regular students rose from the late 1960s until the mid 1980s from about 1.9 to about 2.3. By 1999–2000, the ratio had gone back down to 1.9 (Parrish et al., 2004). Although the ratio per student had gone down, school systems still spent about twice as much on special education students as on regular students, and the proportion of the former had increased dramatically.

In 2001, NCLB required, for the first time, that students with disabilities (SWD, a subset of special education) be tested and included in accountability measures alongside all other students. There were to be no excuses: SWDs were held to exactly the same standards as everyone else. School districts could provide alternative assessments only to a very small percentage of students, but even these alternative assessments had to be directly linked to the standards to which all students were being held. Regular and special education teachers across the United States complained loudly that many SWDs were not capable of taking regular assessments. School administrators complained that including the scores of special education students in the overall average scores of schools and districts was unnecessarily lowering ratings. The governmental response, though, was essentially, "We don't want excuses. All children can achieve well, and can achieve well on the same tests."

It may have seemed obvious to the planners that this kind of mandate would lead to uniform excellence. However, those carrying out the plans experienced the demand as futility. One of the authors was once a special education teacher forced to administer standardized multiple-choice achievement tests lasting several hours to young adolescents reading three or four (or more) grade levels below the reading level of the test. All of the students were classified as "educationally mentally retarded." Though working with this group of students was generally a wonderfully rewarding experience, forcing them to take a state-mandated standardized test was one of the more frustrating exercises in which the author ever engaged. After staring blankly at indecipherable marks on the page, most students simply put their heads down after about 5 minutes of grimacing and went to sleep. Since some of his students had severe emotional and behavioral disorders, too, the author spent much of the time simply trying to keep these students in their seats. While this is, admittedly, a single anecdote, it does represent the experience of other teachers who found it utterly unrealistic to expect uniform standards among highly varied student populations.

The Problem of Uniform Standards

The difficulties with NCLB went beyond the mandate to fully include all special education students. Local creativity and innovation have been stymied as school personnel try first to figure out what NCLB means, and then try to craft plans to implement it. According to education policy expert Christine Rossell of Boston University, who extensively analyzed the act: "Navigating the law's parts and sub-parts can be a mindnumbing exercise, even for those experienced at working with education law. One has to read it many times to figure out what it says and that is only the beginning of its technical and conceptual problems" (Rossell, 2005, p. 2).

Critics who recognized the redistributive basis of NCLB were disturbed by the program's concentration on what were presumed to be the weakest-performing subgroups. Schools could be penalized if any groups failed to meet preset goals. For example, NCLB mandates that all students must achieve a given state's "proficient" level in "challenging" academic standards by 2014. As already noted, "all" includes everyone from students with severe learning disabilities to Limited English Proficient (LEP) students. However, LEP students are those who by definition score low on English tests. As noted in a report by Professor Rossell (2005), "If you define a group by their low test scores, that group must have low test scores or someone has made a mistake" (p. 2). Thus, it is logically impossible to ever close the achievement gap between LEP students and those fluent in English, because as soon as a LEP student becomes proficient in English, he or she is reclassified as a fluent English student. Trying to close this gap is logically on par with lifting every student to above average academic achievement.

The law stipulates that schools that fail to meet "Average Yearly Progress," or AYP goals set by their respective states, are designated "Schools in Need of Improvement," and are provided "extra help" to improve (U.S. Department of Education, 2005). This extra help can include tutoring for students as well as the assistance of teams of professional educators who are brought in to fix the school's problems. Though these measures may seem like sound educational practice, in reality they are as likely to disrupt and set back the project of education as to advance it. Teachers in the field report that these teams of professionals who are charged with helping failing schools improve are often staffed with central office personnel who fled from their previous classroom positions. But even competent and dedicated educational specialists can add little to the day-to-day efforts of teachers, other than complicate an already difficult job.

More fundamentally, the very premise on which this extra aid to failing schools is predicated is faulty. The basic premise of NCLB is that failing schools are caused by failing staff. If this is true, why is it that almost all failing schools also happen to be low-income schools serving high populations of at-risk children? Is it simply a coincidence that all the "good" teachers are in the highest-achieving schools, and all the "bad" teachers are in the lowest-achieving schools? This would be extremely unlikely. For such a scenario to be true, it would imply that teachers have 100% control over the academic achievement of their students. We know from much research, however, that how a child performs in school is highly correlated with the child's family socioeconomic status and the average socioeconomic level of the child's classmates.

This last point has been particularly problematic for the policy of transferring students out of failing schools. From the perspective of planners, it makes sense to conclude that if one school seems to be failing, as reflected in the test scores of its students, then students should have the opportunity to move to a better school. However, this overlooks the role of the students themselves in making "good schools" and "failing schools."

The events at Dewey High School in Brooklyn can provide us with an example of why school transfers have not worked as planned. This school has struggled to distinguish itself as one of the best high schools in New York City and, indeed, was ranked by *U.S. News and World Report* as one of the top 505 high schools in the entire country (Freedman, 2008). Students in Dewey have been accepted into Ivy League colleges, including Harvard. However, Dewey High's preeminence as an outstanding place to receive an education is being threatened by the influx of students abandoning a nearby failing high school (Freedman, 2008). According to award-winning social studies teacher Chung Chan at Dewey High, "When I was first here, we had no discipline problems." But Chung added that since Dewey began taking on the weaker students from the failing sister high school, "we've had an influx of students who are unprepared. It's destroying our entire school." Students who are striving to achieve at Dewey now report regular disturbances and disruptions, like kids roaming the halls and regularly disrupting other teachers' classrooms.

According to a Harvard-bound senior, "There are more police here than I've ever seen in my life. It feels like a jail. It doesn't feel like a school." The administration of Dewey has been complaining about the overcrowding caused by accepting so many students from the failing high school. However, rather than being praised for creating an obviously successful school, the central office felt that Dewey could be doing an even better job since it was operating at "only 118% utilization" (Freedman, 2008).

The transfer policy did not work out as planned at Dewey or in other schools because the schools exist within the larger society and reflect the problems of the larger society and its institutions. Students bring varying experiences and levels of preparation with them from their own communities and households. We can see the problems of trying to remake basic social institutions through the schools by looking more closely at the latest version of efforts to remake families through education policies.

The Problem of Restructuring Families through Schooling

The No Child Left Behind legislation did recognize the role that the society outside of schools, especially family, plays in the educational success of children. However, rather than acknowledge that the family domain marks a major limitation in the effectiveness of any public schooling efforts to boost academic achievement, the education bill glosses over this inconvenient truth by attempting to reshape families, much as the assimilationist programs of the War on Poverty had sought to do. Believing that public schools can artificially manufacture the critical family involvement ingredient in student school success, the bill mandates in Section 1118 that in order to receive Federal funding under the act, local education agencies shall implement "programs, activities, and procedures for the involvement of parents in programs assisted under this part consistent with this section. Such programs, activities, and procedures shall be planned and implemented with meaningful consultation with parents of participating children" (NCLB, 2002).

As was earlier the case with the culture of poverty approach of the Great Society programs, the "meaningful consultation" with parents doesn't refer to the parents of educationally successful children, but rather refers to educational authorities trying to involve the parents of children failing in school. The implication of this provision of NCLB is that government can somehow re-create the family involvement that leads to higher academic outcomes, and should intervene to do so. Critics of NCLB may object that this assumes governmental authority over the families of the disadvantaged, and also assumes the power of educational planners to reshape families and communities at will.

THE PROFESSIONAL REACTION
TO NO CHILD LEFT BEHIND

While those in the educational profession largely sympathized with the goals of NCLB, critics of the legislation came from nearly every point on the ideological spectrum. The American Educational Research Association (AERA) is the profession's chief organization for conducting empirical research in schools. One of the authors has been attending the annual meeting of this research group for more than 20 years. Though not a definitive measure of the membership's discontent and hostility to NCLB, the best-attended and most lively session he ever witnessed was in a packed Montreal ballroom at the 2005 annual meeting, where five leading educational researchers took turns castigating the act from several different angles. No one had a kind word for the education law. The standing-room-only crowd spilled into the ballroom's foyer, and periodically erupted into wild applause as the scholars tore into the unpopular act and its consequences.

The American Society for Curriculum Development (ASCD) is the leading organization for researching and developing effective school curriculum. This association has a widely read online newsletter that periodically surveys its readership via an online survey. In a 2006 online survey responded to by 5,183 readers, members were asked, "How has the NCLB affected your school district?" Fully 49% of respondents answered the question "negatively," while only 35% answered "positively" (ASCD, 2006). When asked in the same survey if the achievement gap was closing, 47% answered "no," and only 31% answered "yes." Again, while not a random sampling of educators, the results still suggest that many education experts believe the bill is actually hurting American public education, not helping it.

Many teachers and educators objected to the focus on standardized testing, often without recognizing that this was a direct result of the focus on outcome-based equity that had emerged in the late 20th century. Related to this objection, critics complained of the narrowing of curricula that came from the concentration on basic, testable areas. Still other opponents of NCLB were disturbed by the extent of Federal control of education promoted by the program. Although the Federal government publicized it as "decentralized," NCLB actually imposed a great deal of central direction on education through its mandates. Many researchers and educators shared the concern we already alluded to that NCLB operates on the premise that schools have complete control over the academic performance of students, irrespective of their family background and circumstances. While NCLB resulted in all of these criticisms, though, few of the critics recognized that the uniformity, the Federal centralization, the excessive assumptions of institutional control, the utopianism, and the egalitarian redistributionism were all logical developments of long-term trends in unexamined beliefs about the role of schooling in the American polity. Though on the surface President Johnson's Great Society and President Bush's conservatism seem on polar opposites of the political spectrum, both actually reflect the same underlying faith in public education as a means of building an equitable society.

Despite the widespread professional rejection of the legislation, resistance to it has been mainly passive. Refusing to implement NCLB, however much states may disagree with it, can result in the withholding of all Federal funding for education. While several states, including Arizona, Hawaii, Minnesota, New Mexico, Utah, and Wyoming, have considered refusing to cooperate, they have been unwilling to face the loss of Federal funds (National Conference of State Legislatures, n.d.).

MANDATING EQUAL EDUCATION
IN AN UNEQUAL SOCIETY

No Child Left Behind, like earlier educational reform programs, derived much of its justification from claims of an economic need to raise educational standards and distribute educational benefits more widely. More education would both provide economic opportunity and supply the needs of a modern economy. In his critique of schooling as a "sorting machine," Joel Spring (1989) objected to this idea of education as a process of economic placement. According to Spring, this drew students from unequal positions and directed them to unequal positions, perpetuating the existing social and economic structure. Spring proposed, instead, a radical approach to education of the sort associated with the work of the Brazilian Paulo Freire. Schooling should not aim at channeling students into the existing society, but at leading students to question, criticize, and ultimately subvert the social structure as it is in order to create a new, freer, and more equal society.

Although the solutions of Spring's radical approach to education may be problematic, the approach does raise some excellent questions that return us to the heretical objections to American faith in education that we looked at in the first chapter. Criticizing education as a sorting machine can help us see that the demands of an economy are rarely the same as the occupational desires of all individuals. Preparing individuals for an economy, therefore, means sorting them into occupations that will not meet every person's desires or aspirations. Even if the competition for

opportunities could somehow be equalized for one generation, the resulting inequality of outcomes would produce inequality of opportunities for
the next generation. Radical critics of education as a sorting process have
realized both that people who come out of an unequal environment will
have unequal chances and that any system of education that serves the
requirements of that environment will direct them to unequal positions.
A differentiated economy, moreover, may require differentiated training
and expectations, so that training people for the economy may entail highly
differentiated training.

Since education occupies such a central place in our civic faith, our
answers to questions of equality of life chances and to questions of the
efficiency of our economy always tend to be "more education." As a part
of his project for a national industrial policy, for example, former Secretary of Labor Robert B. Reich argued that "one goal we should consider is
universal, high-quality K through 14" education (Reich, 2002, p. 74). Reich
failed to recognize that credentials constitute a form of currency that can
be used to "purchase" occupations. The more currency we print, through
universal K through 14 education, the more a 2-year college or vocational
education degree is downgraded to the current value of a high school
degree, or the former value of some secondary school. On this point, prominent educational sociologist Pamela Barnhouse Walters has observed that
"by allowing unfettered growth in enrollment, states provide elites with a
way of escaping the intent of egalitarian reforms—and thus the reforms do
not significantly reduce class differentials. When social equality is achieved
at the level of the school system that was formerly the place of consequence
(for example, secondary education), expansion just pushes the consequen-
tial sorting to the next level (for example, higher education). What matters
in the educational competition is not absolute level of attainment, but relative attainment" (Walters, 2000, p. 257).

Walters is describing the process of credential inflation. If we could
obtain a 100% high school graduation rate, this would not create greater
equality, it would simply make high school graduation meaningless as an
economic asset. Students would need to employ higher credentials in their
efforts to occupy positions of varying desirability. As the demand for postsecondary education increases, so does its cost, with the most elite institutions of postsecondary education becoming ever more valuable as a
means of standing out from the great multitude of competitors. Some
readers may object that holders of a high school diploma have skills that
dropouts do not have. This is extremely questionable, though, since the
skills of high school graduates have arguably gone down as the credential
has become more widespread. In addition, there is a difference between
skills that are actually needed to perform a task and skills that simply

differentiate individuals in a competitive market. Even if credential holders have greater skills than non–credential holders at any particular point
in time, those skills will be worth less when more people have them than
when fewer people have them.

Figures 8.2 and 8.3 illustrate the rapid increase of educational credentials in the United States and the corresponding rapid increase in costs of
university education, respectively. As shown in Figure 8.2, from 1975 to
2006, the percentages of Americans aged 25 and over with 4-year college
degrees or more doubled, from under 14% to 28%. However, during much
of this period of the credentialization of the American public, income distribution became less equal, not more equal (Jones & Weinberg, 2000). It
is true that the gap between the college-educated and others grew greater
during this time, but this does not mean that income inequality would
disappear, or even lessen, if we could disperse college degrees throughout
the population. University degrees have taken on the value that high school
diplomas had formerly, and people have had to find new ways to get ahead
in the competition.

One of the ways in which the pursuit of credentials has been ratcheted
upward, as Walters (2000) perspicaciously understood the process, was

Figure 8.2. Percentages of the Population Over 25 with 4 Years of College or
More, 1975–2007

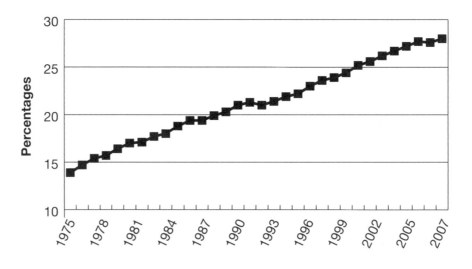

Source: U.S. Census Bureau, 2007.

Figure 8.3. Average Tuition and Fees of Public and Private Universities 1974–75 to 2006–07 (in Hundreds of 2007 Dollars)

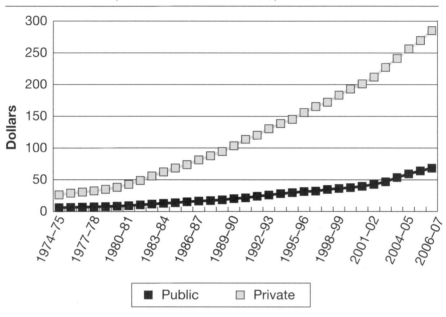

Source: National Center for Education Statistics, 2007.

through more graduate education. However, this has also happened through the chase after degrees from more elite institutions. As Figure 8.3 shows, during the same period that college degrees were reaching the hands of more people in the United States, college costs shot up. Private college costs, moreover, rose at a much greater rate than those of public institutions.

The rising cost of college has been a complex phenomenon, and we do not mean to suggest that it can be reduced only to the hot market created by credential inflation. There are supply-side as well as demand-side factors in these prices. But it is also evident that people would not be paying these much higher costs, especially for private institutions, if it were not worth the sacrifice to them. A more expensive college education in general is justified by the fact that people seeking the kinds of jobs considered desirable by most Americans now cannot be obtained merely with a high school diploma. With college degrees more abundant, degrees from more prestigious institutions and from institutions that hold out the possibility of elite contacts become more desperately sought.

If the competition for credentials is growing more intense, though, some might suggest that this in itself means we should help more people compete by helping them gain those credentials. After all, it might be argued, didn't the G.I. Bill fuel the American economy during the 1950s? Here, it is essential that we distinguish the career ambitions of individuals from the demands of the labor market. Many American young people would probably like to be movie stars or rock musicians. This doesn't necessarily mean that we need more entertainers, or that we could conceivably make everyone a celebrity. The 1950s saw a fortuitous consistency between the career ambitions of young postwar adults and the labor market. Government funding to individuals for higher education largely worked because of a rapid increase in white-collar jobs. This was the structural mobility that we saw in Chapter 5. But what were the demands of the labor market at the end of the 20th and the beginning of the 21st centuries, when we were proposing to leave no child behind?

Figure 8.4 shows that some of the fastest-growing jobs in the United States in the 21st century were going to be in fields that required only short-term, on-the-job training. Some of the job areas expected to grow most rapidly, for example, were personal and home health care. According to a publication by the Bureau of Labor Statistics, "Occupations that usually require only short- or moderate-term on-the-job training, while not growing as quickly as those usually requiring more formal education, will continue to account for about half of all jobs by 2016. These occupations require little, if any, postsecondary training. Among such occupations are retail salespersons, food preparation workers, and personal and home care aides, all of which are expected to add numerous jobs over the coming decade" (Dohm & Shniper, 2006). If we did manage to extend access to higher education to our entire population and to push all subgroups in the nation through advanced levels of education, who would do half the jobs in the country?

Education commentator Gerald W. Bracey, writing in the pages of the education publication *Phi Delta Kappan*, has been outspoken in pointing out that our economy does not have jobs available for more people with high-level skills, and that most students do not need to acquire high-level skills to do the jobs that need to be done:

> For many years now, Dennis Redovich, who runs the Center for the Study of Education and Jobs in Wisconsin and the United States, and I have been screaming about what we might call the "high-skills hoax"—the notion that *everyone* [emphasis in the original] must have high skills. It's not that we don't recognize a civil rights issue in the debate—everyone should have the *opportunity* [emphasis in the original] to develop the skills to land a high-paying

Figure 8.4. Projected Numbers of Positions in the Fastest-Growing Occupations in the United States (in Thousands of Job Positions), According to Educational Requirements of Jobs, 2006–2016

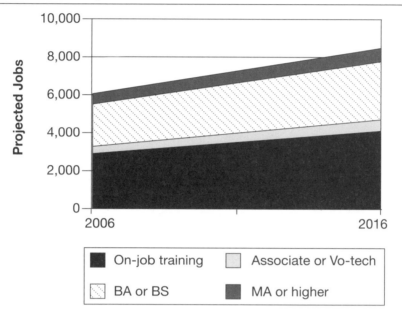

Source: Dohm and Shniper, 2006.

job. However, we understand the law of supply and demand, and we know about what jobs are actually being created. In fact, if everyone became highly skilled, the wages of skilled labor would fall, and the unemployment rates for skilled workers would rise, a condition conducive to social unrest. (Bracey, 2006, p. 93)

Creating a shortage of low-skilled or unskilled workers could, of course, lead to rising wages for those at the bottom, if the United States did not share a long and permeable border with a nation to the south that has much lower wage levels. As a result, much of the nation's working class is now a working class that must be imported. According to our calculations from data in the 2006 American Community Survey of the U.S. Census Bureau, immigrants in that year constituted 23% of workers in the construction industry, 22% in furniture and fixtures, 38% in laundering, cleaning, and dyeing, 21% in miscellaneous personal services, 29% in hotels and lodging, 20% in auto repair and garages, and 43% in private household employment, as well as 29% in agriculture (Ruggles et al., 2008). The belief that no American child should ever be left behind simultaneously raises expectations beyond realistic levels for natives, and creates a vacuum drawing in new workers and fueling the debate over undocumented migration.

We should also note, though, that not everyone needs equal skills or equal levels of education. Figure 8.4 indicates that the demand for jobs requiring postsecondary education, as well as those requiring only on-the-job training, will increase in number and remain relatively constant as a proportion of high-demand occupations. In the economic race, some will have to get ahead and some will have to be left behind. This should remind us that planning is not only limited by what government can do through education, but by what government should do, even if it can.

If one believes that preparing students for the labor market is a legitimate goal of education, and if half the jobs in that labor market are in low-paid, low-skilled occupations, then the curriculum should logically be preparing half the students for positions that will pay them little and require limited formal education. From this perspective, though, it should also not be concentrating exclusively on basic literacy and numeracy, since the job market will also call for people in high-end positions. Advocating efficiency in meeting labor demand means accepting a sorting process and it means accepting class inequality, generally correlated with social origin.

If, on the other hand, we are truly interested in creating the kind of equal opportunity that will end all family and class advantages for students, so that individuals may end up anywhere in the system, regardless of where they start out, then we are by definition arguing for downward mobility, as well as upward mobility. In truth, it is difficult to imagine the intangible advantages middle- and upper-class families convey to their children being redistributed to children of the socially and economically marginalized. But if one faces the issue honestly, putting aside our simultaneous faith in mobility and equality, one would have to admit that efforts to cancel out family advantages of necessity require that those in the middle and upper classes sacrifice the life chances of their own children. At the same time, by encouraging everyone to compete for the same limited set of privileged positions, we raise expectations so that no one will want to do the less desirable jobs and we will have to import new workers, whose children will grow up in the United States and look with disdain on the jobs of their parents.

None of this means that we need the inequality of distribution of benefits that we currently have. There may be ways of achieving greater equality of condition, so that the income and benefits gap between garbage collectors and surgeons is less than it is today. But this would not be a matter of equality of opportunity to become garbage collectors or surgeons, and it would not involve the schools.

2001 AND THE RENEWAL OF CIVIC SOLIDARITY

As the administration of George W. Bush attempted to create a society of universal inclusion through standardized testing, older aspects of the educational civic faith took on new life. The crisis that began in the 1960s had involved an intensified emphasis on the egalitarian and social reconstructionist side of the American creed. It had linked this intensified emphasis to the membership of Americans in historically marginalized or oppressed categories. In this version of the creed, the model civilization to be realized by Americans would be one in which all citizens are equal (in political rights or economic opportunities) as individuals, but their equality is threatened on the basis of group membership. Therefore, in the name of individual equality, the government must take action to establish equality among groups. Much of this action would take place in the school, the core institution of the American faith.

Clearly, the Bush Administration continued to pursue this side of the late modern American creed in its own way. In the previous sections, we have tried to describe how this faith formed the administration's approach to the problem of inequality in American society through the No Child Left Behind project. In describing the policies as derived from a civic religious creed, we do not intend to belittle or deride the policies or their goals. Belief can be a source of motivation, and it can propel people to act together to solve their shared problems. But faith can also blind us to logical inconsistencies and unite us behind words that reverberate with emotional resonance, such as "equality," that turn out to be complicated and paradoxical concepts when carefully analyzed. In discussing the difficulties that we see in the Bush educational program, and in redistributive educational planning in general, our goal has been to point out contradictions that have been obscured by commitment.

There has been another side to American civic religion, though, one that was a predominant current from the Progressive Era onward. This is the civic solidarity side, the binding of citizens into one nation. This flowed into the current running from the 1960s, with the insistence on inclusiveness and the efforts to assimilate the less advantaged into the American mainstream. But belief in civic solidarity and belief in the redistributive inclusion of disadvantaged categories of people also ran counter to each other in some important respects. The drive toward inclusion that began with the civil rights era also, paradoxically, valued diversity. The many who were to become one also remained many. The inclusive strain of American civil religion was, further, based on the idea of individual rights, although (again paradoxically) it saw the need to protect and promote these rights on the basis of group membership. An insistence on unity of belief for the sake of solidarity could be at odds with rights, as we saw in the cases of the Jehovah's Witnesses penalized for refusing to say the Pledge of Allegiance during the interwar period.

Civic solidarity could reach its greatest pitch when civil religion openly rooted itself in theistic religion, explicitly giving divine sanction and divine protection to the nation. As we saw in Dr. King's best-known speech, the different elements of American civil religion—the sacredness of individual rights, the quest for equality among citizens, the need for inclusion, the movement toward a promised land—could always be brought together in a theistic setting. But God appeared in sacred beliefs about the nation with the greatest clarity when Americans felt an existential threat to the polity.

The "under God" phrase was introduced to the Pledge of Allegiance, the basic national credo, at a time when Americans saw themselves as faced with the danger of godless Communism and perceived a need to intensify expressions of civic solidarity, and also to make clear the divine sources and purposes of the United States. Religion had remained a popular political issue in the United States, even as many Americans advocated a strict separation between recognized religions and the state. George W. Bush had announced his candidacy for the presidency at a prayer breakfast, and identified Jesus Christ as his favorite political philosopher. His public christianity won support from large segments of the electorate and helped him gain many of the votes that enabled him to eventually claim success in the disputed 2000 election.

A little less than a year after that still-debated election, the 2001 attacks on the World Trade Center and the Pentagon brought a new sense of threat to the nation and a new desire for solidarity. This had immediate consequences for the practice of civic religion in American schools. In his 2005 book, *To the Flag*, historian Richard Ellis reported,

> Today, at least thirty-five states have state laws requiring the Pledge of Allegiance in public schools. Roughly a quarter of these states—Arkansas, Colorado, Connecticut, Minnesota, Missouri, New Hampshire, Pennsylvania, Tennessee, and Texas—enacted their laws within two years of September 11, 2001. Moreover, September 11 spurred a number of other states to strengthen existing Pledge requirements, often, as in the case of Illinois and Utah, by requiring the Pledge of Allegiance not only for elementary school students but for high school students as well. Even where no change was

mandated by the legislature, local school boards and schools often, on their own initiative, responded to September 11 by instituting a daily Pledge. (Ellis, 2005, p. 207)

The sense of national solidarity, expressed through patriotic ceremonies and especially through the recitation of the Pledge, was deeply felt by young people inside the schools. "As a surge of patriotism has washed over the country in the wake of the terrorist attacks," wrote one reporter less than 3 weeks after the attack, "nowhere has the revival been more omnipresent than in schools. Hallways and classrooms have been decorated with bunting and posters of Uncle Sam . . . Teachers and principals report that once slouching students now stand at rapt attention and virtually shout a pledge they used to mumble" (Sack, 2001, p. B1). The September 2001 assault had brought a revived sense of the sacred unity of the nation, and a revived sense that the schools were the places to cultivate and express this unity.

By the 21st century, though, the doctrine of inclusion had become firmly established in the American creed, and for many this meant the inclusion not only of non-Christian religions, but of those opposed to theistic faiths. Michael Newdow, an atheist, filed a lawsuit in 2000 on behalf of his daughter, maintaining that the recitation of the Pledge in her school violated her rights. In 2002, the Ninth Circuit Court of Appeals in California ruled that requiring students to recite the Pledge with the words "under God" was an unconstitutional endorsement of religion. Judge Alfred T. Godwin, in the majority opinion of the 2 to 1 ruling, wrote that the pledge in its current form conveys a message to unbelievers "that they are outsiders, not full members of the political community, and an accompanying message to believers that they are insiders, favored members of the political community" (quoted in "Excerpts from the federal court ruling," 2002, p. A20). Theistically based solidarity and inclusiveness were held to be mutually incompatible.

In the political climate of the time, this was an enormously unpopular decision. The Supreme Court avoided passing judgment, while maintaining the Pledge in its current form in schools, by ruling in June 2004 that Newdow, a noncustodial parent, did not have standing to bring suit on behalf of his daughter. Nevertheless, the issue continued to stir controversy. In July 2006, the U.S. House of Representatives, by a margin of 260 to 167, voted to take away from the courts the right to make decisions about the wording of the Pledge. Republican House Speaker Dennis Hastert of Illinois explained that "by protecting this phrase in our country's Pledge, we are protecting and revering the faith on which our country was founded" (quoted in Bellantoni, 2006, p. A10). A similar bill, sponsored by Republican Senator Jon Kyl of Arizona, went to the Senate Judiciary Committee, where it was delayed.

The controversy over the Pledge of Allegiance essentially concerned whether civil religion should explicitly claim theistic religion as a foundation. It was not a challenge to the expression of civil religion per se, since the debate about the Pledge in the 21st century focused only on the two most recently added words. It did not, therefore, represent opposition to the surge of national solidarity after September 11, or to the ritual affirmation of that solidarity. It did, however, indicate the continuing tensions within the American creed.

Many Americans continued to see the United States not only as a land of destiny, but as one whose destiny had been divinely ordained. One of those was the nation's leader, whose religious views had contributed to his political success. "Speaking at a school in Nashville, Tennessee, in September 2002," wrote Richard Ellis (2005, p. 217), "George W. Bush explained that the thirty-one words of the Pledge 'help define our country.' In a single sentence, Bush continued, 'we affirm our form of government, our unity as a people, and our reliance on Providence.'" Ellis pointed out that in a letter written to the Ninth Circuit Court over the legal controversy over the "under God" phrase, President Bush reiterated the long-expressed belief that Americans are God's chosen people, with the mission of serving as a "beacon of liberty" to the rest of the world (Ellis, 2005, p. 217).

Other Americans would disagree with the President about who had chosen us or whether we should acknowledge the choosing. But when suddenly stricken, Americans of all ideological and religious inclinations seemed to feel the conviction that their country was a special place, with a sacred history and a future goal. They would commemorate that history and they would seek that goal where President Bush had proclaimed the affirmation of our reliance on Providence: in the school.

A 21ST-CENTURY CIVIL RELIGION

The roots of educational policy in the early 2000s, we have argued, came out of the turn in the civil religion of education in the 1960s and 1970s. The No Child Left Behind legislation, the primary official expression of education under President George W. Bush, was based on legislation enacted during the War on Poverty. Many of the distinguishing traits of NCLB, such as the efforts at extensive Federal direction of education, the emphasis on bringing the least advantaged into the mainstream, and the commitment to preparing all for middle-class occupational positions, were lineal descendants of the War on Poverty and illustrations of the post-1960 civil religion of education.

We have argued that NCLB set unrealistic goals precisely because of the belief that schooling could create the American Promised Land. Some of the ends of education have been unrealistic because they were based on theories that everyone should be able to learn the same materials, with little qualification from experience. Some of these ends have been logically contradictory, such as maintaining schools as places for competitive upward mobility and simultaneously expecting that no one will be left behind. Others assumed that producing people with degrees would automatically create appropriate positions for those people, ignoring structural changes in the American economy and ignoring the fact of credential inflation. Higher education for everyone may be desirable if we see this as a matter of individual personal development. But to the extent that we see schooling as a means of filling necessary positions in our job market, trying to push the broad mass of our population toward higher education is not only not needed, it is counterproductive.

At the same time that these post-1960 manifestations of education as a civil religion continued to mark and complicate schooling in the new millennium, older versions of the faith were still present. Schools had never ceased to be centers of national solidarity. Perhaps a resurgence of this aspect would have occurred without the traumatic events of September 11. With the attacks of that day, though, the Pledge of Allegiance came once again to the forefront, alongside No Child Left Behind.

American Civil Religion
and the Schools

NOW, at the end, we can look back and ask again, what is the American civil religion and what does it have to do with our schools? More specifically, what do beliefs about schools tell us about beliefs about the nation? What are the common elements running through American educational ideology that make it possible to describe this as a shared faith, underlying and cutting across political disagreements? How can we place the most recent developments in debates about schooling within the tradition of this shared faith? What are the consequences of our commitments and assumptions?

DEVELOPMENT AND NATURE OF THE FAITH

Drawing on Robert Bellah's classic description of American civil religion, we have suggested that the belief in education developed as a central part of the belief in the nation. The civic creed of education went through a stage of an early commitment to schooling as way to express and convey a sense of the sacredness of American nation and government before the Civil War, to a means of integrating citizens into an industrial power from the late 19th through the mid-20th century, to a commitment to egalitarian social reconstruction from the 1960s onward. In discussing this last turn in the creed of education, we have attempted to demonstrate how the same tenets motivated policymakers from the supposedly liberal administration of President Lyndon B. Johnson to the supposedly conservative administration of President George W. Bush.

America's civil religion was one part of a more general sacralization of nation-states that began as these political entities took shape and became focal points of belief and commitment from the late 18th century onward. Jean-Jacques Rousseau, at the time of the origin of the modern nation-state, put the term "civil religion" into use with his call for a political faith that would link individuals into a community of believers. "Political religions," the demanding sectlike belief systems of authoritarian and would-be totalitarian states, and "civil religions," the more open denominational systems of moderate governments, can be seen as two ends of a continuum, and even liberal democracies like the United States can sometimes veer toward the political religion end when times of stress encourage citizens to stress national solidarity.

Schooling has been a part of the civic faiths of many nations. In the United States, though, it was linked to the long-standing image of Americans as moving toward a special destiny, and the peculiarly American version of the faith in education was shaped by the nation's history. In the country's formative period, from the Revolution to the Civil War, education was linked to the competing visions of a geographically and ideologically divided land. The localism associated with Jefferson's educational plan and the federalism expressed in Webster's "Federal Catechism" offered striking alternatives of the kind of social order Americans should create, although both were imbued with characteristic American tenets, such as belief in American democratic exceptionalism and in achieved rather than ascribed status. During the period of the common schools, the most active educational advocates were supporters of the federalist trend. Individuals such as Mann and Barnard saw schools as ways to preach the doctrine of a unified nation, to mold inhabitants into citizens, and to reshape society into an idealized egalitarian form. Rituals and ceremonies celebrating the American state became centered on schools. Widespread and freely available schooling also became part of the image of American democracy. The nation's divisions both prevented schooling from becoming a truly nationwide faith and, at the same time, promoted the association of schools with democratic, unified government, since the common schools were most successful in the northeastern part of the county.

American civil religion made its first great turn in the years following the Civil War. To the established idea of the New World as the New Israel, veneration of the Founding Fathers, and prewar rituals of political community were added new national holy days, a martyrology of the war dead and Abraham Lincoln, and a new mythology of the nation-state. The trauma of war provided imagery and memorial occasions for reverence of the body politic and, more importantly, the war resulted in a unified country. Further, the decades after the struggle saw a booming industrial and urbanizing economy that drew in vast numbers of immigrants. This was the time of the rise of the public school system, when schooling became mandatory throughout the nation. The schools became temples of a civic cult dedicated to celebrating and enhancing national solidarity. Responding to the rapid social and economic changes of the time, policymakers and educators sought to employ the schools to reshape the behavior of Americans according to an ideal image of what the unified nation would become, giving special attention to the assimilation of immigrants and children of immigrants.

The term "Progressivism" describes both political trends in the late 19th and early 20th centuries and a pioneering movement in public education. The Progressive movement in education was, in fact, closely linked to the political unification of the nation, and that unification motivated the spread of public schools. Belief in the importance of the nation-state and in cultivating popular dedication characterized both political and educational Progressivism. Out of the Progressive era came not only a system of public schools across the nation, but also the central creed of American civil religion, the Pledge of Allegiance, which was aimed first and foremost at students. Recitation of the Pledge in schools became the most important ceremony of the civic faith.

The Progressive goal of creating a new Promised Land in America drew on the orientation of the era toward rationalized and scientific procedures. Educators and public activists sought to create the society of the future by careful planning and empirically based methods, as well as inculcating reverence for the nation. Both child-centered education and education for social efficiency, the two main trends in Progressive educational theory, reflected faith in scientific manipulation as a way to create better people and a better society. This belief in the efficacy of scientific method could be seen in the work of prominent figures such as Edward L. Thorndike and John Dewey. It also led to attempts to organize classrooms and schools along rationalized, systematic lines in order to produce adherents to the American creed, in the form of efficient workers and active, cooperative citizens.

The systematization of the schools outlasted what we normally think of as the Progressive era. During the time between the two world wars, America settled into the role of a developed industrial society, even while it experienced the challenges of the Great Depression, and it largely closed its doors to the immigration of earlier years. This was the period of the stabilization and institutionalization of the school system created between the Civil War and World War I. The social efficiency trends that had grown out of Progressive educational theories and practices achieved predominance in a setting now dedicated to factories and to implementation of management and design plans exemplified by the ideas of Frederick Winslow Taylor.

This interwar time of stabilization did not lack divisions or controversies in ideas about schooling. We can call the two main ideological divisions in education "traditional" and "Progressive," although both came out of the Progressive Era and were shaped by different aspects of Progressivism. Advocates of traditional education favored basic courses, delivered in a standardized fashion. Progressive educators, on the other hand, drew more on the heritage of the child-centered approaches and supported more varied course work, oriented toward the interests (or perceived interests) of children.

These two trends in educational ideology tended to be associated, also, with political ideologies. Traditionalists tended to be among the many Americans who leaned toward emphasizing the intensification of national solidarity in schools through promoting the Pledge of Allegiance and rituals of commitment to the nation-state. Progressives, such as Harold Rugg and George Counts, generally advocated social reconstruction through education, the use of schools as mechanisms for building the ideal society of the future. Counts, in particular, recognized that rituals of solidarity in the schools promulgated a religious adherence to the state, and he was highly critical of such practices. Nevertheless, the Promised Land that Rugg, Counts, and their associates sought to build through social reconstruction by schooling was also an aspect of the American civil religion of education, and these Progressives described and defended their ideals using reverential references to the sacred ideals of American life on public holy days such as Washington's Birthday. Ultimately, the traditionalists and the Progressives of the interwar period represented two sectarian tendencies of a single civic faith.

The decade and a half following World War II saw the apparent end of Progressive education, symbolized by the demise of the Progressive Education Association in 1955. Much of this was a result of the fact that so much of the program of the Progressive educators had been absorbed into the mainstream. However, it was also a consequence of the close association of the Progressives with social reconstruction, and particularly with the goal of socializing students in order to have them fit into future cooperative social order. Two tendencies militated against those who were still labeled as Progressives: the increased emphasis on education as a means of upward mobility, which undercut the life adjustment approach of education as socialization, and public suspicion of social reconstruction during the Cold War.

Criticism of Progressive educators at this time was part of increased scrutiny of institutions of learning, a scrutiny that resulted from the intensified role of schools in American economic life. White-collar jobs became more widely available than ever before in the job market of the 1950s. Schooling became the way to fill the growing numbers of jobs requiring technical and managerial skills, enhancing the American view of education as the avenue to mobility and raising expectations for mobility through schooling. In addition, the status of the United States as an economic and military superpower led the government to become much more involved in promoting education, especially at the level of colleges and universities. That same superpower status put the United States into a geopolitical and ideological struggle with the Soviet Union and the Communist world in general. This struggle contributed to the involvement of the Federal government in schools for the sake of competition with the rivals on the global scene, and it greatly intensified the demand for national solidarity. As the urge for solidarity grew, civil religion drew closer to explicitly theistic religion, symbolized by the addition of the words "under God" to the Pledge that American students recited daily. Thus, the Cold War years simultaneously drove faith in education as the answer to social and individual problems and placed new stress on schools as temples of the cult of the nation.

In retrospect, the late 1940s and the 1950s can be seen as bringing to a close the second period of American civil religion that began with the unification and industrialization of the country in the closing decades of the 19th century. Those years after World War II also foreshadowed the great change in beliefs about national purpose that would commence in the 1960s. With the proliferation of upward mobility, American belief in equality increasingly became belief in equality of opportunity, and this was to be achieved through the schools. African Americans, long denied access to many opportunities, began to acquire a more audible public voice and became the clearest instance of the country's failure to ensure equality of opportunity. The most significant product of the doctrine of equality of educational opportunity during the 1950s became the effort to obtain racial equality in education.

The shift in civil religion of the 1960s can be traced to two primary sources: an affluent consumer society in which the distribution of goods and opportunities became the focus of concern, and the televised moral drama of the civil rights movement. The most marked characteristic of the shift was the concentration on excluded and disadvantaged segments of American society. In addition to offering a revised version of the social reconstructionist dream of the Promised Land, this concentration reworked older assimilationist approaches to achieving national unity by aiming to incorporate the outsiders into the social and economic mainstream.

If the Pledge of Allegiance summarized the main thrust of civil religion shaped by the Progressive era, Dr. Martin Luther King Jr.'s "I Have a Dream" speech summarized the reorientation of this religion at the beginning of the second half of the 20th century. This second creedal statement, like the first, has been reverentially memorized and recited in classrooms nationwide. The speech invoked the long-established holy references to the Founding Fathers and the sacred texts from the country's origin, linking the new concentration on inclusion and equalization to older traditions.

Official educational policy, resulting from the legislative framework of the War on Poverty and judicial decisions on education based on the civil rights perspective, came out of the new form of the faith and reinforced that new form. Bringing the poor, minorities, and the excluded into the center of American life became the new assimilation, and it was the new version of fulfilling the promise of American life. The assimilationist view, and the almost exclusive concern with groups seen as disadvantaged, permeated programs such as Head Start and laws such as the Elementary and Secondary Education Act.

Even as political administrations became more conservative than President Johnson's, during the late 20th and early 21st centuries, beliefs about education and American life continued along the tracks set down in the civil rights era. As in earlier years, the national faith in education meant that schools became focal points for worries about the state of the nation in general. With the growth of a global economy, Americans developed anxiety over competitiveness in the international market, and when Japan rose as a perceived economic threat in the 1980s, Americans directed their anxiety toward the schools, repeatedly arguing that their nation was falling behind in the economic competition because it was failing to keep up in the scholastic competition. Americans entered the 1980s with a broader concern about social and political decline as their lives fell short of expectations for social equality and universal prosperity, and this broad concern was also translated into worry about the schools. The alarm over the quality of education intensified calls for clear standards and measurable outcomes for students, expressed in the 1984 *A Nation at Risk* report. As a result of the shift in beliefs about nation and schooling that began in the War on Poverty years, the alarm over excellence also became an alarm over equity. Standardized curricula and standardized testing became strategies for building an inclusive, egalitarian society, as well as for addressing the country's perceived decline. This commitment to building the City on a Hill through tests and curricula led directly to the ambitious mandates of Goals 2000 at the end of the century.

The No Child Left Behind legislation passed under the administration of President George W. Bush was a logical continuation of Goals 2000. It was also a lineal descendant of Great Society programs and projects, based on a reauthorization of the Elementary and Secondary School Act of 1965. Following the civil rights–era reorientation of national beliefs about the kind of Promised Land in the destiny of the United States, the NCLB program aimed at resolving the problems of the society by ending inequalities in educational outcomes. Standardized curricula and testing made up the main strategy for eliminating educational inequalities, since the legislation mandated testing all students, with particular attention to disadvantaged groups. If any group failed to meet standards, schools would be penalized and alternative educational approaches provided to failing students. Teachers and educators were expected to bring special education students, including disabled students, up to the same measurable standards as all others.

While egalitarian social reconstruction was the dominant trend in American faith in education by the early 21st century, the two terms of President George W. Bush also saw a renewed enthusiasm for rituals of national solidarity. After the tragedy of September 2001, ceremonies of patriotism and the Pledge took on a new vibrancy in American school life.

PROBLEMS AND PARADOXES

Schooling has been at the center of American civil religion in two ways. First, schools have been ways of inculcating the creed. Ceremonies and rituals take place in educational institutions, and these are the places where we pass on the values we consider most important, such as patriotism, inclusiveness, and equality. But the schools have also been included within the creed. We can achieve the Promised Land of prosperity, social order, and equality by means of education.

The national faith in education has had many positive consequences. By the early 20th century, Americans had achieved a high level of literacy, providing the broad range of citizens with access to information and ideas. The common sense of nationhood that emerged in the late 19th century had been reinforced by the rituals of the schools, and reverence for the nation fostered a sense of belonging and helped to maintain the legitimacy of the state. The turn toward a creed of inclusiveness and equalization in the late 20th century gave the schools an important part to play in turning away from the drastic racial inequities that scarred much of American history.

The religious commitment to schools as places for propagating devotion and for realizing social ideals has also had negative consequences, though. Some of the negative consequences can be traced back in the history of this commitment. Although we do consider some of the long-standing difficulties of our educational creed, our concentration is on consequences for the present, since our main interest in looking back at the past has been to achieve some critical understanding of the present.

The faith in schooling as the answer to every problem has turned us away from other possible answers. In the years just after the Civil War, the Freedmen's Bureau concentrated heavily on education, overlooking the fact that access to land and economic opportunity may also have been valuable, perhaps even more valuable, to newly freed slaves. As the United States built up its system of formal education over the decades, it generally moved away from apprenticeships and similar types of training outside the classroom. Even during the great boom in white-collar employment during the period following World War II, when the kinds of jobs being offered in increasing numbers were those associated with diplomas and degrees, few seriously considered the possibility that diplomas and degrees were not necessarily the only way, or even the best way, of preparing people for those jobs. By the end of the 20th century, it had become an article of faith that more credentialization for more people would meet the challenges of the times, so that policymakers were arguing that the way to increase American competitiveness was by ratcheting up the expected minimal expected level of credentials from the high school diploma to the 2-year college degree.

Closely related to this first problem, faith in schooling has not only led us to overlook alternatives to schooling, but to overlook the issue of whether established forms of schooling really do fit our needs. This difficulty, we suggest, became especially evident in the late 20th and early 21st centuries, after the white-collar boom in the middle of the 20th century. Jobs involving management and the handling of information in the United States did increase in numbers in the decades following that white-collar boom, although we may, again, question whether formal schooling was always the best way to prepare people for those occupations. However, the United States had also become a service economy with, according to Bureau of Labor Statistics reports and predictions, growing needs for people in service jobs (Dohm & Shniper, 2006). Although the United States had moved away from a blue-collar economy, it still required many blue-collar types of jobs, such as workers in the construction industry.

The type of educational system produced by our historically developing faith did not just fall short in producing the diverse workforce needed for a diverse economy. The expectations created by this system actually directed Americans away from tasks essential to our society and our economy. Over the decades, but especially after World War II, the Promised Land of our country came to be seen as one of upward mobility through education for everyone, with upward mobility commonly defined as movement into white-collar professional positions. Within the school system, Americans increasingly saw elementary education as preparation for secondary education, secondary education as preparation for college education, and college education as preparation for professional employment. Even readers who disagree with Bureau of Labor Statistics on the future demand for occupations will surely agree that we will not live in an economy in which everyone will be in the professions.

Expectations that everyone should move along the educational trajectory have affected socioeconomic inequality in the United States in ways that we suggest are unfortunate. There is now a certain amount of social stigma attached to not having a college degree and a most definite stigma attached to not having a high school diploma. Moreover, these expectations mean that anyone who does a job "below" the level identified with one of these credentials will suffer from low social status.

In talking about the movement of immigrants into the American economy, commentators often say that immigrants take the low-paid work that Americans do not want. But why are some occupations low-paid and why are Americans unwilling to do them? A large part of the answer, we argue, is that our national faith in education has also become a set of beliefs about what kinds of economic and social positions are desirable and admirable. By promoting occupations associated with high levels of education, we systematically undervalue occupations associated with little formal education. The competition for the former pushes wages up, while the avoidance of the latter pushes wages down. Paradoxically, promoting upward mobility in this way can actually increase inequality. In addition to creating a vacuum that pulls in immigrant workers willing to take the undervalued jobs, the intense competition for the overvalued professional jobs helps to push up college costs, especially costs at the elite private institutions that may give an extra competitive edge to degree holders.

Our belief in schooling as the way to improve our society has lifted expectations of the schools, as well as shaped expectations about socioeconomic status. Seeing schools as the answer to individual and social problems, Americans have tended to see existing imperfections as consequences of school failure. In the Progressive era, when proselytizers for the faith in education were lifting expectations, sociologist Albion W. Small described educators as "makers of society" (Small, 1896, reprinted in Cohen, 1974, p. 2188). But if educators were to "make society," this meant that all real or perceived social shortcomings could be seen as failures or errors of educators. Across the years, teachers and school administrators have, variously, been seen as failing to inculcate sufficient patriotism to face foreign threats; failing to produce a population sufficiently educated for geopolitical competition with the Soviets or economic competition with the Japanese; and failing to simultaneously eliminate social inequalities, create universally high standards of literacy and numeracy, and promote individual upward mobility. By the time of the No Child Left Behind legislation, it had become official government policy to blame and penalize schools automatically for all less than desired student outcomes.

The issue of expectations placed on schools raises questions of power: How much power can schools exercise over their society, and how much should they exercise? On the first question, the main reason that we see American expectations of schooling as unrealistic is that our society does not exist inside the school system; rather, the school system exists inside the society. As early as the time of the common school movement, Horace Mann and other believers in the civic role of schools claimed enormous power for schooling in creating the ideal social organization. The faith in education of the Progressive Era reflected in Albion Small's attitude continued the idea that the educational system could be a place for engineering the social order. This faith formed a substantial part of the views of John Dewey and social reconstructionists such as George Counts and Harold Rugg. By the late 20th century, programs such as the ESEA legislation, Head Start, school desegregation, and educational affirmative action went far beyond aiming to improve opportunities for individuals and sought to employ schools to restructure the whole of American society according to the ideals of the post–civil rights era turn in civil religion. Similarly, advocates of standardized testing argued that schools could use tests to identify and eliminate gaps in educational outcomes and thereby eliminate inequalities among people from different racial, ethnic, and socioeconomic backgrounds.

Schools, however, do not stand at some Archimedean point outside the society. They exist inside the society and reflect the larger society's complications and controversies. In the late 20th century, for example, policymakers recognized that the school achievement of students was closely associated with social circumstances outside the schools. Racially and economically isolated communities, peer groups with low educational aspirations, and single-parent families were all negatively related to educational performance. Moreover, concentrations of students from disadvantaged backgrounds tended to create school environments that were not conducive to high performance. Therefore, believing in the power of schools to address social problems, policymakers sought to redistribute students, through busing or changing school attendance boundaries, in order to put the disadvantaged in contact with relatively more advantaged students. However, the families of relatively more advantaged students then tended to seek sanctuary in gifted or magnet classrooms, to request permits to move to other schools, to move to other school districts, or to enter private school systems. Meanwhile, the children who go to school from economically disadvantaged and racially segregated neighborhoods return to those same neighborhoods at the end of the school day. Inequalities in the larger society had more power to determine events in schools than schools had to reshape the larger society (see Bankston & Caldas, 2002; Caldas & Bankston, 2007).

The ability of schools to achieve social goals has also been limited by the fact that those goals have often been contradictory. Americans have generally ignored these contradictions in the same way that believers in other religions have ignored logical conflicts within their creeds. Perhaps the most egregious example of contradictory goals can be found in the paradoxical ideology of equal opportunity that became a guiding principle of educational policy in the second half of the 20th century. Equal opportunity means equal competition for unequal life situations. But equality in competition entails beginning from the same situations. If we ever could establish true equality of opportunity at one point in time, this state of affairs would lead to its own opposite in a single generation.

We can understand many of the educational programs from the late 20th century onward as efforts to square the circle of equal opportunity. Our school system and our economy are still highly competitive and generally measured on linear scales of success, through standardized testing or through the types of jobs that policies of upward mobility encourage Americans to seek. It is a race that is expected to have no losers, though, with literally no children left behind.

The question of how much power schools should exercise over their society is one of the most vexing and difficult of all. The phrase "paradox of democracy" refers to a common problem in attempting to design democratic societies. The concept of a liberal democracy is based on the idea that citizens should make their own decisions about how their society should be organized and how they should be governed. But what if the decisions they make are not conducive to democracy? One answer is to use undemocratic means, such as expert social planning and indoctrination, to shape citizenry and create the proper conditions for democracy.

Since the period of the common schools, American educational theorists have sought to use schooling as a tool for social design and control. Indeed, this is precisely one of the reasons that it makes sense to see education as a core part of an American civil religion, since Rousseau had proposed the creation and maintenance of a political community through public beliefs as the rationale for civil religion. As the public school system took root across the nation during the Progressive Era, the goal of creating the ideal society by shaping its citizens and the goal of welding the people more closely into a unified national community of belief came to imbue educational theory and practice. While schools continued to be under local control, under the charge of elected school boards, experts, educational theorists, and policymakers became more influential in employing schools to attempt to form the kind of citizenry the authorities believed the country should have.

During the decades between the two world wars, schools became factories for the design and management of an industrial workforce. Those who sought to use schools to intensify national solidarity and those who dreamed of schools as laboratories for social reconstruction shared the faith in design and management of the public. In the heated atmosphere of the Cold War, the stress on shaping a patriotic citizenry through the schools at times moved American civil religion toward becoming a political religion. From the 1960s onward, educational programs have taken quite seriously the goal of turning educators and educational lawmakers into "makers of society." Schools have been cast as places to reshape the cultural backgrounds of students, direct their social contacts, and eradicate socioeconomic, racial, and ethnic inequalities. At times, these efforts at redesigning society have been reminiscent of Bertolt Brecht's 1953 quip that the East German people had apparently lost the confidence of their government, so the government should "dissolve the people and elect another one" (Judt, 2005, p. 177). Creating a new society is precisely the attempt to dissolve the people as they are and to appoint the people as one would like them to be.

Ultimately, we argue that the key place of education in our civil religion has led Americans to overestimate what education can or should do. The answer is not to abandon our faith in the nation's future or to conclude that schools have no part in that future. But faith must be tempered by reflection, examination, and careful criticism. We need to be cautious in our assessments of what formal schooling can do. Schools can make available to students the skills of literacy and numeracy. They can provide access to practical skills, from the most basic to the most advanced, and to the rich cultural heritage of humanity. They can offer training in techniques of reasoning and analysis. While good teachers may make the offerings of schools appealing to many students, even the youngest pupils are people with their own wills, talents, and interests, who cannot and should not be made to learn or shaped to any plan for new people in a new utopia. Finally, we, as a nation, may want to be more skeptical about accepting claims that the hallways of American schools can or should lead to anyone's vision of the Promised Land.

References

553 social scientists. (2006). Brief of 553 social scientists as amici curiae supporting respondents, Parents Involved in Comty. Sch. v. Seattle Sch. Dist. No. 1
et al. (Nos. 05-908 & 05-915), 5–9.

Address of Governor Yates at the Normal University. (1861, January 31). *Chicago
Tribune*, p. 2.

Address to the people of Massachusetts. (1848, September 20). *Emancipator and
Republican*, p. 1.

Aikin, W. M. (1942). *The story of the Eight-Year Study: With conclusions and recommendations.* New York: Harper and Brothers.

American Educational Research Association. (2006). Brief of the American Edu-
cational Research Association as amicus curiae supporting respondents,
Parents Involved in Community Schools v. Seattle Sch. Dist. No. 1 et al.
(Nos. 05-908 & 05-915), 5–19.

Anderson, B. R.O.G. (2006). *Imagined communities: Reflections on the origin and spread
of nationalism.* Brooklyn: Verso.

Anonymous parent. (1950, December 22). Harry Gold (letter to the editor), *The
Washington Post*, p. 24.

Antin, M. (1912). *The Promised Land.* Boston: Houghton Mifflin.

Anti-slavery lectures. Address by Rev. Henry Ward Beecher. (1855, January 17).
New York Daily Times, p. 5.

Asbury, E. A. (1953, June 23). Good teacher held chief foe of reds. *New York Times*,
p. 18.

ASCD Smartbriefs. (2006, December 14). Retrieved December 14, 2006, from
http://www.smartbrief.com/ascd/

Bankston, C. L. (2006). *Grutter v. Bollinger*: Weak foundations? *Ohio State Law
Journal, 67*, 1–13.

Bankston, C. L., & Caldas, S. J. (2002). *A troubled dream: The promise and failure of
school desegregation in Louisiana.* Nashville, TN: Vanderbilt University Press.

Bellah, R. N. (1967). Civil religion in America. *Daedalus, 96*, 1–21.

Bellah, R. N. (1975). *The broken covenant: American civil religion in the time of trial.*
New York: Seabury Press.

Bellamy, E. (1898). *Looking backward: 2000–1887.* New York: Houghton Mifflin.

Bellantoni, C. (2006, July 20). House votes to protect pledge. *Washington Times*,
p. A10.

Bennett, M. J. (1996). *When dreams came true: The GI Bill and the making of modern America*. Washington, DC: Brassey's.

Bergman, P. M. (1969). *The chronological history of the Negro in America*. New York: HarperCollins.

Berkowitz, P. (2002). John Rawls and the liberal faith. *Wilson Quarterly*, Spring, 60–69.

Berube, M. R. (1994). *American school reform: Progressive, equity, and excellence movements*. Westport, CT: Praeger.

Billington, J. H. (1980). *Fire in the minds of men: Origins of the revolutionary faith*. New York: Basic Books.

Bloom, B. S., Davis, A., & Hess, R. (1965). *Compensatory education for cultural deprivation*. New York: Holt, Rinehart, and Winston.

Bossey, S. (2000). Academic pressure and impact on Japanese students. *McGill Journal of Education, 35*(1), 71–89.

Bound, J., & Turner, S. (2002). Going to war and going to college: Did World War II and the G.I. Bill increase educational attainment for returning veterans? *Journal of Labor Economics, 20*, 784–815.

Bourne, R. S. (1916). *The Gary schools*. Boston: Houghton Mifflin.

Bowles, S., & Gintis, H. (1976). *Schooling in capitalist America: Educational reform and the contradictions of economic life*. New York: Basic Books.

Bowles, S., & Gintis, H. (2000, April 13). *Schooling in capitalist America: Revisited*. Symposium conducted at the meeting of the American Education Research Association, Seattle, WA.

Bracey, G.W. (2006). Research: The high skills hoax. *Phi Delta Kappan*, 88 (September), 93–4.

Brown v. Board of Education II, 139 F. Supp. 468, 469, (1955).

Burleigh, M. (2005). *Earthly powers: The clash of religion and politics in Europe from the French Revolution to the Great War*. New York: HarperCollins.

Caldas, S. J. (1993). A multivariate re-examination of input and process factor effects on public school achievement. *Journal of Educational Research, 86*, 206–214.

Caldas, S. J., & Bankston, C. L. (1997). The effect of school population socioeconomic status on individual student academic achievement. *Journal of Educational Research, 90*, 269–277.

Caldas, S. J., & Bankston, C. L. (2007). *Forced to fail: The paradox of school desegregation*. Lanham, MD: Rowman and Littlefield.

Caldas, S. J., & Bankston, C. L. (2008, January). A re-analysis of the legal, political, and social landscape of desegregation from *Plessy v. Ferguson* to *Community Schools v. Seattle School District No. 1 Et Al. Brigham Young University Education and Law Journal*, 1, 217–256.

Caldas, S. J., Bankston, C. L., & Cain, J. (2007). A case study of teachers' perceptions of school desegregation and the redistribution of social and academic capital. *Education & Urban Society, 39*(2), 194–222.

Callahan, R. E. (1962). *Education and the cult of efficiency*. Chicago: University of Chicago Press.

Cassius M. Clay's Address. (1845, February 27). *The Farmer's Cabinet*, p. 2.

Chang, M. J. (2001). The positive educational effects of racial diversity on campus. In G. Orfield (with M. Kurlaender) (Eds.), *Diversity challenged: Evidence on the impact of affirmative action* (pp. 175–186). Cambridge, MA: The Civil Rights Project, Harvard University, and Harvard Educational Publishing Group.

Church, R. L. (1976). *Education in the United States: An interpretive history.* New York: The Free Press.

Clark, K. W., Chein, I., & Cook, S. W. (1952). The effects of segregation and consequences of desegregation: A social science statement in the Brown v. Board of Education Supreme Court case. *American Psychologist, 59,* 495–501.

Cohen, S. (Ed.). (1974). *Education in the United States: A documentary history.* (Vol. IV). New York, Random House.

Coleman, J. S., Campbell, E. Q., Hobson, C. J., McPartland, J., Mood, A. M., Weinfeld, F. D., & York, R. L. (1966). *Equality of educational opportunity.* Washington, DC: U.S. Department of Health, Education, and Welfare.

Commission on Higher Education. (1947). *Higher education for American democracy: A report.* Washington, DC: Author.

Committee for Economic Development. (1985). *Investing in our children: Business and the public schools.* New York: Author.

The common school system of the State of New-York. (1851, September 19). *New York Daily Times,* p. 3.

Common Schools in the State of Ohio. (1839, May 10). *The Ohio Statesman,* p. 3.

Compulsory education. (1890, January 5). *New York Times,* p. 4.

Conant, J. B. (1959). *The American high school today.* New York: McGraw-Hill.

Counts, G. S. (1930). *The American road to culture.* New York: John Day.

Counts, G. S. (1939). *The schools can teach democracy.* New York: John Day.

The Courier. (1799, July 17). p. 1.

Crawford, J. (1992). *Hold your tongue: Bilingualism and the politics of "English Only."* Reading, MA: Addison-Wesley.

Cremin, L. A. (1961). *The transformation of the school: Progressivism in American education, 1876–1957.* New York: Knopf.

Cristi, M. (2001). *From civil to political religion: The intersection of culture, religion, and politics.* Waterloo, Ontario: Wilfred Laurier University Press.

Daniels, L. A. (1988, September 7). Illiteracy seen as threat to U.S. economic edge. *New York Times,* p. B8.

Decoration Day. It was celebrated in Chicago as never before since in its situation. (1890, June 3). *The Weekly Inter-Ocean,* p. 2.

Dewey, J. (1899). *The school and society.* Chicago: University of Chicago Press.

Dewey, J. (1926, January). Individuality and experience. *Journal of the Barnes Foundation,* 1–6.

Dewey, J. (1928a, December 5). "What Are Russian Schools Doing?" *The New Republic.* Reprinted in *John Dewey: The Later Works, 1925–1953: Volume 3: 1927–1928* (J. A. Boydston, Ed.). Carbondale, IL: Southern Illinois University Press, 1984.

Dewey, J. (1928b, December 12). "New Schools for a New Era." *The New Republic.* Reprinted in *John Dewey: The Later Works, 1925–1953: Volume 3: 1927–1928*

(J. A. Boydston, Ed.). Carbondale, IL: Southern Illinois University Press, 1984.

Dewey, J. (1934). *A common faith*. New Haven, CT: Yale University Press.

Dewey, J. (1959). Progressive education and the science of education. In M. S. Dworkin (Ed.), *Dewey on education* (pp. 113–126). New York: Teachers College Press.

Dewey, J., & Dewey, E. (1962). *The schools of tomorrow*. New York: Dutton. (Original work published 1916)

Dohm, A., & Shniper, L. (2006, November). Occupational employment projections to 2016. *Monthly Labor Review*, 86–125.

Durkheim, E. (1947). *The division of labor in society* (George Simpson, Trans). New York: MacMillan. (Original work published 1893)

Durkheim, E. (1965). *The elementary forms of religious life*. New York: The Free Press. (Original work published 1915)

Education. (1825, April 5). *Vermont Gazette*, p. 3.

Education. (1830, December 11). *Macon Weekly Telegraph*, p. 199.

Education. (1845, May 27). *Macon Weekly Telegraph*, p. 2.

Education in Maine. (1823, March 4). *American Mercury*, p. 3.

Educational address of Prof. J. M. Bloss before the teachers. (1890, January 9). *Topeka Weekly Capital*, p. 10.

Ellis, R. J. (2005). *To the flag: The unlikely history of the Pledge of Allegiance*. Lawrence, KS: University Press of Kansas.

Esteem for institutions is rated in Gallup Poll. (1983, September 12). *New York Times*, p. B13.

Excerpts from the federal court ruling on the Pledge of Allegiance. (2002, June 27). *New York Times*, p. A20.

Fenn, R. (2001). *Beyond idols: The shape of a secular society*. New York: Oxford.

Fine, B. (1953, June 29). Fearful teachers shunning controversy, survey finds. *New York Times*, p. 1.

Finke, R., & Stark, R. (1992). *The churching of America: Winners and losers in our religious economy, 1776–1990*. New Brunswick, NJ: Rutgers University Press.

Fitzpatrick, J. L., Sanders, J. R., & Worthen, B. R. (2004). *Program evaluation: Alternative approaches and practical guidelines* (3rd ed.). New York: Allyn & Bacon.

Flag salute mandatory. (1935, November 3). *New York Times*, p. E7.

Flesch, R. (1955). *Why Johnny can't read: And what you can do about it*. New York: Harper.

Fletcher, S. (1823, March 24). Report of the school committee for the town of Concord, 1822–1823. *New Hampshire Patriot*. p. 3.

Foner, E. (1988). *Reconstruction: America's unfinished revolution, 1863–1977*. New York: Harper & Row.

Foster, S. J. (2000). *Red alert! Educators confront the "Red Scare" in American public schools, 1947–1954*. New York: Peter Lang.

Freedman, S. J. (2008, May 7). Failings of one Brooklyn high school may threaten a neighbor's success. *The New York Times*. Retrieved May 9, 2008, from http://www.nytimes.com/2008/05/07/education/07education.html?pagewanted=1&ei=5070&en=1844fb8e7f543cec&ex=1210824000&emc=eta1

The freemen's great want. (1870, April 1). *New York Times*, p. 4.

French, M. (1997). *U.S. economic history since 1945*. Manchester, UK: Manchester University Press.

From the Connecticut Courant. (1805, January 11). *New-York Commercial Advertiser*, p. 2.

Furman, B. (1955, January 9). Schools lauded on "American Way." *New York Times*, p. 74.

Furman, B. (1958, August. 23). Senate votes aid to science study. *New York Times*, p. 16.

Galbraith, J. K. (1958). *The affluent society*. New York: New American Library.

Gallup, G. (1953, May 9). Public in 3-to-1 vote favors "Under God" in U.S. Oath. *The Washington Post*, p. 11.

Gentile, E. (1996). *The sacralization of politics in Fascist Italy* (K. Botsford, Trans.). Cambridge, MA: Harvard University Press.

Gentile, E. (2006). *Politics as religion*. Princeton, NJ: Princeton University Press.

George Washington University—Center for Equity and Excellence in Education. (2008). *About GW-CEE*. Retrieved July 3, 2008, from http://ceee.gwu.edu/About_CEEE.html

Goal of growth: Assets must be widely shared. (1962, January 23). *Chicago Daily Tribune*, p. C6.

Goals 2000: Educate America Act (P.L. 103-227) (1994).

Goodman, P. (1966). *Compulsory mis-education and the community of scholars*. New York: Vintage Books.

Gordon, E. W., & Wilkerson, D.A. (1966). *Compensatory education for the disadvantaged, programs and practices: Preschool through college*. New York: College Entrance Board.

Green v. County School Board of New Kent County, Virginia. 391 U.S. 430, 88 S.Ct. 1689. (1968).

Grutter v. Bollinger, 539 U.S. 306 (2003).

Grutter v. Bollinger, 539 U.S. 306, 350 (2003) (Thomas, J., concurring in part and dissenting in part).

Handy, R. T. (1980). A decisive turn in the civil religion debate. *Theology Today*, 37(3), 349.

Hanushek, E. (1986). The economics of schooling: Production and efficiency in public schools. *Journal of Economic Literature*, 49(3), 1141–1177.

Harrington, M. (1962). *The other America: Poverty in the United States*. New York: Macmillan.

Hindelang, M. J., Gottfredson, M., & Gaofalo, J. (1978). *Victims of personal crime*. Cambridge, MA: Ballinger.

Hirsch, E. D. (1987). *Cultural literacy: What every American needs to know*. Boston: Houghton Mifflin.

Hofstadter, R. (1955). *The age of reform: From Bryan to F.D.R.* New York: Knopf.

Holton, W. (2007). *Unruly Americans and the origins of the constitution*. New York: Hill & Wang.

Honor the Stars and Bars. Flag Day will be elaborately observed by public schools. (1896, February 21). *Sioux City Journal*, p. 5.

Illich, I. (1971). *Deschooling society.* New York: Harper & Row.

Japan Ministry of General Affairs. (1987). *Roujin no seikatsu to ishiki [Awareness of the elderly and their lifestyles].* Tokyo: Chuou Houki.

Japan Times, September 18, 1994, p. 3.

Jaycox, F. (2005). *The Progressive era.* New York: Facts on File.

Jencks, C. (1972). *Inequality: A reassessment of the effect of family and schooling in America.* New York: Basic Books.

Jenks, W., & Lauck, W. J. (1913). *The immigration problem: A study of American immigration conditions and needs.* New York and London: Funk and Wagnall's.

Johnson's message to Congress outlining broad program of educational gains. (1965, January 30). *New York Times,* p. 20.

Jones, A. F., & Weinberg, D. A. (2000, June). *The changing shape of the nation's income distribution, 1947–1998.* Washington, DC: U.S. Census Bureau (Current Population Reports P60-204).

Jones, M. A. (1992). *American immigration* (2nd ed.). Chicago: University of Chicago Press.

Judt, T. (2005). *Postwar: A history of Europe since 1945.* New York: Penguin Press.

Kaestle, C. (1983). *Pillars of the republic: Common schools and American society, 1780–1860.* New York: Hill & Wang.

Kanigel, R. (1996). Frederick Taylor's apprenticeship. *Wilson Quarterly, 20*(3), 44–51.

Kay, J. (1993). *Foundations of corporate success.* Oxford: Oxford University Press.

Kennedy, J. F. (1974). President Kennedy's special message to the Congress on education. In S. Cohen (Ed.), *Education in the United States: A documentary history (Vol. 5,* pp. 3348–3350). New York: Random House. (Original work published 1961)

Keyes v. School District No. 1, Denver, 413 U.S. 189 (1973).

Kimball, R. (2000). *The long march: How the cultural revolution of the 1960s changed America.* San Francisco: Encounter Books.

Lee, V. E., Brooks-Gunn, J., Schnur, E., & Liaw, F. (1990). Are Head Start effects sustained? A longitudinal follow-up comparison of disadvantaged children attending Head Start, no preschool, and other preschool programs. *Child Development, 61,* 495–507.

Lemann, N. (1999). *The big test: The secret history of the American meritocracy.* New York: Farrar, Strauss, and Giroux.

Lilla, M. (2007). *The stillborn God: Religion, politics, and the modern west.* New York: Knopf.

Lindsay, M. (1955, January 10). School ferment betokens new era. *The Washington Post and Times Herald,* p. 12.

Linklater, A. (2007). *The fabric of America: How our borders and boundaries shaped the country and forged our national identity.* New York: Walker & Company.

Lynd, R., & Lynd, H. M. (1929). *Middletown: A study in contemporary American culture.* New York: Harcourt Brace.

MacMullen, E. N. (1991). *In the cause of true education: Henry Barnard and nineteenth-century school reform.* New Haven, CT: Yale University Press.

Mann, H. (1957). Twelfth annual report (1848). In L. A. Cremin (Ed.), *The repub-*

lic and the school: Horace Mann on education of freemen (pp. 79–111). New York: Teachers College Press. (Original work published 1848)

Many questions. (1950, January 8). *The Washington Post*, p. L5.

Marty, M. E. (1996). *Modern American religion: Vol. 3. Under God*. Chicago: University of Chicago Press.

Marwick, A. (1998). *The sixties: Cultural revolution in Britain, France, Italy, and the United States, c. 1958–1974*. Oxford: Oxford University Press.

Massey, D. S., & Denton, N. A. (1993). *American apartheid: Segregation and the making of the underclass*. Cambridge, MA: Harvard University Press.

Matusow, A. J. (1984). *The unraveling of America: A history of liberalism in the 1960s*. New York: Harper & Row.

McGerr, M. (2003). *A fierce discontent: The rise and fall of the Progressive movement in America, 1870–1920*. New York: Free Press.

Meredith v. Jefferson County Board of Education, 551 U.S. (2007).

Mettler, S. (2002). Bringing the state back in to civic engagement: Policy feedback effects of the G.I. Bill for World War II veterans. *American Political Science Review*, 96, 351–65.

Minersville School District v. Gobitis, 310 U.S. 586 (1940).

Modern immigration. (1900, August 13). *Chicago Tribune*, p. 6.

Muse, B. (1956, April 8). The county will calmly close schools. *Washington Post and Times Herald*, p. E2.

N.A.A.C.P. sets advanced goals. (1954, May 18). *New York Times*, p. 16.

National Commission on Excellence in Education. (1983). *A nation at risk: The imperative for educational reform*. Retrieved online at http://www.ed.gov/pubs/NatAtRisk/risk.html

National Commission on Excellence in Education. *A nation at Risk Report* retrieved December 7, 2006, from http://www.ed.gov/pubs/NatAtRisk/recomm.html

National Conference of State Legislatures. (n.d.). "No Child Left Behind: Quick Facts 2004–2005." Retrieved December 15, 2006, from http://www.ncsl.org/programs/educ/NCLB2005LegActivity.htm#legactivity04

New York observes Washington's birthday. (1901, February 23). *New York Times*, p. 7.

The New Orleans riot. (1867, March 6). *San Francisco Bulletin*, p. 3.

New York Daily Times. (1851, October 15). No title, p. 4.

No Child Left Behind (NCLB) Act of 2001. Pub. L. No. 107-110, § 115, Stat. 1425 (2002).

Nyad, D. (1989, May 28). How illiteracy makes athletes run. *New York Times*, p. S8.

Oakes, J. B. (1940, June 4). Flag salute rule in schools held valid by court. *Washington Post*, p. 4.

Oakeschott, M. J. (1996). *The politics of faith and the politics of skepticism*. New Haven, CT: Yale University.

Office of Head Start. (2006). Administration for Children and Families, U.S. Department of Health and Human Services, "Head Start History," retrieved October 16, 2006, from http://www.acf.hhs.gov/programs/hsb/about/history.htm

On education. (1802, August 11). *Massachusetts Spy, or Worcester Gazette*, p. 1.

Opening of schools and colleges. (1858, October 2). *Harper's Weekly*, pp. 626–627.

Orfield, G., Eaton, S. E., & the Harvard Project on School Desegregation. (1996). *Dismantling desegregation: The quiet reversal of Brown V. Board of Education*. New York: New Press.

Our California correspondence. (1861, March 31). *Chicago Tribune*, p. 2.

Our school system. (1852, January 17). *New York Daily Times*, p. 4.

Parents Involved in Community Schools v. Seattle School District No. 1 et al., 551 U.S. (2007).

Parrish, T., Harr, J., Wolman, J., Anthony, J., Merickel, A., & Esra, P. (2004). *State special education finance systems, 1999–2000. Part II: Special education revenues and expenditures*. Palo Alto, CA: Center for Special Education Finance.

Patriotic topics in many pulpits. (1903, November 27). *The Philadelphia Inquirer*, p. 2.

Patriot's week to be observed in schools Feb. 12 to Feb. 22. (1926, February 7). *New York Times*, p. 3.

Perkinson, H. J. (1995). *The imperfect panacea: American faith in education* (4th ed.). New York: McGraw-Hill.

The Pilgrim fathers. (1864, December 31). *New York Times*, p. 6.

Pledge revision asked. (1953, April 22). *New York Times*, p. 38.

Postman, N. (1996). *The end of education: Defining the value of school*. New York: Vintage Books.

President hails revised Pledge. (1954, June 15). *New York Times*, p. 31.

The public school map. (1892, May 21). *Santa Fe Daily New Mexican*, p. 3.

Ravitch, D. (2000). *Left back: A century of battles over school reform*. New York: Touchstone.

Rawls, J. (1971). *A Theory of justice*. New York: Belknap Press.

Reese, W. J. (2005). *America's public schools: From the common school to "No Child Left Behind."* Baltimore: The Johns Hopkins University Press.

Regents of the Univ. of Cal. v. Bakke, 438 U.S. 310 (1978).

Reich, R. B. (1989). *Resurgent liberal: (And other unfashionable prophecies)*. New York: Times Books.

Reich, R. B. (1993). *American competitiveness and American brains*. New York: City College of New York.

Reich, R. B. (2002). *I'll be short: Essentials for a decent working society*. Boston: Beacon Press.

Remarks of E. C. Benedict on city schools. (1852, January 17). *New York Daily Times*, p. 6.

Rhodes, J. M. (1980). *The Hitler movement: A modern millenarian revolution*. Stanford, CA: Hoover Institution Press.

Robbins, J., & Robbins, J. (1955, June 19). The great parent–teacher debate: Are our children learning to read? *Los Angeles Times*, p. G7.

Roberts, K. A. (2004). *Religion in sociological perspective*. Belmont, CA: Wadsworth.

Rossell, C. H. (2005, September). *Making uneven strides: State standards for achieving English language proficiency under the No Child Left Behind Act*. Report prepared for the Lexington Institute, Arlington, VA.

Rossum, R. (2006). A short history of a big mistake. *The American Interest* I (4, Summer), 82–93.

Rousseau, J.-J. (1960). Politics and the arts. Letter to D'Alembert on the theatre (A. Bloom, Trans.). Ithaca, NY: Cornell University Press. (Original work published 1758)

Rousseau, J.-J. (1961). *Émile, ou de l'education* [*Emile: Or, on education*]. Paris: Garnier Frères. (Original work published 1762)

Rousseau, J.-J. (1972). *Du contrat social.* [*The social contract*]. Oxford: Clarendon Press. (Original work published 1762)

Rudolph, F. (1965). *Essays on education in the early republic.* Cambridge, MA.

Rugg, H. (Ed). (1939). *Democracy and the curriculum: The life and program of the American school.* New York: D. Appleton Century.

Rugg, H. (1947). *Foundations for American education.* New York: World Book.

Ruggles, S., Sobek, M., Alexander, T., Fitch, C. A., Goeken, R., Kelly Hall, P., King, M., & Ronnander, C. (2008). *Integrated public use microdata series: Version 3.0* [Machine-readable database]. Minneapolis, MN: Minnesota Population Center [producer and distributor].

Sack, K. (2001, September 28). School colors become red, white and blue. *New York Times,* p. B1.

School celebration at Albany. (1851, September 30). *New York Daily Times,* p. 2.

Schools. (1801, November 12). *The Balance and Columbian Repository,* p. 101.

Schools failing, educators charge. (1937, February 15). *New York Times,* p. 19.

Schools in New-York. (1823, March 25). *Rhode Island American and General Advertiser,* p. 1.

Seeger, M. (1963, December 2). Civil rights action forecast. *Christian Science Monitor,* p. 10.

Shanks, C. (2001). *Immigration and the politics of American sovereignty, 1880–1990.* Ann Arbor: University of Michigan Press.

Shogan, R. (1980, September 23). Each man faces problems. *New York Times,* pp. B1 & B7.

Slavery—the evil—the remedy. (1843, December 28). *The Emancipator,* p. 137.

Small, A. W. (1896). The demands of sociology upon pedagogy. *Journal of Proceedings and Addresses,* 178–81. Reprinted in S. Cohen (Ed.), (1973), *Education in the United States: A documentary history* (Vol. IV, pp. 2185–2188). New York: Random House.

Sobsey, D. (1994). *Violence and abuse in lives of people with disabilities: The end of silent acceptance?* Baltimore, MD: Paul Brookes.

Southern freedmen. (1867, November 8). *Daily Iowa State Register,* p. 2.

The Southern revolution. (1867, April 25). *San Francisco Bulletin,* p. 2.

Spring, J. (1989). *The sorting machine revisited.* White Plains, NY: Longman.

Stack, S. (1992). The effect of divorce on suicide in Japan: A time series analysis, 1950–1980. *Journal of Marriage and the Family,* 54, 327–334.

Stafford, B. S. (1937, April 14). Club leader sounds warning note against Socialism and Communism. *Atlanta Constitution,* p. 14.

Star-Spangled Banner still floats unsullied, patriotism permeates capital's classrooms. (1937, February 4). *New York Times,* pp. 1, 3.

Stark, R., & Finke, R. (2000). *Acts of faith: Explaining the human side of religion.* Berkeley: University of California Press.

Statistics of New-York. (1825, April 2). *Washington Whig,* p. 2.

Stauffer, R. E. (1975). Bellah's civil religion. *Journal for the Scientific Study of Religion, 14,* 390–395.

Strayer, G. D., & Bachman, F. P. (1918). *The Gary public schools: Organization and administration.* New York: General Education Board.

Sullivan, P., & Knutson, J. (2000). Maltreatment and disabilities: A population based epidemiological study. *Child Abuse and Neglect, 24,* 1257–1273.

Swann v. Charlotte-Mecklenburg Board of Education, 402 U.S. 1 (1971).

Sweatt v. Painter, 339 U.S. 629, 848 (1950).

Taylor, F. W. (1911). *The principles of scientific management.* New York: Harper & Brothers.

Text of Mr. Johnson's State of the Union message and his earlier press briefing. (1964, January 9). *New York Times,* p. 16.

Text of the President's message on economic recovery and growth. (1961, February 3). *New York Times,* p. 10.

Thanksgiving sermons. Our country and its destiny. (1852, November 26). *New York Daily Times,* p. 1.

Thayer, V. T. (1965). *Formative ideas in American education: From the colonial period to the present.* New York: Dodd, Mead & Co.

Thomas, M. C., & Flippen, C. C. (1972). American civil religion: An empirical study. *Social Forces, 51,* 218–225.

Thousands of teachers at opening session. (1905, July 4). *New York Times,* p. 3.

Tribute to Washington. Birth anniversary of first president honored with beautiful exercises. (1902, February 22). *Idaho Daily Statesman,* p. 8.

Troeltsch, E. (1931). *The social teaching of the Christian churches.* New York: Macmillan.

The turkey on top. Thanksgiving Day will generally be observed in Philadelphia. Recreation for everybody. (1890, November 27). *The Philadelphia Inquirer,* p. 5.

Tyack, D. B. (1974). *The one best system: A history of American urban education.* Cambridge, MA: Harvard University Press. Quoting John D. Philbrick. *School systems in the United States.* U.S. Bureau of Education: Circular of Information, no. 1. Washington, DC: Government Printing Office, 1885.

Tyler, R. (1987). *Education—Curriculum development and evaluation.* Berkeley: University of California Regional Oral History Office, the Bancroft Library.

Under God. (1957, March 18). *Christian Science Monitor,* p. 16.

United Nations. (1984). *Statistical yearbook.* New York: United Nations.

U.S. Census Bureau. (2000, October). *School enrollment—Social and economic characteristics of students: October 2000* (PPL-148). Washington, DC: Author.

U.S. Census Bureau. (1930). *Statistical abstract of the United States, 1930.* Washington, DC: Author.

U.S. Census Bureau. (1940). *Statistical abstract of the United States, 1940.* Washington, DC: Author.

U.S. Census Bureau, Census of Population and Housing. (1990*). United States*

Summary. Table 4. Population: 1790 to 1990. United States, Urban and Rural, p. 5. Washington, DC: Author.

U.S. Department of Education. (1989). *National Education Goals Report.* Retrived online Decemer 12, 2006, at http://www.ed.gov/pubs/goals/report/goalsrpt .txt

U.S. Department of Education. (2005). *My child's academic success: Facts and terms every parent should know about NCLB.* Retrieved online January 19, 2007, at http://www.ed.gov/nclb/overview/intro/parents/parentfacts.html

U.S. Immigration Commission. (1911). *The children of immigrants in schools.* Washington, DC: Author.

Vatter, H. G. (1996). The economy at mid-century. In H. G. Vatter & J. F. Walker (Eds.), *History of the U.S. economy since World War II* (pp. 3–23). Armonk, NY: M.E. Sharpe.

Vinovskis, M. A. (1999). *The road to Charlottesville: The 1989 education summit.* Washington, DC: National Education Goals Panel.

Voegelin, E. (1986). *Political religions* (T. J. DiNapoli & E. S. Easterly III, Trans.) Lewiston, NY: Mellen Press.

Voegelin, E. (2005). *The collected works of Eric Voegelin: Vol. 5. Modernity without restraint* (M. Henningsen, ed.). Columbia, MO: University of Missouri Press.

Walters, P. B. (2000). The limits of growth: School expansion and school reform in historical perspective. In M. T. Hallinan (Ed.), *Handbook of the sociology of education* (pp. 241–261). New York: Kluwer Academic.

Warden, P. (1952, October 14). A few teachers may be reds, educator says. *Chicago Daily Tribune,* p. 4.

Warner, W. L. (1963). *Yankee City.* New Haven, CT: Yale University Press.

Webster, N. (1800). *The American spelling book.* Wilmington, DE: Bonsal & Niles.

Whalen says reds menace schools. (1930, March 25). *New York Times,* p. 23.

Wong, K., & Nicotera, A. C. (2004). Brown v. Board of Education and the Coleman Report: Social science research and the debate on educational equality. *Peabody Journal of Education, 79,* 122–135.

Index

About the Authors

CARL L. BANKSTON III is professor and chair in the Department of Sociology and co-director of the Asian Studies Program at Tulane University. His previous books include *Growing Up American: How Vietnamese Children Adapt to Life in the United States* (with Min Zhou, 1998), *A Troubled Dream: The Promise and Failure of School Desegregation in Louisiana* (with Stephen J. Caldas, 2002); *Blue Collar Bayou: Louisiana Cajuns in the New Economy of Ethnicity* (with Jacques Henry, 2002); and *Forced to Fail: The Paradox of School Desegregation* (with Stephen J. Caldas, 2005). He has also published over 100 scholarly journal articles, book chapters, and law review articles on topics in education, immigration, religion, family, economics, and social history.

STEPHEN J. CALDAS is professor of education in the Department of Foundations, Leadership and Policy Studies at Hofstra University. He is the author of the book *Raising Bilingual-Biliterate Children in Monolingual Cultures* (2006). He has co-authored three previous books with Carl L. Bankston III, including *Forced to Fail: The Paradox of School Desegregation* (2007) and *A Troubled Dream: The Promise and Failure of School Desegregation in Louisiana* (2002). Stephen has authored or co-authored more than 60 articles and book chapters. His research interests include the social, policy, and legal contexts of education. He also conducts research in socio/psycholinguistics and bilingual education.